LIV ULLMANN

INTERVIEWS

CONVERSATIONS WITH FILMMAKERS SERIES
PETER BRUNETTE, GENERAL EDITOR

Photo credit: Photofest

LIV
ULLMANN
INTERVIEWS

EDITED BY ROBERT EMMET LONG

UNIVERSITY PRESS OF MISSISSIPPI/JACKSON

www.upress.state.ms.us

The University Press of Mississippi is a member of the Association of
American University Presses.

Copyright © 2006 by University Press of Mississippi
Manufactured in the United States of America

First edition 2006
∞
Library of Congress Cataloging-in-Publication Data
Ullmann, Liv.
Liv Ullmann : interviews / edited by Robert Emmet Long.— 1st ed.
    p. cm. — (Conversations with filmmakers series)
    Includes bibliographical references and index.
    ISBN 1-57806-823-1 (cloth : alk. paper) — ISBN 1-57806-824-X (pbk. : alk.
    paper)
    1. Ullmann, Liv—Interviews. 2. Actors—Norway—Interviews. 3. Motion
    picture producers and directors—Norway—Interviews. I. Long, Robert
    Emmet. II. Series.
PN2768.U4A3 2006
791.4302'8'092—dc22   2005052901

British Library Cataloging-in-Publication Data available

CONTENTS

INTRODUCTION

LIV ULLMANN IS OFTEN regarded at the mention of her name as the actress most favored by Ingmar Bergman in his history-making films of the 1960s and 70s. Beginning with *Persona*, she drew international attention, and her period with Bergman would by itself have made an ample career; yet it was to be merely the first phase of her engagement with the performing arts that would reach from one side of the Atlantic to the other. She has starred on the stage both here and abroad and appeared in over two dozen films quite apart from her collaboration with Bergman. She has enjoyed notable success as a writer and been recognized as an award-winning film director.

This volume contains more interviews than is usual for the interviews with film directors series published by the University Press of Mississippi, because Ullmann's career has been unusually diverse and abundant. Her work as a film director cannot simply be lifted out of its context, which is replete with references to her other endeavors and connections that can best be seen in their totality. The interviews collected here reveal her as a constantly working actress of stage and screen, the author of best-selling memoirs that have been translated into twenty languages, Ingmar Bergman's collaborator and sometime lover, caring mother of a daughter fathered by Bergman, tireless worker for refugee women and children in the most impoverished of Third World countries, and for the last fourteen years a film director. She is, in short, a veritable wonder—the subject of a cartoon in the *New Yorker* in which a housewife exclaims to her husband, "I'm getting sick and tired of hearing how perfect Liv Ullmann is."

In the absence of a full-length biography of Ullmann in English, this volume provides a valuable source of information about her life and career. Her Scandinavian background comes up fairly often in these pieces; and what one notices particularly is the sense of displacement in her early years. Her father, Viggo Ullmann, was an engineer whose work took him away from Norway at times; at one such time in 1939 his daughter Liv was born in Tokyo, Japan. The Nazis were then overrunning Norway, which precluded the Ullmann family's return to their home-land. They emigrated to Toronto, Canada, where the father served with the displaced Norwegian Air Force training flying cadets. Tragically, in 1943, he was gravely injured when he walked accidentally into a moving propeller. The Ullmanns then removed to New York City, where he could be treated by specialists; he died shortly before the end of the war in Europe.

His widow, left with little money, booked passage aboard a freighter to Norway for herself and her two small daughters, Liv and Bitten. In Norway they went to live in the port city of Trondheim, where the mother found employment working in a bookstore. In these circumstances, Liv grew up a loner who felt awkward and unattractive. After school she would sit in a corner of the bookstore and read voraciously. She formed a drama club at school, for which she wrote condensed plays from classics, giving herself the best parts; by then she thought of the theater as a place where she could be most alive. "Life to me," she told an interviewer, "was on stage." One would think that the theater was a form of therapy for her loneliness; "It was," she said, "the only way I could talk to people."

At seventeen she went to Oslo, where she auditioned for the National Theatre School and was rejected for admission. Refusing to give up, she took acting lessons at the Webber-Douglas Academy of Dramatic Art in London; then auditioned again at the National Theatre School, only to be rejected once more and told that she had no talent. Yet she did find an opportunity to act with a repertory company in the small city of Stavanger, where she was given the lead in their production of *The Diary of Anne Frank*, in which she earned local acclaim. For the next three years with the Stavanger company, she played a variety of roles from the classics (Shakespeare to Ibsen). In 1960, she was accepted into the National Theatre School; and in the same year, at the age of twenty, she married the Oslo psychiatrist Hans Jacob Stang.

The interviews contained in this collection are drawn from a variety of sources and are of varying lengths. The American Film Institute's "dialogue" with Liv Ullmann is one of the longest as well as one of the most searching; but it is rivalled by the two-part piece in the English paper the *Guardian*, in which Ullmann is interviewed by Shane Danielsen, the artistic director of the Edinborough International Film Festival. Another two-part interview, from the *Christian Science Monitor*, is unique in that Ullmann discusses her approach to the craft of acting at length with David Brooks Andrews, who has probably interviewed Ullmann more often than anyone else. Some of the interviews come from influential periodicals such as *Cineaste* and *Cinema Journal*, while others first appeared in a wide variety of newspapers ranging from the *Village Voice* to the *Boston Globe* and the *San Francisco Chronicle*.

But regardless of where these interviews made their first appearance, one subject keeps coming up—Ullmann's relationship with Ingmar Bergman. It is a relationship with many aspects—as actress, lover, screenwriter, and director. Ullmann has written with startling candor about her five-year liaison with the celebrated director in her memoir *Changing*; but she has more still to say on the subject in the course of the interviews. The memoir and these interviews, taken together, provide the fullest account of the Bergman-Ullmann relationship, both professional and personal, available at the present time.

The interviews include Ullmann's piquant recollections of the well-known figures in the arts with whom she had worked. One, for instance, has to do with a meeting between Ingmar Bergman and Woody Allen, who idolized Begman. Bergman had a great fear of traveling, but he made a brief and exceedingly rare visit to New York to see Ullmann in her Broadway stage debut in *A Doll's House*. When Ullmann, who also knew Woody Allen, mentioned to him that Bergman was coming to New York, he gasped. "I can't believe it," and he beseeched her to introduce him. An elaborate ritual ensued with Allen arriving to pick up Ullmann in a limousine driven by a chauffeur wearing white gloves. When they reached the hotel suite where Bergman was staying, Allen was in a state of nerves. At the door he and Bergman said "hello" to each other, and were then speechless for the rest of the evening. Throughout the dinner neither said so much as a word, as if each had been struck dumb in the other's presence.

What the interviews reveal strongly, however, is what exactly it was that Bergman gave Ullmann as an actress. She was twenty-five when she first met Bergman, who was forty-seven, and much more experienced and accomplished. He introduced her to Italian, French, Russian, Polish, and other national filmmaking, and helped to mold her tastes. He could see her potential and knew how to cultivate it. When *Persona* was being made, she tended to be shy and blushed easily; and she was unsure of what the character she was playing was supposed to be feeling. Indeed, she was unsure of what the film was about. Yet in Bergman's hands she turned in an assured and convincing performance.

But their life together in Stockholm and on the Baltic island of Fårö, where a number of Bergman's films of the 1960s and 1970s were filmed, was not exactly a romantic idyll. It was at times very strenuous and filled with psychological conflict. "Together we were too strong," she tells an interviewer, "too emotional. He was older, more dominant. I fought not to be cancelled by him." In one of the interviews, Ullmann tells of the affinity she feels with Norah in *A Doll's House*, who leaves her husband to become self-sufficient and find her own identity.

The interviews are arranged in chronological order, from the earliest in 1972 to my own in the spring of 2004—a method that makes it clear how Ullmann developed as a person and as an artist, and how she was perceived by the public at particular times. An early flurry of reviews appeared in the 1970s when Ullmann starred in a series of distinguished films for Bergman and made the cover of *Time* magazine. In 1977 she attracted particular attention with her best-selling memoir *Changing*, and as a result gave numerous interviews. It also marked the point at which Ullmann achieved independence from Bergman, becoming a writer as well as an actress. Her forging of a new identity overlaps with the changing-growing-developing-into-new-awareness theme of the book. If Bergman's films give a sense of guilt and debilitating psychic fixation that cannot be overcome, Ullmann's outlook in *Changing* inclines toward an optimism that allows for renewal and hope.

Ullmann came to prominence as the author of books a second time with the publication in 1984 of *Choices*. In a number of the interviews she gave at that time she speaks of becoming less and less interested in performing in the theater, and of being increasingly drawn to alleviating the condition of the handicapped and impoverished—particularly as it affected women and children. In practically every interview of this time she is asked about her work as a UNICEF goodwill ambassador in such blighted lands as Somalia and Ethiopia and about her playing a prominent role in the International Rescue Committee. The interviews she gives at this time are unlike those that appeared earlier insofar as they deal with her personal experience among the downtrodden in such regions as India, Bangladesh, and the Sudan which revitalized her life with a new sense of purpose. Several of the interviewers point out that in her responses Ullmann exhibits a Nordic seriousness and sincerity similar to that in *Changing.* "I am learning that if I just go on accepting the framework for life that others have given me," she tells Kristin Helmore in the *Christian Science Monitor*, "if I fail to make my own choices, the reason for my life will be missing. I will be unable to recognize that which I have the power to change. . . . I refuse to spend my life regretting the things I failed to do."

Another issue involved in the interviews is feminism, since Ullmann has much to say about valuing her femininity while at the same time being effective as a professional woman. She recalls the rigid formulations for girls in authoritarian and traditionalist Norway and takes care to allow her daughter Linn her "freedom." The most searching exploration of the feminist issue can be found, it seems to me, in Molly Haskell's piece in the *Village Voice*, but the subject turns ups as well in other interviews. So, too, does the subject of Ullmann's supportive attitude toward Jewish friends and Jewish issues. As several of the interviewers point out, a tradition of support for the Jews was begun by Ullmann's paternal grandfather, who was sent to the Dachau concentration camp, where he perished, for having helped Jews in Norway to escape from the Nazis.

Ullmann's own encounter with Jewish subject matter began early with her theater debut at eighteen as Anne Frank. Later she welcomed the chance to play Ida Nudel, a feisty Russian Jewish dissident who was exiled to Siberia before being allowed to emigrate to Israel. Elie Wiesel, who survived the concentration camps to become a spokesman for the Jews, became one of Ullmann's closest friends; another was Erland Josephson, with whom she starred in Bergman films. In 1985 she met and married Donald Saunders, a Jewish realtor and hotel owner in Boston, whom she accompanied on visits to Israel. Although remaining a Christian, her inspiring experience of Israel, she told an interviewer, "changed my life."

Ullmann made her directorial debut with her feature film *Sofie* in 1992. A study of a Jewish family in nineteenth-century Copenhagen, *Sofie* marks the beginning of the second half of the book, which concentrates on Ullmann's work as a director. Many aspects of *Sofie* come under discussion, but none is more interesting to note than the distinction she makes between Bergman's outlook and her own. "He looks at the universe as something unforgiving," she tells a journalist, "and I look at the universe as being full of wonderful possibilities in a way. I think his outlook is bleaker than mine." Her second film, *Kristin Lavransdatter* (1995), adapted by Ullmann from Sigrid Undset's celebrated novel set in fourteenth-century Norway, again centers upon a young woman and the choices she makes about her life. An international release, it made a particularly powerful impression in Norway. But as Ullmann acknowledges in an interview, she was forced by producers to make extensive cuts, so that it was not in the end the work she had envisioned.

Her subsequent films, *Private Confessions* (1996) and *Faithless* (2001) were collaborations with Bergman, who wrote the screenplays and asked Ullmann to direct them. The interviews go into these films deeply, but one of the most intriguing points made about them is the conjoining or confluence of Bergman's art and Ullmann's craft. The films add to the procession of female central figures in Ullmann's work and show her tact with social situations; but in her emphasis on facial close-ups and telling silences to create tension, one can see how she has learned from Bergman. And it is Bergman's projection of guilt and inner suffering that dominates both movies. My interview with Ullmann, in which she looks back on the films she has directed and reveals the new work she now has underway, brings us up to the present moment. A parting word about Ullmann, from all accounts of her in the book, is that she is a joy to work with on the set, and that she elicits brilliant performances from her casts not by over instructing them but by allowing them to absorb from her the pleasure of being in touch with an inner self. There is no sloppiness in her films, which are sensitive and textured and civilized.

CHRONOLOGY

1939   Born December 16, 1939, in Tokyo, Japan, to Viggo (an aeronautical engineer) and Janna Ullmann. In same year the Nazis overrun Norway and the family takes refuge in the "Little Norway" colony in Toronto.

1943   White serving with the displaced Norwegian air force her father accidentally walks into a moving propeller, sustaining serious injuries. The family moves to New York where special treatment is available; Ullmann's father dies shortly before the end of the war.

1945   The mother, with Liv and her older sister Bitten, return to Norway, settling in the port city of Trondheim, 250 miles north of Oslo. A lonely child, she aspires to become an actress.

1956   Auditions at seventeen for the National Theatre School in Oslo but is rejected. Studies acting for eight months in London, reapplies to the National Theatre and is again rejected on the grounds that she has "no talent."

1957   Acts in repertory for several years in the small city of Stavanger, making stage debut in title role in *The Diary of Anne Frank* to rave reviews.

1960   Is finally accepted as a member of the Norwegian National Theatre Company; marries psychiatrist Hans Jacob (Gappe) Stang.

1965   Is introduced to Ingmar Bergman by her friend Bibi Andersson, and the two are starred together in *Persona* (1966), which makes her internationally famous. Ullmann and Bergman divorce their marital partners and begin a five-year relationship outside of marriage for which Ullmann is treated severely in the Norwegian media.

1968   Initial collaboration with Erland Josephson and Max von Sydow in Bergman's *Hour of the Wolf*. Linn Ullmann, the daughter of Bergman and Ullmann, is born during the making of the film. In the same year Ullmann also stars with Max von Sydow in Bergman's film *Shame*. Wins National Board of Review Award and New York Society of Film Critics Award for *Hour of the Wolf* and *The Shame*.

1969   Stars with Bibi Andersson and Erland Josephson in Bergman's *The Passion of Anna*.

1972   Stars with Harriet Andersson in Bergman's *Cries and Whispers*. Also stars opposite Max von Sydow in Jan Troell's *The Emigrants*, receiving Oscar nomination as Best Actress. Wins Golden Globe Award for *The Emigrants* and New York Critics Circle Award for both *Cries and Whispers* and *The Emigrants*.

1973   Is featured with von Sydow again in Troell's *The New Land*, sequel to *The Emigrants*. Stars with Bibi Andersson and Erland Josephson in Bergman's *Scenes from a Marriage*. Also makes Hollywood debut in musical version of *Lost Horizon* (in which she sings). The picture receives savage reviews. Wins National Society of Film Critics Award for *The New Land* and National Board of Review Award for *Scenes from a Marriage*, for which she is also nominated for a BAFTA Award.

1974   Stars in film *The Abdication*, former vehicle for Greta Garbo, about Sweden's Queen Christina. Nominated for a Golden Globe Award for *Scenes from a Marriage*.

1975   Has American stage debut in New York in the American Shakespeare Festival revival of Ibsen's *A Doll's House*.

1976   Stars opposite Erland Josephson in Bergman's *Face to Face*, and is nominated again for Oscar as Best Actress; wins BAFTA Award and National Board of Review Award.

1977   Plays title role in Eugene O'Neill's *Anna Christie* on Broadway, for which she receives Outer Critics Circle Award, and publishes her memoir *Changing*, which becomes an international best seller.

1978   Is featured in Bergman's *Autumn Sonata*, playing the daughter of the Ingrid Bergman character, and has lead in Ingmar Bergman's *The Serpent's Egg*.

1979   Makes Broadway musical debut in the Richard Rodgers–Martin Charnin adaptation of *I Remember Mama*.

1980   Begins her long-standing association with UNICEF as its goodwill ambassador. Wins Venice Film Festival Pasinetti Award for Best Actress for *Richard's Things*.

1981   Begins her second career as a screenwriter and director with the "Parting" segment of the anthology feature *Love*.

1982   Returns to Broadway playing Mrs. Alving in Ibsen's *Ghosts*.

1984   Appears in Richard Dembo's *Dangerous Moves*, Swiss foreign intrique movie which won Oscar for Best Foreign Film. Publishes her second memoir, *Choices*, about her work with UNICEF in Third World countries.

1985   Marries Donald Saunders, well-to-do Boston realtor and hotel owner.

1987   Stars in Luis Mandoki's *Gaby: A True Story*. Wins Donatello Prize for Best Actress for *Moscow Adieu*.

1990   Nominated for Golden Globe for Best Actress for *The Rose Garden*.

1991   Appears with Max von Sydow in *The Ox*, debut as director of Bergman's celebrated cinematographer Sven Nykvist.

1992   Makes *Sofie*, her feature directorial debut about Jewish family in nineteenth-century Copenhagen; also co-writes the screenplay. Wins Montreal World Film Festival Special Grand Jury Prize for her direction.

1995   Co-writes and directs her second feature film, *Kristin Lavransdatter*, from Sigrid Undset's epic novel of fourteenth-century Norway; Erland Josephson featured, with Sven Nykvist as cinematographer. Wins Montreal World Film Festival Award for her direction of *Kristin Lavransdatter* and for exceptional contribution to cinematic art as actress and filmmaker.

1996   Directs *Private Confessions* from script by Bergman; von Sydow featured, with Nykvist as cinematographer.

2000   Nominated for Cannes Film Festival Golden Palm Award for her direction of *Faithless*.

2001   Directs *Faithless* from script by Bergman, and with Erland Josephson portraying Bergman.

2003   Receives Lifetime Achievement Award from the Copenhagen International Film Festival.

FILMOGRAPHY

As Actress in Films Directed by Ingmar Bergman

Persona, 1966 (as Elisabet Vogler)
Hour of the Wolf, 1968 (as Alma Borg)
The Shame, 1968 (as Eva Rosenberg)
The Passion of Anna, 1970 (as Anna Fromm)
Cries and Whispers, 1972 (as Maria and the Mother)
Scenes from a Marriage, 1974 (as Marianne)
Face to Face, 1976 (as Dr. Jenny Isaksson)
The Serpent's Egg, 1977 (as Manuella Rosenberg)
Autumn Sonata, 1978 (as Eva)

As Actress in Films by Other Directors

The Night Visitor, 1971, Laslo Benedek, director (as Ester Jenks)
The Emigrants, 1972, Jan Troell, director (as Kristina)
The New Land, 1972, Jan Troell, director (as Kristina)
Pope Joan, 1972, Michael Anderson, director (as Joan)
40 Carats, 1973, Milton Katselas, director (as Ann Stanley)
Lost Horizon, 1973, Charles Jarrott, director (as Catherine)
The Cold Sweat, 1974, Terrence Young, director (as Fabienne Martin)
The Abdication, 1974, Anthony Harvey, director (as Queen Kristina)
Zandy's Bride, 1974, Jan Troell, director (as Hannah Lund)
Leonor, 1975, Juan Buñuel, director (as Leonor)
A Bridge Too Far, 1977, Richard Attenborough, director (as Kate ter Horst)
Richard's Things, 1980, Anthony Harvey, director (as Kate Morris)

The Wild Duck, 1983, Henri Safran, director (as Gina)
The Bay Boy, 1984, Daniel Petrie, director (as Mrs. Campbell)
Dangerous Moves, 1984, Richard Dembo, director (as Marina Fromm)
Gaby: A True Story, 1987, Luis Mandoki, director (as Sari)
The Rose Garden, 1989, Fons Rademakers, director (as Gabriele Freund)
Mindwalk, 1990, Bernt Capra, director (as Sonia Hoffman)
The Ox, 1991, Sven Nykvist, director (as Mrs. Gustafsson)

Feature Films Directed by Ullmann

1992
SOFIE
Producer: Lars Kolvig
Director: **Liv Ullmann**
Screenplay: **Liv Ullmann** and Peter Poulsen, from Henri Nathansen's
novel *Mendel Philipsen and Son*
Cinematography: Jörgen Persson
Editor: Grete Møldrup
Art Direction: Peter Høimark
Costume Design: Jette Termann
Production Design: Peter Høimark
Set Design: Magnus Magnusson
Makeup: Cecilia Drott
Sound Re-recording: Petter Fladeby
Color
Running Time: 146 minutes
Cast: Karen-Lise Mynster (Sofie); Ghita Norby (Frederikke); Erland
Josephson (Sofie's father); Jesper Christensen (Hojby); Torben Zeller
(Jonas); Henning Moritzen (Frederick Philipson); Stig Hoffmeyer
(Gottlieb); Kirsten Rolffas (Jonas's mother); Lotte Hermann (Aunt Pulle);
Jonas Oddermose (Aron age 3); David Maym (Aron age 7); Jacob Allon
(Aron age 12); Kasper Barfoed (Aron age 18); Anne Werner Thomsen
(Rose Philipson); Sanne Grangaard (Fanny Philipson); Elna Brodthagen
(Sofie's grandmother); Elin Reimer (Belse); Lone Herman (Malle); Peter
Hesse Overgaard (Harry Hirsch); Peter Schrøder (Lagen); John Hahn-
Petersen (Colin); Hardy Raen (Larsen); Maurstad (Josephine); Claus

Bue (Kelner); Bent Lexner (Rabbi); Daniel Hertz (Julius); Anna Szaff
(Dina age 9); Lea Louise Leitner (Dina age 6); Anetta Lutchen-Lehn
(Mrs. Hjortekar); Johannes Våbensted)

1995
KRISTIN LAVRANSDATTER (Norwegian)
Producer: Esben Høiland Carlson, Gören Lindström
Director: **Liv Ullmann**
Screenplay: **Liv Ullmann**, from the novel by Sigrid Undset
Cinematography: Sven Nykvist
Non-Original Music: Henryk Mikolaj Gorecki
Editor: Michal Leszczylowski
Costume Design: Inger Pehrsson
Production Design: Karl Juliusson
Production Manager: Arve Figenschow, Gudny Hummelvoll Andersen
Assistant Director: Bjarne Bjørndalen
Visual Effects: Bente Santi Helle
Sound Editor: Baard H. Ingebretsen
Color
Running Time: 144 minutes
Cast: Elisabeth Matheson (Kristin Lavransdatter); Bjørn Skagestad
(Erlend); Erland Josephson (Broder Edvin); Lena Endre (Eline
Ormsdatter); Sverre Anker Ousdal (Lavrans); Henny Moan (Ragnfrid);
Rut Tellefson (Ulv); Jørgen Langhelle; (Simon Darre); Gisken Armand
(Ingbjorg); Berard Arnø (Ung Erlend); Gina Green (young dancer); Anne
Kokkinn (Duchess)

1997
PRIVATE CONFESSIONS (Swedish) ENSKILDA SAMTAL
Producer: Ingrid Dahlberg
Director: **Liv Ullmann**
Screenplay: Ingmar Bergman
Cinematography: Sven Nykvist
Non-Original Music: Johann Sebastian Bach (from "Brabdenbrugische
Konzerte Nr. f-dur, ur sats 2, adagio," and cantata "Jesu Bleitbet Meine
Freunde No. 147")
Editor: Michal Leszczylowski

Costume Design: Inger Pehrsson
Production Design: Mette Möller
Makeup Artist: Cecilia Drott
Color
Running Time: 144 minutes
Cast: Pernilla August (Anna); Max von Sydow (Jacob); Samuel Fröler (Henrik); Anita Björk (Karin Åkerblom); Vibeke Falk (Ms. Nylander, housekeeper); Thomas Hanzon (Tomas Egerman); Kristina Adolphson (Maria); Gunnel Fred (Märta Gärdsjö); Hans Afredson (Bishop Agrell); Bengt Schött (Stille, verger)

2000
FAITHLESS (Swedish-German) TROLÖSA
Producer: Kaj Larsen, Johan Mardell
Executive Producer: Maria Curman
Director: **Liv Ullmann**
Screenplay: Ingmar Bergman
Cinematographer: Jörgen Persson
Editor: Sylvia Ingemarsson
Costume Designer: Inger Pehrsson
Art Director: Göran Wassberg
Makeup Artist: Cecilia Drott, Elisabeth Ekman
Production Manager: Elisabeth Liljequist
Production Manager, Paris: Jacques Foussat
Assistant Directors: Gunnlaugur Jónasson, Roland Lindmark
Sound Editors: Tomas Krantz, Bo Persson
Casting Director: Maria Kiisk
Color
Running Time: 155 minutes
Cast: Lena Endre (Marianne); Erland Josephson (Bergman); Krister Henrikssson (David); Thomas Hanzon (Markus); Michalle Gylemo (Isabelle); Juni Dahr (Margareta); Philip Zandén (Martin Goldman); Thérèse Brunnader (Petra Holst); Marie Richardson (Anna Berg); Stina Ekblad (Eva); Johan Rabaeus (Johan); Jan-Olof Strandberg (Axel); Björn Granath (Gustav); Gertrud Stenung (Martha)

LIV ULLMANN

INTERVIEWS

Liv Ullmann: Dialogue on Film

AMERICAN FILM INSTITUTE/1972

LIV ULLMANN, FOUR MONTHS fresh from filming Ingmar Bergman's *Cries and Whispers*, was in Los Angeles to perform in Ross Hunter's musical version of *Lost Horizon* when she spoke to Fellows at the American Film Institute's Center for Advanced Film Studies.

Ms. Ullmann's career has been extensive. From her starring performances in such films as *Persona, The Passion of Anna* and *The Shame*, she has branched out to perform in *The Emigrants, Lost Horizon*, and *40 Carats*. As this issue was going to press, Ms. Ullmann had just been nominated for an Academy Award as Best Actress for her role in Jan Troell's *The Emigrants*.

At Ms. Ullmann's seminar, Fellows moved from questions about the filmic intricacies of director Ingmar Bergman to those seeking the person behind the famous face. Is an actress a liberated woman? Can an actress affect politics?

The transcript of Ms. Ullmann's March 1972 seminar is reprinted here in full, edited only for clarity.

INTRODUCTION: *Our guest today is Liv Ullmann. Over the past two weeks we have seen three films:* The Shame, Persona, *and* The Passion of Anna. *Let's start off with an obvious question which is: How does Ingmar Bergman work with and direct his actors?*

LIV ULLMANN: He is very different from what most people seem to believe. He has a reputation of a demon, which is totally untrue. He

From *Dialogue on Film*, vol. 2, number 5—March 1973 © 1973 by the American Film Institute. Reprinted by permission.

depends very much on his actors. He knows whom he has hired. He listens to them and he watches them. He tries to get out of them what they have to give, not what he would want to do in a similar situation. He is a fantastic listener and he has a fantastic manner of looking. He sees what you are trying to express and he builds on that. He helps get it out of you. He also makes very good scenery. Do you call it scenery? I mean the movements of the scene are always telling in itself very much of the scene. He doesn't explain very much.

QUESTION: *Do you mean his blocking of the scene?*
ULLMANN: Yes, his blocking of the scene, in that blocking actually is what he wants the scene to be like and then it is up to the actor to film it.

QUESTION: *Where does he actually sit?*
ULLMANN: He sits very close to the camera. You feel him very much and if he is not close to the camera, you tend to act towards him. He always is very, very close to the camera and he is terribly inspiring. I don't know what he is doing, but it is something that makes you want to give everything you have. You feel that there is somebody who is really there.

QUESTION: *Does he tell you that or is it something you have to feel out?*
ULLMANN: He hates to discuss and analyze. He feels that if you have chosen your profession as an actor, then you know a little how to act. He feels that you are fairly intelligent. He sort of feels that an analysis would take away the fantasy. He knows that is the way an actor creates. The actor has to use his own fantasy and imagination.

QUESTION: *How many takes does Bergman usually shoot of a scene?*
ULLMANN: It depends. Sometimes he uses the first take. Sometimes we go on for twenty, thirty, or forty takes until you are completely exhausted.

QUESTION: *Does he allow rehearsals?*
ULLMANN: Yes, he allows technical rehearsals. As I said before, the blocking is very important. But then he likes to take on the first emotional rehearsal because sometimes that is the best take.

QUESTION: *I am interested in a scene in* Persona *where Bibi Andersson sits down and tells you the story about your marriage and your boy. Could you take that as an example?*

ULLMANN: That was very strange because he did that with two cameras. There was one on Bibi when she told my story, and there was one camera on me while she was telling the story. It was supposed to be cut up, using the best from each. But when he saw it as a whole, he didn't know what to pick. So he used them both. Many people have tried to analyze why he does this. The real reason is that he felt that both told something there which he felt was important. He felt that he couldn't choose which one was most important so he had both.

QUESTION: *So that scene actually wasn't in the script that way?*

ULLMANN: No, not at all.

QUESTION: *I am interested in your experience with Jan Troell in* The Emigrants. *How long did that shooting last? Was it very exhausting, being that it was a three and a half hour movie?*

ULLMANN: The truth of it is as it stands today it is a seven and a half hour movie. There is a sequel. He did them both at the same time and we spent one year doing them. He took such a lot of material. Ingmar has already cut so he knows what he wants. Jan Troell is his own photographer, so he goes along with the camera all the time. He has to take every scene from every angle. That means that it is very long and very tiresome.

QUESTION: *Have you seen the film since it was cut?*

ULLMANN: Yes, I have seen both films.

QUESTION: *Are you satisfied?*

ULLMANN: Honestly, I love those pictures. I think he is a great poet. He really is a very timid, very quiet man. He said absolutely nothing. He went along with his camera. We never knew what was going to be on the screen.

RESPONSE: *It was really an incredible story that he managed to tell. I really enjoyed the film and I thought that each frame was a painting. I particularly enjoyed the scene of you on the swing. I thought that his approach to how he handled that was really poetic.*

ULLMANN: I am sure that with that scene I did two days of swinging. If any picture is anybody's, then this is his picture. We didn't know what was happening. When we were doing all the farm work, he really wanted us to do the farm work. We had to learn to wash clothes the way they do it with the horses. He went for days in the fields. You see much more in the second picture. It's fun for a day, but after three days it gets a little tiring. But it was an experience, and for me I think that it was the best experience ever. The cinema is also life.

QUESTION: *The picture had a lyrical quality and I am sorry that it did not get much publicity. Are there any plans for showing it?*

ULLMANN: Yes, Warner Bros. has bought it and they will release both of them. They want on both of them twenty minutes or half an hour away. That maybe will be fine.

QUESTION: *Cuts of twenty minutes?*

ULLMANN: Yes, cuts. The books which the films are based upon are very well known in Scandinavia. We would have missed scenes which maybe you will not miss. Jan Troell himself is cutting the picture.

QUESTION: *So Bergman doesn't actually cover as much as Troell?*

ULLMANN: No.

QUESTION: *What does one of his scripts look like?*

ULLMANN: The last picture that I did for him is *Cries and Whispers*. It is with Harriet Andersson and Ingrid Thulin and me. That was more like a personal letter. It starts, "My Dear Friends: We're now going to make a film together. It is sort of a vision that I have and I will try to describe it." He describes it in fifty pages. That was his script.

QUESTION: *You got the script before the shooting started?*

ULLMANN: Yes. It was like taking off from there. He did all of it in natural light. We had no artificial light. We filmed everything in a big castle. He used big windows. From sunrise until the sun went down, he used the different light. I think it will be exceptional.

QUESTION: *Was it shot in the winter or during the summer?*

ULLMANN: It was shot during the autumn. He made it for his own company. He said, "I am not happy with it. I won't release it, but it is an experience for me. It is my own workship. I am working with my own group. If we are happy with it, then we will release it."

QUESTION: *That is why all the actors with leading roles were also listed as being producers?*

ULLMANN: That is what he did so he didn't have to pay us. We thought we were being producers and we would have things to say. But what it all amounted to was that he didn't pay us.

QUESTION: *Does that mean that you don't have as much say as you would like when you work with Bergman?*

ULLMANN: I have a say as an actress. As I said, he respects everybody that he works with and this includes his actors. In this film we thought that we would have something to say about publicity and when we would quit at the end of the day. But it was all his. It was his picture.

QUESTION: *When was it finished?*

ULLMANN: The shooting finished last December (1971), and it will be released in August (1972).

QUESTION: *He must like it?*

ULLMANN: Yes, he must like it, but he didn't ask us. We haven't seen it.

QUESTION: *How much improvisation is there in a Bergman film?*

ULLMANN: More and more. In my experience it started in *The Shame*. If you remember they are sitting by a table and they are drinking wine and eating. Then they fall down on the grass. That was improvised. We knew what he wanted to say. But the way that we wanted to do it was more or less left up to us.

QUESTION: *That was a change from the way he had directed you before?*

ULLMANN: Yes. He has always been very strict in wanting us to keep to his sentences. There was the dinner party in *The Passion of Anna* where the four tell their own story. That was our own complete freedom. But we had to stick to the character. One day a lady came and she made a beautiful dinner. First it may have been Max von Sydow's turn. He drank red wine and all of us could ask him questions. He had to answer as the character and the camera was on him all the time. He did the same thing with all four of us. Then he cut it together.

QUESTION: *There are scenes in* The Passion of Anna *where he interviews each one of the actors. Did he write those interviews?*

ULLMANN: No. As it was before, in the script he had written what the characters themselves spoke as characters. Then he had written a text. Do you understand what I mean? He broke the picture in four places. The characters sort of came out and spoke as the character.

RESPONSE: *Yes, but you speak as an actor.*

ULLMANN: Yes, because then he didn't really feel that it was good. He took it away, and after the picture was finished he asked us to come to the studio and to speak as the actor. Bibi Andersson used the text which her character had when she was the character.

QUESTION: *You have played different women's roles in Bergman's films. How accurate do you think his interpretations of the different women have been?*

ULLMANN: They are accurate for that sort of woman. I think he has a great understanding for women, maybe even more than for men. I think his women characters, especially in the last years, have been more interesting.

QUESTION: *Does he allow you to tell him more about what you would feel if you were that woman?*

ULLMANN: First of all, he knows which actor is going to play which part when he writes the script. So he knows something of what he is going to get. He is also very open for suggestions. He hates it if you start to analyze, but he is very open to your own kind of interpretation of the kind of woman that he has written.

QUESTION: *Besides acting, have you thought of other things that you would like to do with film? Would you like to do photography or directing?*

ULLMANN: No. I would like to write, but not for film.

QUESTION: *Earlier you were talking about Bergman putting a lot of himself into his women characters.*

ULLMANN: Yes, I think there is very much of himself in both the men and the women. People tend to believe that his pictures are from his own private life, what he's like just in that moment. I don't believe that is true. Of course, he uses his own experience but in a different way. I think he uses his experience of life and people. I don't recognize any real situation or real human being. You suggested that in *The Passion of Anna* I was maybe a part of Anna. There might be parts of you which he puts into the character that he wants you to play. But I never killed my first husband. It is very difficult for us when people think that.

QUESTION: *We know you are here to do a film with Ross Hunter, the remake of* Lost Horizon *as a musical. Why have you chosen to pick that as a project?*

ULLMANN: I will be very honest. I came here to promote *The Emigrants*. I just finished *Cries and Whispers* with Ingmar. It is very sad. It's about someone who is dying of cancer. I've always done terribly sad women, mostly farmers. I know that producers when they hear about me must think, "Oh, no. She's not right for the part." I knew Charles Jarrott and he wanted me in this picture. Ross Hunter said, "No, she's sad." Then they said, "Oh, we would like you to do it. You could be happy. It's a musical." They also pay much more. He said, "Do you sing?" I said, "No." He said, "It doesn't matter." I thought it sounded fun. I am living in Beverly Hills. I always wanted to know how that would be. I have my family here. We have a swimming pool. That is the first part of the deal. The second part is that I wouldn't have done it if it had been *The Godfather* or something which I would really be against. I believe in the naive way of telling a story which I think many people need today. Maybe we all, deep down, dream of a place that is Shangri-La where people live in peace and in love. It is artistic in its way. It has Burt Bacharach. It has a very good cast: Charles Boyer, Sir John Gielgud, and many other people. I am very proud to be among them. I don't think that there is anything shameful about saying to people, in a naive way, that we can still hope for a Shangri-La. That's my excuse.

QUESTION: *How often do you get out here to do films in Hollywood?*
ULLMANN: I've already told you my problem with the producers. I've gotten several offers from directors and some of them I didn't want to do. Others stranded on the producer. In a way it is very good to be with Ingmar Bergman but you also get a reputation of being neurotic and bad looking and all of that. I have worked some, but I am not overwhelmed.

QUESTION: *As an actress, what do you look for when a project is presented to you?*
ULLMANN: The director.

QUESTION: *The director more than the script?*
ULLMANN: Well, if he's a good director, he wouldn't accept a bad script. Of course, I do look at the script. I don't want to be naked and I don't want to be in any violent pictures. I've done that once. But if it is a good director whom you respect, he usually offers you the kind of script that you would like to do.

QUESTION: *The one violent film that you did was in English, wasn't it?*
ULLMANN: Yes. To be honest I did two films. Both of them have the same name. One of them is called *Visitors of the Night* and the other one is called *The Night Visitor*. I am not very proud of either of them.

QUESTION: *Two different films?*
ULLMANN: Yes. One of them with Terence Young and the other with Laslo Benedek. I like him very much as a director.

QUESTION: *The one with Per Oscarson, how do you feel about that?*
ULLMANN: I haven't seen it, but I am not very proud of it.

QUESTION: *Where was it shot?*
ULLMANN: It was shot in Denmark but I have not seen it. I understand that in its way, it is a thrilling picture. But I am not sure how much

violence we should show on the screen nowadays. I saw *The Godfather* the other day and I hated it. I am shocked that the critics and everybody says that it is so marvelous. The audience applauded when the more fantastic murders were shown. I don't like that. I don't see the purpose.

QUESTION: *Have you seen any of the work of Sam Peckinpah?*
ULLMANN: No, but I have heard of him.

QUESTION: *I was just curious if you could compare the violence in Peckinpah's films with Francis Ford Coppola's violence.*
ULLMANN: On the other hand, I have seen Kubrick's last picture, *A Clockwork Orange*, and there I think the violence is done in a very artistic way. He wants to tell you something, and to me I think it is a masterpiece. It is not violence for violence's sake, violence for having fun. When the audience is applauding, I think it is terrible. It is frightening.

RESPONSE: *Perhaps that is what you didn't like about* The Godfather. *He didn't tell you anything new about violence. He just showed you violence.*
ULLMANN: Kubrick's film was made with artistry and with feeling. I had the same feeling with the book. I was terribly entertained.

QUESTION: *There is a kind of ensemble company about Bergman. How much do the actors feed into him in the preparation of the script? I am speaking of anything they do aside from improvisation and for the camera.*
ULLMANN: Nothing. We have nothing to do with the script. He is writing a script now which we are going to shoot in the fall. He just asks you, "Do you want to be in my next picture?"

QUESTION: *He doesn't show you the script at all?*
ULLMANN: Not before it is finished. Of course, you can suddenly say, "No," but I don't think that has happened.

QUESTION: *On* Cries and Whispers, *was the letter that you received beforehand the only preparation for the film?*
ULLMANN: But there were actually fifty pages, and we used the letter in the filming. He described his visions.

QUESTION: *Did everybody get the same letter?*
ULLMANN: Yes.

QUESTION: *Then was it all improvised?*
ULLMANN: Yes. But it was very clear. He said, "I see a room, a red room. There are three women dressed in white and they are moving slowly around." That is a scene. From there on he made the blocking.

QUESTION: *But the dialogue wasn't in the letter?*
ULLMANN: Very little. He said, "I feel that they are talking about love and about being afraid." But the dialogue was not blocked out.

QUESTION: *You people all know each other as you have been working together for a long time. How much of the real feelings that you have about each other are used by him in terms of realities in the scene? Does he make use of your own personal feelings about each other?*
ULLMANN: No. I don't think so.

QUESTION: *He just goes for the imaginary situation?*
ULLMANN: Yes.

QUESTION: *He does not get results from real relationships outside?*
ULLMANN: Bibi Andersson and I are close friends, but except in *Persona* we have not worked closely together. The same is true with Max von Sydow. Ingrid Thulin and I have no relationship with each other.

QUESTION: *So it's primarily the imaginary situation that you work on.*
ULLMANN: Yes, absolutely.

QUESTION: *What happens to you when you are making a film? Are you living together, like on the island?*
ULLMANN: We are forced to. In the summer this island has a big sand shore.

QUESTION: *Beach?*
ULLMANN: Yes, a beach. There are a lot of tourists there. Usually when he has made pictures there, he has rented all the small tourist houses.

Each crew member has a little tourist house. They bring their families. It's not that we live together. We all have individual lives apart from the set.

QUESTION: *On pictures like* Persona, *how many weeks before shooting started did you get the script? Also how long did you rehearse before the shooting started?*

ULLMANN: We did not rehearse at all. We got the script, actually, because he had been very sick. They did not know if they were going to make the picture at all. They just asked Bibi Andersson and me to be free for the summer, and they would pay us something if the picture didn't come off. Then he finished the script and it was decided very shortly before, three weeks before, that they would make the picture. Then we had one meeting at Bibi Andersson's house where he told us some of his visions about the script. That was all done before we started. To me it was very difficult because I didn't know him before. I was terribly shy and frightened because he was sort of a god to me.

QUESTION: *So, in fact, you rehearsed with the technical crew before the shooting started. Was it just before he shot?*

ULLMANN: Just before each shot. He never has rehearsals before the actual shooting starts.

QUESTION: *That scene in which you created a great mood where you were humming when you went out in the country in that particular picture, was that the first take? You were peeling mushrooms and humming.*

ULLMANN: He got the idea of that actual situation when we were sitting in between takes with our big hats. We were humming. He said, "This is wonderful. It looks relaxed. I want this in the picture." So that was perhaps the only time when he used a personal relationship.

QUESTION: *The scene where he uses the two cameras, how long did you rehearse before the first take?*

ULLMANN: Not very much. It was a very long dialogue for Bibi Andersson. He doesn't believe in rehearsing long dialogues.

QUESTION: *Were you surprised to see the ending of the film?*

ULLMANN: Of *Persona?* Yes, very much. Very much of that picture happened at the cutting table. This scene was not in the script. Also the scene where the two faces come together, we did not know about that either. He took us once to the cutting room. We hadn't heard about this. He said, "I want you to watch something." We saw this strange face. I thought, "Oh, God. Bibi is fantastic. She looks completely neurotic." At the same time, Bibi thought, "How did Liv do it?" Suddenly we saw that it was half of each. It was really frightening. That was also an idea that he had thought of during the shooting.

QUESTION: *Were the effects, the picture of the film breaking, and the excerpt from the early Swedish comedy in the script?*
ULLMANN: No.

QUESTION: *He put them in later?*
ULLMANN: Yes. It might have been in his special script, however. But it was not in ours.

QUESTION: *His special script?*
ULLMANN: Yes, he sometimes does that.

QUESTION: *What is his special script?*
ULLMANN: It is more or less a technical script between him and Sven Nykvist, his photographer.

QUESTION: *What kind of dialogue does he carry on with Nykvist?*
ULLMANN: Not very much. They have worked together for a long time. Sven Nykvist is not verbal at all. They sort of feel each other. Nykvist knows what Ingmar wants. They sort of go along touching each other. I can't really describe it. It's the way friends work when they know each other very well. You don't have to speak very much.

QUESTION: *When does Bergman bring Nykvist into a production? Will he show him the script earlier than the actors?*
ULLMANN: Not that I know of. I think we all get it at the same time. They prepare together. They experiment a lot with colors and lights. On this last picture with the natural light from the windows, they lived in this castle for three weeks and experimented. They woke up very early in the morning and took pictures.

QUESTION: *This was before the shooting started?*
ULLMANN: Yes.

QUESTION: *Do you look at your own dailies?*
ULLMANN: Not with him. He says that he doesn't mind, but I think that he would mind. Also, I trust him. Mostly though I don't watch them. If I am working with a director that I am not sure of then I would like to look at them. But mostly it is better not to do it.

QUESTION: *When you do watch the dailies what do you look for?*
ULLMANN: Well, I don't like to do it if it is a good director. If you feel that he has gotten the best that you can give him, then you would rather have the fantasy that that is what you gave. It is always a disappointment to see the dailies. What you think you expressed is not there. There is something else there. When you don't trust the director, however, you have to go to see if he is leading you in the right way. You have to see if he is making you do too much or too little. You have to see if he is photographing it well.

QUESTION: *Are you looking at the dailies on* Lost Horizon?
ULLMANN: There I am supposed to be beautiful and loving and I think I will trust him.

QUESTION: *What is the part that you are playing in* Lost Horizon?
ULLMANN: I play the woman that Peter Finch finds in Shangri-La and he falls in love with. It's a love story. Also, she is wonderful with children. She is really a part of Shangri-La.

QUESTION: *She comes to the valley?*
ULLMANN: No, she lives there and she never wants to leave.

QUESTION: *Did you see the original version?*
ULLMANN: No.

QUESTION: *Perhaps you can tell us a little bit about some of the techniques you employ as an actress. Do you function as an actress using the techniques of Stanislavsky? If you don't use his techniques, then what are some of the ways in which you approach a particular role? What is your background and training as an actress?*

ULLMANN: Well, I went to a theater school in England. I am a stage actress primarily. Everyone has read Stanislavsky and I believe that he is a good help for an actor. To be an actor today I think that you have to use your experience in life. You have to use your psychological feelings about people. I wouldn't say that I know what sort of an actress I am or what kind of school I belong to. I try to portray a character the way I see it. I try to be as human as I can. I feel that it is very important that what you do is human. You want people to be able to recognize what you are doing, if not in themselves, then in somebody on the street.

QUESTION: *How did you prepare for the role in* Persona *where you didn't have dialogue to either play with or against?*

ULLMANN: That was a script that I had to read many times. It was very difficult for me because I was twenty-four at the time. I had experienced a lot which I didn't know about then. The way that I prepared was to read the script many times, to try to block it into sections. I would try to think, "This is the section where this is happening to her, and now he goes a little further with this section." That is the way that I very often work. I divide the manuscript into sections which always makes you know where you are at the shooting.

QUESTION: *Perhaps we can talk about some specific scenes and what you tried to present within the context of a certain scene. For instance, there is a dialogue in* The Shame *where you and Max von Sydow are drinking a bottle of wine and are having a conversation about having a child. What specifically within the context of the character did you go for and how did you go for it?*

ULLMANN: To me it was the last time when these people were happy. It was the last time when they had a sort of hope in their lives. What was important for me to express in that scene was love for him. Whatever the character said and did there was done primarily to express that. Also I tried to take out of it everything which was also a part of her character, but which would come later on in the picture. But if you didn't know this about her, I feel that the tragedy that these people would never have hope again in life wouldn't be so big in them, if you didn't know that they had love and happiness and hope in them at one time.

QUESTION: *There was an interesting intoxication about the scene. How did you approach the particular feeling in this scene?*
ULLMANN: I don't know. Sometimes it is a help when a scene says that you are in a specific mood. That takes you more or less away from the way that you would have reacted in that particular situation. You have a little background if you know that "here I am a little drunk" or "here I am a little afraid." Even if this isn't supposed to show too much, all the time it is in the background and it is sort of a pillar which helps you to act out the scene.

QUESTION: *Have you worked in very many stage productions and in any directed by Bergman?*
ULLMANN: Yes. I worked six years in Norway. I am Norwegian so I wanted to work on the stage in Norway. I worked with Bergman in *Peer Gynt.*

QUESTION: *His directing must be very different.*
ULLMANN: Yes, it is. There he speaks much more. He really speaks. He is fantastic. You should meet him. He is a verbal genius. The actors in Norway just adore him. The biggest actors will take small parts just to work with him. I learned more from that stage play than I ever learned anywhere.

QUESTION: *Which do you enjoy more, acting on the stage or acting in film?*
ULLMANN: I used to say acting on the stage, because that is where I belong. But I think I have been fortunate to work with very good directors in pictures. The directors in theater in Norway are not very good. So in a way working in film has been more fun.

QUESTION: *Do you find that you employ different techniques acting in film than acting for stage?*
ULLMANN: Yes. That is also something that I now like about pictures. What I feel I want to express is something human, something natural.

On the stage when you play the classics, sometimes you feel that there is a big gap between you and the audience. Everything has to be so much bigger, so much farther from life. This is even true if what you say is for people today.

QUESTION: *What is the longest run that you have ever been in?*
ULLMANN: We play repertory theater at the National Theater where I am so that would be a year. But then you don't play every day.

QUESTION: *When you are shooting a movie and you have a very intense scene and the sun goes in and you have to wait an hour or an hour and a half, how do you maintain your intensity?*
ULLMANN: By trying to relax completely. I may try to read something.

QUESTION: *So you don't think about it? What you are saying is that you try to get away from it?*
ULLMANN: Yes, I try to get away from it if the sun is apparently to be away from one hour. It will ruin everything if you sit and concentrate. Then you will use up the spirit. The best thing is to really relax with something which doesn't demand anything. You could play cards or something like that.

QUESTION: *Then how do you trigger yourself to get back into that situation again? Would this be true even with a change of setup?*
ULLMANN: I think of it in this way. If you have worked with it and thought it out at home the way you would like to do it and you have concentrated on it, I feel that it stays with you.

QUESTION: *So in taking time off, you can do that?*
ULLMANN: Yes and that is part of the fun of it. Of course, sometimes it doesn't work. When they retake and retake and something happens all the time, then suddenly it's dead and gone and you never get it.

QUESTION: *In terms of takes what is the best take for you? A first take? A second take? A twelfth take?*
ULLMANN: If I know my lines, it would be the first take.

QUESTION: *Do you find that your reactions diminish from that point on?*

ULLMANN: Yes, that is what I feel.

QUESTION: *How much preparation do you do on your own, before the film begins? How much reading do you do and how much thinking?*

ULLMANN: It depends upon the script. In the film *The Emigrants*, my character is taken from the time when she is seventeen until the time she dies at the age of forty-five. At that time she was quite old because she had worked so hard and had had so many children. You really have to block it out, especially in terms of the aging and what happened to her. I had to know about her body and everything. Every day I knew just where I was. One day I was seventeen and the next day I was forty-five. You really have to know your script. You have to know how many children you have and what has happened before.

QUESTION: *How do you go about that? Do you talk to yourself and look at yourself in a mirror?*

ULLMANN: No, never. That is too embarrassing. I read the script and I try to think it out. I don't try out things. That's not good.

QUESTION: *You seem to be a very sensitive person. I was wondering if in the ensemble with Bergman, if everybody is pretty much that way?*

ULLMANN: Yes, maybe.

QUESTION: *What kind of a relationship do you have with Sven Nykvist as well as with the rest of the ensemble?*

ULLMANN: We are very good friends. We have worked together on so many pictures, also apart from Ingmar. We are very good friends. Sven Nykvist is very timid and shy.

QUESTION: *Is he also sensitive?*

ULLMANN: Yes, he is very sensitive but he never comes out with it. He is a perfectionist. On one picture he and Ingmar were looking at the daily rushes and he had done something wrong with the light. Ingmar had said that he should not have used one of the lights and Nykvist had insisted. Ingmar was right and when they saw the rushes he was very angry because they had to shoot it once more. Ingmar told Nykvist that he was an idiot. Nykvist was so timid that he didn't say a word.

QUESTION: *I thought that* The Shame *was one of the finest anti-war films ever made.*
ULLMANN: I felt very much that it was an anti-war picture. I thought that I was doing something that was very important. That is the difficult thing with acting today. You sometimes feel that it is really stupid. But in *The Shame* I felt that I was doing something which was important for human beings.

QUESTION: *Bergman and the other actors felt this way too?*
ULLMANN: Yes. I think that everybody felt a part of it. I am very sorry that in Sweden they were very much against the picture, especially the left wing. They felt that he didn't take sides. That is what the picture was all about: You can't take sides.

QUESTION: *Do you find it easier or more difficult to approach roles that are not contemporary? This would include costume dramas or classical parts.*
ULLMANN: I would actually prefer the modern people, the ordinary people. But I have mostly done costumes. In the theater it has been only costume parts and in pictures too. I perfer to do modern things.

QUESTION: *Why?*
ULLMANN: Again those parts are closer to what I want to express. I want to make contact and I feel that the cinema is one of the few places left where people can meet and be together. Between the screen and the audience I feel that there can still be a contact. They can speak and understand each other. The audience can go out from there and maybe have found a new approach to life. I think that communication between people is so little.

QUESTION: *Do you enjoy seeing your finished films with an audience? Do you ever go and see your films to see the audience's response?*
ULLMANN: Not very often. I have done it once or twice if it has been a festival. But it's terrible. If somebody turns a little you think, "Oh, they're bored." It's really terrible. I don't like to do that.

QUESTION: *Did you shoot the scenes of* The Emigrants *in sequence?*
ULLMANN: No, we jumped all the time.

QUESTION: *But you traveled didn't you?*
ULLMANN: Yes. We started the principal shooting in Sweden. We were in America for two months and then went back. In America we shot things from their first years in America and twenty years later. We had great difficulties because she gets children all the time. She had nine children in the end. I had to know the script to know if I was five months pregnant or six months pregnant and maybe I already had three children.

QUESTION: *Did you ever have the experience in a scene when you wanted to be moved or you wanted something to happen and it didn't happen? How do you deal with something like that when the situation itself doesn't move you? Usually do you find that it always does?*
ULLMANN: No, it doesn't always. It's terrible because there really is little that you can actually do, except use your training as an actor to try to express what you would feel if you were moved by it.

QUESTION: *Is that the way you approach it? If it's not there, you try to behave as if it is there?*
ULLMANN: Yes.

QUESTION: *And then it will usually come?*
ULLMANN: Sometimes it does. But other times it looks fake. When the camera is close to your face, it really shows what is fake and what is not.

RESPONSE: *Hopefully the director sees that too.*
ULLMANN: Hopefully, yes. That is why you have to go and see the rushes if it is a bad director. He doesn't always recognize these things.

QUESTION: *Have you ever told a director that you don't think that you made the right decision?*
ULLMANN: Yes. Sometimes he feels like "she won't get it." He will say, "It's OK. We'll keep that." Then he will do it a week later. Sometimes if he is a bad director, he will say, "It's good enough," and he will keep it in the film.

QUESTION: *With Bergman, is it rare that you have to mention that you don't think you had a good take?*

ULLMANN: Oh no. We mention it very much there because we trust him so much. He will listen. What he will do, because he is a good director, is that he will change the blocking of the scene. He feels that if the actor can't express it or doesn't know how to, if it is an actor who knows his job, then it might be something wrong with the blocking. Maybe you should be standing instead of sitting. Very often he is right. Very often a change of scene helps you to get the feeling that you didn't have.

QUESTION: *Which Bergman film did you enjoy working in the most? Do you have a preference?*

ULLMANN: I think *The Shame* meant most to me. *Cries and Whispers* I also thought was very good.

QUESTION: *Do you see the ones that you are not in?*

ULLMANN: I have seen all of them.

QUESTION: *Did you see* The Touch?

ULLMANN: Yes.

QUESTION: *Did you talk to Bergman about what you thought of it?*

ULLMANN: Yes.

QUESTION: *Is there a certain charisma about Bergman within the ensemble of actors? Do they put him on a certain level because of the aura about him, even though they know him very well?*

ULLMANN: Yes. There is something about him. This is not always in private. In private he is very amusing. But there is something about him. It's magic. There is something when he is sitting by the camera. You feel that you are a part of something. I can't really explain it very well. But he has an aura about him. It's his eyes and his ears. You know there is something there.

QUESTION: *Are you nervous when you work with him? Are you always trying to outdo yourself?*

ULLMANN: No, I feel relaxed. I know that he will help and he will know what I am trying to express. If I don't do it, then I know that he will help me. He will never say that I am phoney or bad. He has a respect for actors and for everybody. A bad director very often doesn't have that respect.

QUESTION: *Have you ever played Hedda Gabler?*
ULLMANN: No, I haven't. But I would like to some day. I would love that.

QUESTION: *Do you know why he decided to do an English version of* Hedda Gabler*?*
ULLMANN: I think that he certainly wanted to try to go outside of Sweden and do something. He admires Maggie Smith and I know that Laurence Olivier had written to him many times to try to get him to come over.

QUESTION: *Are you tempted to do anything else besides acting? Do you think that acting will meet all of your challenges and expectations?*
ULLMANN: I would like to write. When I write I feel that I am . . .

QUESTION: *More at ease?*
ULLMANN: No, not more at ease. I feel I give it more time. I give it every time of my life. With acting I want to be proud of it and I like the day to end. But when I write I feel that I can go on.

QUESTION: *What do you write when you write?*
ULLMANN: I write what I feel about different things. When I am here I write about Hollywood and my approach to life. I have written to some newspapers, and I am trying to write a book about what I feel like being a human being today. I am not a good writer. I am not saying that. I just feel that it is a fun way of expressing myself.

QUESTION: *Have you ever written any short stories or scripts?*
ULLMANN: No, I've only written essays.

QUESTION: *Do you feel that there is a difference between acting and writing, in the sense that with acting you are forced to act at the moment that the camera rolls? When you write, you are free to write when the inspiration comes to you. Do you feel that freedom?*

ULLMANN: Yes, I feel it is a wonderful freedom. At the same time it is more difficult. There is nobody there to really push you to do it. If you are lazy, then you may not do it as much as you should.

QUESTION: *You said before that you don't think that you will be writing a screenplay. Can you tell us why you feel that way?*

ULLMANN: I don't know how to do that sort of writing.

QUESTION: *If you looked at some scripts and gained a familiarity of style and format, would you then attempt to write a screenplay?*

ULLMANN: No, I don't think so. My way of writing is more reactions to things. I describe things more than developing persons from the beginning to the end.

QUESTION: *Will you elaborate more on how Bergman helps you when you are having trouble with a scene? Also what do you look for from a director? When the scene's not working he might change the blocking. Is there something else that he might do?*

ULLMANN: He really sees what I am trying to express, even if I am doing it very badly. He can say, "I see what you are trying to do and you are not doing it now. What if you do this?" He will give you a different blocking.

QUESTION: *A piece of physical action will help you?*

ULLMANN: But it won't help if he starts to say, "You are thinking this and this and this. Count to three and then you can start." Then that doesn't help completely. But if he in a relaxed way says, "Why don't you try and walk when you do this? Drink your coffee first and then speak." It's like you are a child. He helps you to do the right thing without telling you why he is doing it.

QUESTION: *What about discussions or analysis of the character motivations or what the character is feeling? Do you get into that kind of discussion with Bergman?*

ULLMANN: Of course, we do it a little but not too much. He hates that. He feels that you can discuss away your fantasy. I feel that he is right.

I would hate to work with actors where you had to sit down and talk about the background of the character. Then I would feel phoney.

QUESTION: *But don't you do that yourself? Don't you conjure up an imaginary background for the character you are portraying?*
ULLMANN: No.

QUESTION: *You don't?*
ULLMANN: Maybe I do subconsciously, but I try to act out what is in the script. I try to capture what sort of a person it is.

QUESTION: *Then you don't verbalize it at all?*
ULLMANN: No.

QUESTION: *When you are considering the development of the character, do you visualize the character in your mind?*
ULLMANN: Yes, I think I do.

QUESTION: *Do you also feel the emotions?*
ULLMANN: Yes. Sometimes I want to do it immediately, if it is something that is very tempting to act. The first time that you read the script you can see how you will do some scenes.

QUESTION: *Are you conscious of an improvement in your ability to portray a character since you started acting? Do you feel that it is much easier for you to get into another person or into a situation? Have you seen things that have made you able to do that?*
ULLMANN: Yes, and I know quick technical ways of doing it. I have also had a greater experience in acting and a greater experience in life. I am also better on concentrating, which is very important. In films there is such a small amount of time when you must be there. If you can't concentrate then, it is lost.

QUESTION: *What is an example of one of your quick technical ways?*
ULLMANN: There is a way that I have learned now that I can very easily do something very coldly which would look real. When I was younger I would struggle very much because I used to think that I needed the tears.

In *The Passion of Anna* where she is telling her story, there is just one close-up of that. He did it first in five or six scenes. I did not know how to do it. Then he said, "We'll try a close-up." I knew what to do then by using my face. Ingmar has worked so much with close-ups. I knew certain things that I could do with my face which would express certain things. I knew how to look in the camera so I would look as though I was expressing certain things. Because of that experience I found that with the close-up I could express more quickly something that I couldn't express in four or five different scenes when I walked around the room and showed my teeth and tried everything. Here I just used my face and it was right.

QUESTION: *Does Bergman talk to you while the camera is running?*
ULLMANN: Sometimes. In that scene, which runs for many minutes, in the middle of it he said, "Start all over again." He didn't want to cut. He felt the emotion was coming. We started over again immediately.

QUESTION: *Does he cover a master and then cover the same thing in close-ups?*
ULLMANN: Sometimes, but not always.

QUESTION: *Do you have any favorite writers that you enjoy reading?*
ULLMANN: Yes. Graham Greene. I don't know what to say would be my favorite. I love to read, and I'm not very selective.

QUESTION: *How do you feel about the younger Swedish directors such as Bo Widerberg?*
ULLMANN: I have not seen his picture.

RESPONSE: *It's fantastic.*
ULLMANN: Yes, I hear that it is very good. They have great talent in Sweden.

QUESTION: *Why is it that you have never worked with Bo Widerberg?*
ULLMANN: Well, he has never offered me anything, and he is also against Ingmar.

QUESTION: *Why is he against Bergman? Is it a difference in philosophy?*
ULLMANN: I don't know. Bo Widerberg is very, very talented. He makes wonderful pictures, but he is very ungenerous to other people

who make pictures. He doesn't like most of the established films. He thinks they are fake. I think he is very ungenerous.

QUESTION: *Moving from close ensemble filmmaking of Bergman to Ross Hunter and Columbia Pictures. The last bastions of Hollywood production must have been quite a change for you. How have you reacted to the scale of the production?*

ULLMANN: It is bigger. I have never seen a producer like Ross Hunter. Mostly the producers don't appear in Sweden, and he is there all the time. He is very happy. He is like a boy. He is childishly in love with this project. That is very inspiring. I think we are most organized in a way. If it's to start at a certain time, then it starts. If you have to be there at a certain time, then everyone is there on time. Here, the people come too late, and sometimes they don't even come at all.

QUESTION: *When you say "we" are you talking about Sweden? In Sweden, is it more organized than it is here?*

ULLMANN: Yes. I feel that it is more organized. So many people here are really doing the same thing and they don't really communicate.

QUESTION: *Have you found it harder or easier to act in that setting? Of course, this is a very different picture than what you have done before.*

ULLMANN: I'm not sure that I know how to answer that. If it was something very serious dramatically, then I would find it harder. But since it is this kind of picture, I find it to be easier. They serve you all the time.

QUESTION: *When you say "they serve you," are you talking about the crew and the director?*

ULLMANN: Yes. It's different.

QUESTION: *Do you feel like a star?*

ULLMANN: Well, yes. You get some strange serving which you are not used to. If you are dressed in beautiful clothes and look beautiful, it's much easier. But in a way you feel a little homeless. I am more happy at home. But then most of the crew here is European so it really shouldn't be that different.

QUESTION: *If you could make just one more film, and you would make no more films after that, and you couldn't make that film with Bergman, what director would you choose to make that picture with?*

ULLMANN: I was very taken with Stanley Kubrick's picture. I was horrified but I think he is a sort of genius. He takes out from the actors something which is different.

QUESTION: *Have you ever written to him to say that you would like to do a picture with him?*

ULLMANN: No.

QUESTION: *Have you ever met him personally?*

ULLMANN: No, and I haven't seen his other pictures. This is the only one that I have seen. I can't say why I liked this one so much, because I really didn't like it. You can dislike something and it can still get to you. It was a masterpiece. Actually, I have seen one of his other pictures. I saw *Dr. Strangelove.*

QUESTION: *What is it that is different that you feel he gets out of his actors? Let me start by asking: Did you see Malcom McDowell in* If?

ULLMANN: Yes. He is not the same person and still he is the same person. Just the first shot when he was sitting there with this eye. This boy has an expression which is not ordinary. It's not his own experience. I expressed myself badly. It is something strange in the picture. It is different. He is a thinker, Kubrick is.

QUESTION: *I would be curious to know how Kubrick would direct an actress and how he would handle a woman's role. In most of his films, the women's roles are either very small or very cold or very remote. This is opposed to Bergman who understands women.*

ULLMANN: Kubrick hates women. I am sure. But he can make an interesting part for a woman and I would love to do it.

QUESTION: *In* The Emigrants, *was the dialogue an old-fashioned sort of speech in Swedish? How did you get yourself into that era? Did you do research?*

ULLMANN: Oh yes. I especially had to do that because I am Norwegian. This was a Swedish picture where they also spoke Swedish dialect. I had to study and learn that dialect.

QUESTION: *Was that dialect different from modern day Swedish?*
ULLMANN: Yes. It was difficult for everybody actually. All of us had to study. It is a strange sort of language. I hear that they want to dub it here in America. Then the whole point will go away. These people came to America and they didn't know how to express themselves. If they speak English, then it misses the whole point.

QUESTION: *Are there linguistic differences between Norwegian and Swedish? Is it easy for you to work in Swedish?*
ULLMANN: It is a little difficult. They are too close in a way. It's like Italian and Spanish. It's easier in a way to work in a completely different language. I speak my own language sort of. It's not really good Swedish. It's with an accent.

QUESTION: *Was your theater school in England?*
ULLMANN: Yes.

RESPONSE: *In* The Night Visitor *you came off speaking the most natural English of anyone.*
ULLMANN: Really? Max von Sydow speaks very good English.

RESPONSE: *It seemed more real to me.*
ULLMANN: Well, that's interesting. I like to act in a different language. I did a picture in England called *Joan*. It was a very verbal picture. I think it would have been much more difficult for me to do that in Swedish or in Norwegian than it was for me in English. I think it takes more away from myself and my ordinary life to go into another language.

QUESTION: Lost Horizon *is obviously in English. Have you been trying to avoid your accent? Are you speaking stylized English?*
ULLMANN: They don't mind. They don't like extremes. But they don't mind a little accent which shows that I am not from here. They don't like heavy accents. I have to work on it.

QUESTION: *Have they written anything into the script which says that you are a descendent of Scandinavian parents?*

ULLMANN: Yes, they say that I came there with my mother and my father when I was two years old. But then, of course, I shouldn't speak with an accent. No, they don't say anything.

QUESTION: *Are you planning to do your own singing?*

ULLMANN: I don't know, but apparently nobody does their own singing.

QUESTION: *What kinds of things did you feel you learned from the acting school in England which have been particularly valuable to you?*

ULLMANN: They trained you in reading Shakespeare. I learned verse speaking. That is a very difficult thing on the stage, because that is something which is in between you and the character and the audience. When you are trying to express a normal feeling and you have to express ten words more because of the long verse, then it is very good to have technical training. You have to know how to speak those verses.

QUESTION: *What is the women's movement like in Sweden and Norway?*

ULLMANN: In Sweden I think the women have felt liberated for a very long time. In Norway this is not true so much. We are about thirty years behind. But Norway did something fantastic. There is the possibility when you vote for the new government that you can take off the names on the top and write your own name. The women in Norway decided secretly that they wanted to have women in the government and into the local things. All of the women took away the men's names and put down women's names. So, for the first time in the history of Norway, in almost every big city there is a majority of women in the government. You know, it came as a surprise. Nobody knew. The voting happened and the next day the newspapers were full of it. They don't know how it happened. The women had just spoken to each other secretly. Nobody knew that it was so well organized. It's a sensation.

QUESTION: *So there is no official women's liberation organization?*

ULLMANN: No. There were the groups from the Norwegian Women's Liberation and there were also groups from the farming women. I think it is much more healthy. It was every kind of woman.

QUESTION: *Are the men accepting this? Do they like it?*
ULLMANN: No, they don't like it. But women have to prove that they can do something too.

QUESTION: *Do you have any children?*
ULLMANN: I have a daughter.

QUESTION: *How does being an actress interfere with you being a mother and a wife? Does being an actress interfere in your personal life?*
ULLMANN: I am a working mother. Of course, then you are not together as much with your children as if you were home. I think it may be healthy. I couldn't be with my child all day. I wouldn't know what to play with her all day. But I feel that it is very important that you have a normal life, a private life. To me, that is more important than my job. I think it is from your normal life and your normal relationships that you create and work in any job that you have. I try to make it as normal as possible.

QUESTION: *Does it interfere if you are more well known than your husband? Does it affect your married life?*
ULLMANN: Once he was more well known than I was, and before that I was married to a psychiatrist. Now I am the godmother to his child in his marriage now.

QUESTION: *Norway has never produced any directors whose films have been seen in the rest of the world. What is your explanation for that?*
ULLMANN: I don't really know. It is very strange. The government very easily gives you money for a script. Almost anybody can go with a script and they can be lent money from the government, which they don't have to pay back if the film is a failure. But there is no real great talent there who the younger people can learn from. In Sweden for such a long time there have been famous names associated with filmmaking. I have wondered why this is so myself. There are no good directors in Norway.

QUESTION: *Are there any women directors either in Norway or Sweden?*
ULLMANN: We do have one in Norway. She is quite good.

QUESTION: *What is her name?*
ULLMANN: Anja Breien.

QUESTION: *Has she been making films recently?*
ULLMANN: She has made two pictures, one which was shown in
Cannes last year. I think it was shown outside of the competition.
Many nice remarks were made about her film but it is not an inter-
national picture.

QUESTION: *Do you know what film she has made recently?*
ULLMANN: *Rape.* It sounds different in English. What she means is
rape by the government. It is a boy who is taken to prison and is treated
unjustly by the system.

QUESTION: *Isn't it strange that in Sweden the women have more priviledges
than women in other countries, and yet you don't find them taking positions
as directors?*
ULLMANN: But you see, I think many women want to sit home. They
want to be married and have alimonies. I think that absolutely in
America they should work for themselves. I have the feeling that a great
part of this liberation is attacking the man. I think that we must find
out what we want. I don't think you can do this by attacking the other
sex. By saying, "He is no good," will it be any better?

QUESTION: *Could you tell us something about the financial crisis that was
so bad in Sweden a year ago? Could you tell us about the change that happened with the new president of the Svenska Filminstitutet? Are things better
now or worse?*
ULLMANN: I think that things are worse. I think that Harry Schein
who was president was a good man. The quality hasn't been better now.

QUESTION: *Is it easier or harder for young Swedish directors to get money
from the film institute?*
ULLMANN: Maybe it is easier, but that can also be the death of
Sweden's film institute. Nobody looks at those movies because many of
them are not talented film people. They are talented politicians.

QUESTION: *How big is the film industry in Norway? Are there films made in Norway for Norwegians or do they mostly watch American and Swedish films?*

ULLMANN: We make movies. We have also started to co-produce with Americans. Charlton Heston is there making a picture right now. They have very good technical equipment, very good. What they really lack is great talent. I think that by co-producing maybe they can establish themselves as a film country. They can learn from the people who come because they can make it so much cheaper there.

QUESTION: *The Norwegians only make five pictures a year. Where do the bulk of their pictures come from? From the United States? From Sweden?*

ULLMANN: I would say that half come from the United States and the rest come from England and France and Italy and Sweden.

QUESTION: *Did you see any of Susan Sontag's films? I was wondering how the Swedish respond to her?*

ULLMANN: They didn't see them at all. They got very bad reviews.

QUESTION: *How about Mai Zetterling's film* Loving Couples *which used most of Bergman's company? Could you tell me how Swedish people reacted to that and how you personally felt about it?*

ULLMANN: I actually liked *Loving Couples*. I didn't like the film she made later. The critics were quite favorable to her and so was the audience in Sweden. But later it was much more obvious that she took too many ideas from other people. She wasn't creating on her own. I liked *Loving Couples*.

QUESTION: *Do you think that it is a case with actors and actresses who go to directing, that they tend to utilize more experiences from other people rather than their own experiences?*

ULLMANN: That could be, but she wrote it. I don't think she is a writer. I think she is very talented as a film director.

QUESTION: *Is this the first time that you have been in a discussion session in the United States?*

ULLMANN: Yes.

QUESTION: *Do you think that the people of this country, as a whole, pry into people's private life too deeply?*
ULLMANN: I haven't felt that these were personal questions.

QUESTION: *I mean that you as an actress and we as people who want to know you, do we go too far?*
ULLMANN: No, I don't have that feeling.

QUESTION: *Do you have that feeling with certain directors?*
ULLMANN: No, I wouldn't say that. There is always one point where you have to go into each other a little bit. You have to get to know each other to be able to work together. Even in a discussion like this, I think it is nicer if people can be open with each other when they meet. I don't think it is prying. I think it is communication.

QUESTION: *Do you think there is more of a lack of communication between people of this country than there is between people in Sweden?*
ULLMANN: It is difficult for me to say, because I don't know too many people here, and I have met some people here whom I think are not like the rest of them. I find it very difficult to communicate with women who stay at home all day, for example. They seem to be very rich and are very high strung. I feel very awkward with them, even if I feel that they are very friendly and want to be very nice.

QUESTION: *If you were an American, what would you do as an actress to improve the world situation? What could you do?*
ULLMANN: I am not a politician, so I couldn't start going around. I am not verbal in politics. I really wouldn't know what to do. Whenever I was interviewed I would try to say what I meant. Hopefully, because I am an actress, some group of people would read what I said.

QUESTION: *Do you think a film like* The Shame *would have a greater influence than most films?*
ULLMANN: In my creative work, I would like to be in pictures like *The Shame*. Hopefully, films like that could influence people. I think it is very difficult. It is very difficult to know what to do as an individual in the world today.

QUESTION: *Isn't that the problem with women's lib? If women want to get into a position of power, they have to create an identity that was never there before.*
ULLMANN: Yes, you are right.

RESPONSE: *But that is very difficult. Women don't know how to do that. They don't want to take on a masculine role.*
ULLMANN: Yes, but there is where I think we do wrong. I don't think that we have to take a masculine role. We can take our own human role, what is good and bad in being feminine. We know things that they don't know.

RESPONSE: *Yes, but they have a whole way of communicating and relating and the whole verbal thing. Men on a political trip do this.*
ULLMANN: Listen to how they speak. Listen to politicians. They just speak. When I went to the gymnasium the boys would just speak. I am not saying that every man is speaking. I am sure that we have some sense, too. If we are not that verbal, then we have to train ourselves a little. We have things to say too. They are not that fantastic.

RESPONSE: *You may have very valid things to say but you have blond hair and blue eyes and you are sexy. They don't listen to what you are saying. They just look.*
ULLMANN: Do you really think that they don't listen to what you say?

RESPONSE: *It depends upon the man.*
ULLMANN: That is unfair to the men—that they are not intelligent.

RESPONSE: *I don't think that it's that they are not intelligent. It's a conditioned reflex. The same is true with Hollywood movies too.*
If you ask a man or a woman in the United States if they want a woman to be the Vice President, they will say, "No." This is something that I think is part of the system. Here we can't take off the men's names.
ULLMANN: So you are saying that it is very much an American problem rather than a European problem?

QUESTION: *That's what I would like to know. Here all these women are getting into positions of power in Norway. How are they relating to the people that they are representing?*

ULLMANN: I think that people listen to them. I never thought that people don't listen to a woman. I think that must be more an American problem.

QUESTION: *I think women have a lot more time in America. Many women are able to think more. There are many factors involved and time is one of them. I get the impression from certain Swedish films that this is also a part of Swedish life. In* The Emigrants *survival is so important. That doesn't happen to us today. Are people more free to consider who they are than they were in the past?*

ULLMANN: Yes, I think they are. I think that here in America they have even more free time. If I was in a house here in Beverly Hills with the machinery and everything, I wouldn't have to do anything. What do they do? I am not sure that they sit down and think. Everything is too perfect. You are not active. People when they had more to do during the day were also active. When you are active things go on in your head too.

QUESTION: *In terms of time, how much of the year do you work? How do you pace yourself? What do you do between films? Do you feel that you work too much and sort of exhaust yourself and your creative forces?*

ULLMANN: Yes. One shouldn't go from one picture to another. That is not good.

QUESTION: *Between films what do you do?*

ULLMANN: I write and I am with my friends. I don't like to do nothing for too long a time. I mean I don't like to go too long without a job.

QUESTION: *How many weeks of the year are you acting and active in your profession? Half of the year?*

ULLMANN: Oh, no. It varies. I would say that I do around two pictures and one stage play a year. That can differ as far as time is concerned. Two pictures and a stage play is good. Three months on each picture is half the year, and the theater is the other half of the year. That is what I am doing this year.

QUESTION: *So you are active in one or the other most all the time?*
ULLMANN: Yes. Sometimes I have one or two months in between. That is the ideal.

CONCLUSION: I think this is a good place to end. Thank you very much for coming up to talk with us.

Liv in London

JOAN JULIET BUCK/1972

IN LONDON TO FILM *The Abdication,* Liv Ullmann turns out to be a humorous, sunny soul. "Producers always think of me as Swedish Neurotic in Rags, until *Lost Horizon.* One very famous producer ran my films and said that, from the way I dressed, he could tell I'd never be a star. Well, I always played rag women and you never saw my legs, not for years. People thought there was something wrong with them."

She is wearing an elegant rust jersey pantsuit. "From this you think I know something about clothes? Well, I don't know anything. I got this at that shop in Los Angeles and it makes me look like I know."

Her daughter, Linn, runs in and asks, "What are you doing in my room?" Liv answers, "This is not your room and, anyway, I'm paying for it so leave us alone" in the firm tones of one who speaks to children as though they were adults. Hugs follow and Linn goes back to her room.

The phone rings. A doctor. "Oh, yes, the cancer," exclaims Ms. Ullmann, who then discusses cancer at length on the line. It turns out she had a sore throat. Cancer has nothing to do with it "but one must make sure," she says to the doctor.

"If I take that, will it be fattening? No? Good."

Having been assured that iron shots are not fattening, she sits down and sips at her non-fattening vodka. The costumes for *The Abdication* were made months ago and she is afraid a relaxed life and lots of food in the intervening time may have added bulges. "I should think more about it because I love food and get fat easily—but now for the film

From *Women's Wear Daily,* August 8, 1972. © 1972 by *Women's Wear Daily.* Reprinted by permission.

I have to care. I never went to the United States because of my figure and beauty. I mean I've just played Gene Hackman's mail order bride who turns out to be unattractive and almost past childbearing age, so it's not for my beauty I was chosen.

"I loved playing *Pope Joan* because how often does a woman get to be a pope and wear those robes and feel saintly? But I'd really like to do a modern love story to make women cry. And I want to play George Sand very badly. It's a project I'm working on now because I think it's better to be in on it from the beginning and not wait for your agent to turn up with *Lost Horizon*."

About this experience she can only say she enjoyed the shooting. "Ross Hunter was great fun. We thought we were doing the picture of the century and even now he's in Australia marveling about the film. For me it was good to see how that kind of film is made so I'll know every aspect of the business. We have all heard about Hollywood and if Sir John Gielgud could do it, so could I. But he claims he didn't know it was a musical."

She went to the United States for ten days to promote *The Emigrants*—"and prove I wasn't Neurotic Swedish. And when I was there I got *Lost Horizon* and *40 Carats*. The other movie I would have got anyway because I'm in rags in it, which is my type-casting. I'm ashamed about *Lost Horizon*, but I stayed in a big rented house in Hollywood and the film was full of famous actors and how could we know what it was going to be like? I had fun and now I'm paying for it."

Having been denied the simple vanities of costumes and makeup in the stark Bergman films she was delighted with the fripperies of *40 Carats* and says a good set of costumes can help greatly with a role.

"But I don't believe in this thing of becoming the character. Queen Christina is difficult and involved. The script is strange and I'm reading a lot about the period to prepare myself."

"I can't read novels while I'm working because I get too involved in them."

She feels guilty about enjoying her work so much. "It's one of the few jobs that you carry over from childhood, but you do learn your craft more craftily than a child."

The stay in the United States has marked her in certain ways. "How can you live in California and not believe in astrology? I can spot an

Aries, an Aquarius or a Cancer," she says, laughing. On a deeper level, her view of life is tinted by amusement, eagerness.

"I believe in a kind of destiny. You have a lot of choices. Breaking the pattern can be the most soul-saving thing. Sometimes it's like everyone getting involved in the same traffic accident. What I thought my life would be when I was eighteen? Well I thought I'd marry young, which I did and stay married, which I didn't. And have children, live faithfully and be in the Norwegian theater and lead a decent life."

The eyes sparkle wickedly at the word Decent.

"I felt life decides for you fortunately and positively. And then my life led me into a completely different kind of existence. I didn't think I'd be what I am now, but the only values that have changed are the ones that I would have outgrown anyway."

She will not discuss the Queen Christina part, but mentions Mme. Bovary and Isak Dinesen as characters she would eventually like to play.

"And I'd love to work with Eric Rohmer—he explores women thoroughly. He makes films the way people write books—the right way."

As for superstitions, she says, "I'm so much superstitious that if you ask me do I believe in God? I don't dare say no, in case he hears."

Garbo, Bergman and Now, Liv Ullmann

BOB LARDINE/1972

THERE'S THE SPRAWLING $300,000 house, and of course, the gleaming pool. There are also the rolling lawns and lush gardens; the exquisite Hawaiian lanai; the neat, well-stocked patio.

And sitting amidst this Beverly Hills splendor is Norway's (Liv) *Ullmann*, one of the world's finest actresses. Most film experts consider her a worthy successor to those other Scandinavian greats: Greta Garbo and Ingrid Bergman.

She's here to sing and dance in the $8 million movie musical, *Lost Horizon*, though admittedly she warbles off-key and is on the clumsy side. But her impeccable acting credentials convinced the director, Charles Jarrott, she could do anything.

Later this year, Liv (pronounced "leave") will be starring in *Forty Carats*, a solid-gold role that was supposedly craved by Liz Taylor, Joanne Woodward and Julie Christie.

With her foreign-made pictures (*The Emigrants, Pope Joan, The New Land, Cries and Whispers*) playing across the U.S., Liv's undoubtedly the hottest "new" actress around today. But instead of enjoying her unique status, Liv sulks and confesses she's uncomfortable in her gilt-edged surroundings.

"I'm easily ashamed by such excesses. If I lived here all the time, I'd be continually embarrassed by this big house, the luxurious cars and everything else. Nobody has these things in Norway. It's a strict socialist

From *New York Daily News*, September 10, 1972, p. 36+. © 1972 by *New York Daily News*, Reprinted by permission.

country, and no one is supposed to own so much. If I drove a big car, it would be impossible for me to be happy in Norway. My friends wouldn't like me any more. Of course, I have more than the average Norwegian woman—a house and a modest car. But everyone has that here."

Liv's made many friends here and ordinarily would be extremely happy except for the strong smell of money that pervades everything.

"Actors are grossly overpaid in America, and I think it can harm a performer if he's paid too much. As for Californians in general, I find them extremely friendly and generous. Maybe it doesn't come from the heart. I really don't care. Just so they smile. In Norway and Sweden, people are more honest—but they don't smile."

She confesses bewilderment over the superrich community in which she lives—Beverly Hills. "You never see anyone. Nobody in the streets. Nobody at the windows of houses. It is as though a lot of cars were living here, not people. Maybe the residents are trying to shut off life, trying to close their eyes to the real world. It's terrifying that people live in all this glory and don't enjoy it. Just this afternoon, for example, my daughter, Linn, was bicycling by the house. A policeman knocked on my door and warned me that I should take her inside. He said: 'There's always the chance that a man in a car might grab her.' "

The fears of Beverly Hills residents both fascinate and repel her. "I was driving through the town with a friend at about seven one night when we happened to see a man, wearing sunglasses, walking slowly through one of the streets. My friend immediately drove to the nearest police station and reported that a strange man was in the vicinity. I was shocked by what he did. I couldn't understand what was wrong with taking a walk in the evening. When you're in love, that can be a delightful experience."

In Norway, Liv found it relaxing and healthful to take long trips on foot. "On Sundays in particular, almost everyone hikes up the mountains. But I've abandoned walking in this town because no one else moves. Even when they have to go to the post office, they take the car. Now I've gotten into that bad habit—and it shows. I'm at least five pounds overweight (125), and I blame it all on non-exercise and Chinese food. I happen to be crazy about chow mein and those other delights. In Norway, they only have two Chinese restaurants and they're quite ordinary. They're all good here, and I eat Chinese food almost every time I go out."

Unlike most Norwegians, Liv is an inept skier. "I'm not the sporty type, not an outdoor girl. I'd rather curl up with a good biography than go out on a snowy slope."

This visit to California marks Liv's second trip to the West Coast. She was here a little more than a year ago to accept an honorary Academy Award for Swedish director Ingmar Bergman.

When the call came to return to Hollywood, Liv expressed amazement. "I couldn't understand why they chose me for *Lost Horizon*. I told them I wasn't a great singer. They said: 'We'll work it out.' And then I told them I was really very clumsy, especially on the dance floor. I never like to get up and dance because I'm so awkward. They said: 'Don't worry about it.' Finally, I told them that outside of having sung on stage in a Brecht play, I had never done a musical. All my experience has been with serious, dramatic works. They just said: 'You'll be fantastic.' "

Immediately after she landed in this country, producer Mike Frankovich signed her for *Forty Carats*. Again, Liv was flabbergasted.

"I thought that when Mike approached me for the movie he wanted me for the daughter role. After all, I figured I looked young. (She is thirty-two.) But just when I was about to tell him that I was too old for the part, Mike offered me the mother's part. The screen play is much more serious than the stage version, and I really feel close to the woman I'll portray."

Frankovich's desire to feature Liv in a movie is understandable. There are few directors in the world who wouldn't consider it a privilege to have her presence in a film. Not that she's the most beautiful actress around.

Her face looks as though a double-barrelled shotgun filled with freckles had hit it full blast. It's an honest face with unblinking, cold eyes. But it's a face that for some strange reason doesn't smile too often.

But gorgeous women are a glut on the show business market anyhow. Actresses like Liv are as rare as Eskimo chess grandmasters. Her performances in seven Ingmar Bergman pictures (*The Passion of Anna*, *Shame*, etc.) indicate the heights that the acting profession can attain.

"I've always appeared in sad, tragic stories on stage and screen," she says. "The switch to comedy and musical roles represents a fantastic change for me."

Liv is content just as long as a part tests her abilities. She has never wanted to be anything but an actress from as long back as she can remember. That happens to be age seven when she was living in of all places—New York City.

"I wasn't very charming as a child," she says. "But I always got attention. And I learned that the way to do it was through acting. Later, I discovered it was the way to make people laugh and cry—and I liked that."

Liv was born in Japan, where her father's civil engineering job had taken him. Her Norwegian parents fled to Canada when the war broke out, and then traveled to New York. Liv's dad died in the city, whereupon her mother took the youngster to Trondhagen, Norway's third largest city.

"The only thing I can recall about my childhood years in New York is the Statue of Liberty," says Liv.

In Norway, she dutifully attended school and upon graduation trekked to London to study dramatics for a year. Liv's relentless pursuit of acting perfection had officially begun.

There was a tough three-year grind of repertory, then a stint with the subsidized Norwegian National Theatre. Confident and ambitious, Liv flew to Sweden for a shot at their superior brand of movie-making. She was determined that nothing would interfere with her career—and nothing did, including her marriage to psychiatrist Gappe Stang when she turned twenty.

And then one day in Stockholm, Liv's entire life style changed. She was walking along the street with her friend, actress Bibi Andersson, when they ran into director Bergman, a longtime acquaintance of Bibi. Bergman peered at Liv and said: "I've seen your work and would like to make a picture with you."

Several months later, Bergman cabled Liv in Norway and told her he was featuring her in *Persona*. "I was very honored," says the actress. "He had never permitted a non-Swedish performer to be in any of his films before. Of course, I accepted. I knew full well he was the best director in the world."

Bergman counseled Liv, gave her new insights, never left her side on the set. They were inseparable and soon became lovers. He divorced his fourth wife; Liv left her husband. For five years, they lived together and made great movies together. A year before Liv's divorce became final, she gave birth to Bergman's child. The tow-headed girl, Linn, is now six.

Two years ago, Liv walked away from Bergman, and last year the brilliant director married for the fifth time. The actress remains friendly with Bergman and continues to work in his films.

Upon completion of *Lost Horizon*, Liv flies to Sweden to star in his first full-fledged effort in television, *The Six Faces of a Woman*.

"He wrote it especially for me," reveals Liv. "It will concern a woman in six phases of her marriage. Each segment will be an hour long. We'll rehearse it one week; shoot it the next. Next year, it should come to the United States in English."

With an ill-fated marriage plus a torrid love affair behind her, Liv's not sure that she'll ever marry again. "Once you have promised yourself to a man in front of an altar, you hesitate about doing it again. It's a religious thing with me. I happen to believe in God but don't go to church. The marriage license is meaningless. I believe two people can live happily together without being married." Currently, she's steady-dating writer Jean-Claude Carriere.

Though acting represents Liv's major means of expressing herself, she also writes. "When I feel lost, I'll sit down at the typewriter. I've written several essays that have been printed in Swedish newspapers. And I fully intend to write one on Hollywood when I get back."

It's quite possible she'll also have some devastating comments to put down on paper regarding American politics. Liv says: "I think your war in Vietnam is disgraceful. And I can tell you that anti-American feeling in Sweden runs very high. The Swedish people worry that America may involve the whole world in a war. And I'm not so sure they are wrong. I've seen President Nixon on television and I can't believe it. He talks to Americans as though they were idiots. He tells them that the war is continuing because American soldiers are stationed there. Yet people are getting killed in the war every day. I think Nixon looks like a robot. Everything he says comes out coldly, not from the heart or from any intelligence."

On a topic she's much more knowledgeable about, Liv attacks American films that stress nudity. "I think it's just a lot of crap when directors tell actresses they should go naked because the script requires it. Most films could be done just as well without naked bodies. I remember a scene from a French film. *The Lovers*, in which Jeanne Moreau and an actor were making love. All you saw were two hands meeting. To me, it was much more sensual than an actual closeup of two bodies."

As for Liv herself, she has never peeled off her clothes in any of her twenty-five films—and doesn't ever intend to. "I feel your private life is more important than showing off everything. Once you are naked on film, what have you left for someone you care about? You have to give away so much anyway as an actress. I think this is where you have to draw the line."

The nudity that she glimpsed in *Carnal Knowledge* didn't disturb her. "It was tastefully done." And the violence that she viewed in *Clockwork Orange* didn't upset her, either. "I admire the director, Stanley Kubrick. He's a genius. The violence fitted in, though it was terrifying."

But the actress couldn't believe her blue eyes when she went to see *Prime Cut*. "I never saw anything like it. The film was the worst I've ever seen. It was so stupid. The idea of making sausages out of people! How could Gene Hackman and Lee Marvin have permitted themselves to be seen in it? Surely they must have read the script."

That facet of her profession is never ignored by Liv. She makes certain that every script measures up to her lofty standards.

When she leaves the U.S. for Oslo in December, Liv intends to star in a Brecht play, *The Good Woman*. And why should one of filmdom's peerless actresses labor on stage for little money and less prestige?

Liv seems surprised at the question. "Because basically I'm a stage actress, and I feel it's important to keep your roots. Next year, my time will be limited. My daughter will be starting school, and I will stay closer to home. Hollywood is pleasant, but I can't continue traveling because I want to be with my daughter."

And just then, Liv's lovely youngster, Linn, dashes across the close-cropped lawn and dives into the pool. She swims effortlessly, although she just learned the art a few months ago. Again and again, Linn repeats the routine of diving in the water and crawling out.

It's obvious she's showing off for the strangers on hand. Liv frowns and pulls her daughter to her. "Have you gone Hollywood, Linn?" she asks.

The little girl shakes her head.

"That's good," says Liv. "I haven't, either."

Liv Ullmann: Depth, Beauty, and Serenity

BLONDE HAIR TUMBLED down her shoulders in loose waves. She was all in black. In contrast, her skin, free of makeup, was the white of alabaster, her eyes a penetrating cobalt blue. As she sat with her feet curled up in an easy chair, it was possible to see what had attracted Ingmar Bergman and Secretary of State Henry Kissinger to Liv Ullmann. It was not just her natural fresh-scrubbed beauty.

Surely Bergman's affections (Bergman and Miss Ullmann lived together for five years, a liaison that produced a child, seven-year-old Linn) were aroused by something deeper. Her inner serenity perhaps. Her quiet intelligence. Her lively curiosity about the world around her. Then again, it may have been her complete lack of affectation, for that, in itself, is terribly appealing.

Unlike many film actresses, her career is of less concern to her than her growth and development as a woman. She describes herself as a dependent kind of woman, one who prefers clinging to a man. Forced by circumstances to live alone as an unmarried mother, she is trying to adjust to her independence. This, then, is where Liv Ullmann is now, groping for a new lifestyle that will be agreeable to both her and her child. But more of that later.

At the beginning of our interview, Miss Ullmann wanted only to talk about *The New Land*, the film sequel to *The Emigrants*, Jan Troell's intimate epic about the struggles of a Swedish family determined to settle

From *New York Daily News*, November 25, 1973, p. 7. © *New York Daily News*, L.P., reprinted with permission.

in America. It is a film, Miss Ullmann feels, that requires care and feeding, a nurturing of the public interest.

Troell's epic film was based on a novel by Vilhelm Moberg that is known and loved in Sweden. Miss Ullmann and Max von Sydow—who plays her husband—knew the book so well and were so at ease with each other they slipped into character almost without realizing it.

As it was, both films were made as one, with Troell jumping back and forth in the story. The project, the most expensive Scandanavian picture ever made, took more than a year to do. Troell, Miss Ullmann explains, used a very small crew, a total of fifteen people. Many of the actors, including Eddie Axberg, who plays von Sydow's younger brother, did double duty. For example, Axberg, in addition to acting, carried sound equipment. The crew—as happens when Bergman shoots a film—was like a family. Troell encouraged the intimacy.

He let his actors do intuitively what they felt was right for the moment, while he concentrated on the camera, picking out scenes that would strike him as visually poetic.

Miss Ullmann explained:

"Max and I, without ever talking about it, discovered that when we were facing some kind of trouble, our hands always found each other. It was an unconscious gesture and we never noticed it. But Troell did notice it with his camera, and he used it to show that these people are holding on to each other for strength."

The New Land has been called too dour in its outlook. Only rarely do the characters smile or laugh. "I feel it is very true," she conceded, adding by way of explanation: "In those days, happiness wasn't so enormous. It came in small moments."

Miss Ullmann continued: "I have seen so many action pictures where feelings are so overexposed. Here they are not. This film has to do with the slow continuous life of a struggling people in a new land. It's a very true picture, but you have to relax and get into the rhythm of it. It's unlucky that people don't have more time to take a slow pace."

One of Miss Ullmann's major concerns is that people today do not slow down long enough to communicate with each other. For her, the cinema is "one of the last ways of communication," adding: "Movies can be a wonderful way of making people go out and respond."

Miss Ullmann had watched such a response while attending a Washington preview of *The New Land*. "A lady in front of me started sobbing lowly," she said. "The more she sobbed, the quieter it was in the theater. As a result, it was a better film. I even cried at my own death scene."

"If you give yourself to the picture, it's a kind of experience," Miss Ullmann said. "To me *The Emigrants* and *The New Land* will live long after *The Godfather*. It is a true picture about you Americans, all your hopes and dreams. Maybe it will encourage people to remember what people came to America to find. It may encourage them to return to nature, to the real values."

Communication on the set is Miss Ullmann's basic ingredient for good acting. She became accustomed to it in her years of working with Bergman. The togetherness on a Bergman set was so great, Miss Ullmann said, that "we used to say jokingly that if Bergman gets sick it's okay because we don't really need him." Once, when Bergman had to go to London to shoot scenes for *The Touch*, he sent the star of the film, Bibi Andersson, to direct the scenes because Bergman is terrified of flying. "Bibi did fine," recalled Miss Ullmann.

"It's no coincidence that Bergman always works with the same people." Miss Ullmann said. "It's sort of a workshop. Everybody is a part of it, not only the actors, but the crew as well."

Now for the main question. What was a serious actress, accustomed to the enforced intimacy and the warm conviviality of a Troell or Bergman set, doing in a splashy, superficial Hollywood movie like *Lost Horizon*? When it was announced that Miss Ullmann was going to star in the Ross Hunter musical, those who cherished her deep sensitivity groaned. The feeling was that she had sold out, and that her subsequent buildup as an international superstar would be detrimental to her luminous talent.

It has begun to look as if these fears might be realized, for Miss Ullmann's Hollywood movies *Lost Horizon* and *40 Carats*, (*Zandy's Bride*, a third movie done with Troell, has yet to be released), were hardly critical triumphs. Even so, she has few regrets about her Hollywood experience. "Poor *Lost Horizon*," (as she calls it) delighted her because she thought it was "fun to be in a big Hollywood movie and see what it was like." Besides, she said with a smile, "They gave me a house with a swimming pool."

She was equally grateful for the opportunity to do *40 Carats*. Why? "Because I never had a chance to smile in any of my movies, and artistically it was lovely to be on a set where there were funny lines."

Hollywood, for Miss Ullmann, was a place to work in, nothing more. "You can't live very long in Hollywood because you get used to the big treatment, and that's dangerous," she said.

There is no danger of becoming swell-headed in Norway, and that is where Miss Ullmann will be living for the time being. For one thing she is committed to doing *A Doll's House* on the Oslo stage. But the real reason for her returning home is that her daughter, who is attending school in Norway, is asking why her mother doesn't stay home like other mothers.

Miss Ullmann has mixed feelings about the prospect of living in Norway again. On one hand, she said, "I want to go back, just to go back and stay at home. There's nothing like being able to go into your own kitchen and boil an egg."

On the other hand:

"I don't know if I'll feel happy staying in Norway. It's really cold. You can never be nicely dressed. It's always dark and the snow is dirty. You need several pairs of underpants. People go around hugging themselves against the cold. No one smiles."

With that, Miss Ullmann shivered slightly and said: "I'm terrified of going home." It is not so much the prospect of a grim winter, she explained. Suddenly, her future looks blank. She doesn't know how she will live. The only thing she does know is that "I can't picture myself being happy on the stage in Oslo; I have to do something else." Something else probably will be writing.

Miss Ullmann has always liked to write, and she has a commitment with an American publisher to do a book. She has been working on it for some time.

"Everyone thought I was writing something exciting about Bergman and me, but it was not that," she said. "They are essays. I do have a lot of material, a lot of things I want to communicate out of my experience. How I feel about being a woman today. What I feel, what I want, what I feel other people may want. It's not a woman's liberation book. It's a book written by a woman today."

If Miss Ullmann has learned anything from her experience, her abortive marriage, her liaison with Bergman, it is this: "You must allow people to feel what they feel, to always teach them to be individuals."

It is a lesson that she hopes her daughter will learn, not necessarily with Bergman's help. Of Bergman, she said: "Just now he isn't what I dreamt a father would be."

Bergman's "Everywoman" Speaks about Herself

HOWARD KISSEL / 1974

YOU EXPECT AN INTENSE, brooding woman whose face reflects the struggle within her of all the psychic burdens of Woman, past and present. Instead you find a woman who is enthusiastic to a point almost childlike, whose sensuality is more delicate than it seems possible to convey on the screen, and who disarms not by any feeling of covert suffering but rather by a remarkable sense of openness and vulnerability.

Liv *Ullmann* herself is surprised, even amused, at her cinematic image as Everywoman. When she became an actress, she wanted to be a comedian. She still does.

"I always thought I was a comedian. I don't have the physical apparatus for tragedy—the long nose, the long face. But when I started in the theater, I played women who were unhappy, starving, killing themselves. Then I met Ingmar Bergman who started me doing neurotics. The first ordinary, un-neurotic woman I've played is Marianne in *Scenes from a Marriage*.

"For the last six months, I've been touring as Nora in Ibsen's *A Doll's House*. It was the first time I heard anybody laugh. Comedy is wonderful because you can hear the response. You can't hear people cry. I was supposed to do *Doll's House* for only three months, but I was enjoying it so much I asked to do it another three.

"*A Doll's House* is a funny play—this woman is manipulating all the men around her. I don't feel Nora is a victim. She's asked to wear a mask and not show herself—she's clever enough to use her sweet, squirrel behavior to manipulate people. When she's noble at the end, it's not because she's leaving but because she wants to make something of her life. Up until then, she has been cheating at life—people have expected her to—but she's not going to anymore. She may come back home the next day, but at least she woke up."

Ms. Ullmann will play Nora in a Joseph Papp production next year. In the meantime, her work can be seen in two new films, Bergman's *Scenes from a Marriage*, which opens Sunday at Cinema I, and *The Abdication*, which will open in early October.

Scenes was originally conceived as a six-part series for Swedish television. The film version lasts three hours and concentrates on a couple played by Ms. Ullmann and Erland Josephson. It begins showing their superficially happy marriage, then charts their disenchantment with each other, their emotional breakup and their eventual intellectual reconciliation many years later, when each is married to someone else. The series was an enormous hit in Sweden.

"The film begins with banalities because it is the banalities that ruin the marriage. That is what a lot of married people say to each other to avoid saying anything real. A lot of people were cheated into watching the series because they identified with the people speaking those banalities. These were people who never went to see Bergman's films. The series was repeated three times in Scandinavia. People would stop Ingmar on the street to talk to him about it, they wrote him letters—that has never happened to him before. Many marriages broke up because of the film—but also many married people began really talking to each other.

"The great thing about working with Ingmar is he gives you freedom. He wrote the entire script himself, but he was open to changes. There were things I had to say that I didn't believe, and he let me say something else. Sometimes, though, he wouldn't let me change the lines. At the end she is supposed to say she is happy with life, that she is secure. I think if she is free and her mind is developed, she wouldn't say those things. But Ingmar wouldn't let me change the lines. I asked him if I could say them as if she were trying to believe things she doesn't really believe, and he said that would be all right. He is really like that—he sometimes thinks the actor he has chosen for a part knows more about the character than he does, and he is anxious to see what will happen with it. When we were filming *The Emigrants*, the author of the book talked to us. He remembered when he was writing it that he came into the kitchen to tell his wife what was happening. 'That whore Ulrica has married a minister,' he said, and laughed. The characters were not symbols—part of the act of creation is not knowing what will happen.

"In *Scenes*, there is a sequence in which Ingmar uses some photos of me when I was growing up. He asked me if he could use a few photos, and I said it was all right. I was involved in another project and could not choose the pictures. He wrote to my mother and she sent him the whole lot. It makes the film more personal, and a lot of people have said it is about the breakup of my marriage to Ingmar and that the pictures are the proof. But that is not so. Marianne is not me. Ingmar uses things he knows from my life, but he also uses many other things. It is a movie about a lot of things I know about. I could have written a lot of these things. It's fun when working is like that."

In *The Abdication*, Ms. Ullmann plays Queen Christina, a role many moviegoers associate with Garbo. Does she feel self-conscious about that?

"No. In the Garbo movie, Queen Christina was beautiful, everything about her was beautiful. She abdicated over a man she loved who was killed in a duel. The real Christina was nothing like that. She was not beautiful. She was ugly, appallingly so. She did not care for men. She had no companions. Nobody really knows the truth about her. *The Abdication* tries to show you a woman undergoing a trauma, but when it's over you still don't know all the answers about her. It's a completely different picture."

Liv Ullmann: Ingmar Bergman Star Talks about Life and Art

JOHN CRITTENDEN/1974

QUESTION: *You've said that the most important thing to you as an actress is to be human. What is this quality? What does it mean to be human?*
ULLMANN: I don't really know how to define "human" or why we are here on earth. But I think it's to be in very close touch with your own feelings all the time, maybe not knowing who you are, but at least being in touch with yourself. It doesn't make you special but it makes you closer to your faith and emotions, so they don't come in bits and pieces. Coming out from that can make you very open to people around you; you are in closer touch with people because you are in touch with yourself. It helps me know whom I'm talking with, that I'm not addressing their surface, but talking with somebody real. It doesn't mean you become a great conversationalist, or a great beauty, or a great mind, but it does make you feel very much a part of the living process.

Liv Ullmann is among the most womanly of women, as well as a great beauty. Fittingly, her name rhymes with Eve. Even more fittingly, Liv means "Life" in Norwegian.

Born in Tokyo thirty-three years ago, her first years were spent in Toronto among refugees from Nazi-occupied Norway. Her father, who had been an aircraft engineer, joined the Norwegian Air Force in Canada. He was injured in an accident and moved his wife, Janna, their

From Bergen County [New Jersey] *Record*, September 12, 1974, pp. B1, B19, B24.

daughter, Liv, and Liv's older sister to New York. There he died before the war ended, and Janna Ullmann took her daughters home.

Liv had an unhappy girl-hood in Norway. She was bookish and religious and wrote religious plays. At seventeen, she was off to London for eight months of acting lessons. Back at home and rejected by the state theater school, she joined a repertory theater in a small town. Her first success was in *The Diary of Anne Frank*.

At twenty-one, she married a psychiatrist. At twenty-five, she met Ingmar Bergman, then forty-six, and the marriage was over. He co-starred her with Bibi Andersson in *Persona*, and Liv was established internationally. She also starred for Bergman in *The Shame and The Passion of Anna*. Their relationship was intimate for five years, and she bore him a daughter, Linn, now seven.

Her unwed motherhood was accepted in Sweden, but Norwegians are less liberated. She was viciously hassled. She went on Norwegian television to defend herself. In Sweden the problem was the couple's celebrity. Curious tourists and the press made their lives miserable.

They parted, but are still friends, and have made both *Cries and Whispers* and *Scenes from a Marriage* since then. Bergman has married for a fifth time.

It has been said that both Bergman and her husband were father-substitutes. She has said that, with Bergman especially, she felt they were both living his life. In restaurants, he even ordered her dinner for her.

She has been both successful and unsuccessful without Bergman. She made *The Emigrants* and *The New Land* with Jan Troell, her most distinguished work since going on her own. She's also participated in two disasters: *Pope Joan* and *Lost Horizon*. Although better, *Forty Carats* was snubbed by most critics and audiences.

Last week she was ensconced in a suite on the thirty-eighth floor of the Pierre Hotel in New York. She had come from Norway to do interviews promoting *Scenes from a Marriage,* which opened last Monday, and *The Abdication*, which is about Queen Christina of Sweden and opens Oct. 3.

She is interesting because she is interested. Her attention is complete. She does not shrink. She does not act dumb. She does not act tough. She is soft and lovely, a lady. Her English is nearly perfect. She says yeah instead of yah. She is an extraordinary person.

QUESTION: *Tell me about working with Bergman. Does he tell you exactly what he wants? Do you collaborate? Articles written about him lead one to believe everyone contributes, but the films seem to have such a singular vision.*

ULLMANN: He gives us the material. First, he knows what kind of talent he's working with, maybe not how much or how little he'll get, but he knows something. And then he gives the material. He gives me a character, like the wife in *Scenes from a Marriage*, where he knows I can put in a lot of things he knows about. And then he hopes I will come with things he didn't know. But it would be very uninteresting for him if he told me everything the character is about because then he would not have the benefit of my experience as an actress and a woman—experiences he would not have himself.

That's why he's such a good director. He gives you the room, the place, the situation, and the person. And then he just benefits from whatever else he can get. Of course everything will be in his line, his style, but it will be alive with many of the fantasies, thoughts, dreams, hopes, longings which belong to the people he's working with. He doesn't like to discuss too much. That's why he works so often with the same people.

That makes it exciting. It's almost like playing, in the good sense. If what he'd hoped for doesn't come, of course he'll take thirty takes. It's a collaboration of people who know each other very well and know approximately what they can get. When they surprise each other it's fun, because then we've reached another step. And next time we'll go farther.

I'm going to do a film with him next spring. It's now two years since we did *Scenes from a Marriage*. I know I've learned a lot. I've had the whole Hollywood thing, you know. I just long to put all that into his hands. Do you understand? And I know when I see his script I'll know what has happened to him in those two years. I don't know what line he will be into. It might be new, something fascinating. It's fantastic to be part of it. He now says he will be going in entirely new directions, something he's never tried before.

QUESTION: *It's been reported that for him* Scenes from a Marriage *is an autobiographical film. How true is that?*

ULLMANN: It's not one straight story that is his. He wrote in the fore-word of the published screenplay that it took him thirty years to live it, three months to write. And in those thirty years, you know, there were more than ten years of marriage. There were other people's experiences he dealt with. There were his own. He put all this in, but it's not one straight story. And it's not one straight story which I'm afraid everyone will believe is mine.

QUESTION: *That was the next question.*
ULLMANN: Yeah, but it isn't. No more than that of people I've met here in America who tell me it is their story. There's a general feeling of that because it seems to be so authentic. Everyone feels it is their story.

QUESTION: *How did you do the last sequence? It's such an individual moment, I don't see how you could do it over and over. The part where the wife is saying, "Must we live in confusion?"*
ULLMANN: I didn't retake many of that, I remember. The strange thing is the last scene was the most difficult for me because she was saying so many things that I didn't believe in and I wanted her to have grown more. I maybe wanted to be more of a heroine. I asked to change some of the lines and Ingmar said absolutely no. Then I asked if I could say it as if I'm bewildered and maybe don't believe it.

"Of course," he said, "say it as you want, but you're not changing." I fought so hard with that scene. Maybe that's the reason it looks like that. The character really took over in it.

QUESTION: *It's an entirely different level of consciousness. Like* Persona. *I saw that when it first came out and wasn't up to it. I was very young and didn't understand a thing. I must get back to it. I think I'm ready for it now.*
ULLMANN: Yeah, I tell you something strange. When I did it I was twenty-five, and obviously it couldn't be all in my mind and experi-ence. A lot of things I seriously didn't understand. I just had to do it on feeling, on instinct. I couldn't ask him, because I felt so grateful he was giving me this, that I must pretend. When I see it now, I understand it so much better. I understand the character. But in a way I think it doesn't matter because deep down we can experience even if we don't

really understand. I think you can instinctively play a character without intellectually or by experience already being at that level.

So many more people would appreciate him if they would dare to go in and think he's really simple that he's going to their emotions, not worry about the symbols.

QUESTION: *In* The Abdication, *it's an entirely different kind of performance.*

ULLMANN: Yes, it is. It's a costume picture about a woman who really existed. I've never done any part that I felt so much for. *Scenes from a Marriage* is a fantastic part because it has all the realism. *The Abdication* is an actress in a human being's dream part. I feel that this woman and her torment is what I want to show. She's a more complicated woman than the wife in the other film. I feel like her problems are what in different ways most women and maybe men have in common. In our world today we don't find our place, so we stretch out and people don't want us and then we don't want people. And you have to put this into a costume picture, into Queen Christina. She's a modern woman, yet a woman of all times.

You have to act in a completely different way. You can't be subtle, and yet you must. I care very much for this picture. To me it was a fantastic thing to do. After that, it's one of the reasons I long to work for Ingmar again because I think I learned so much. I had to do things that aren't in me. I would like to do that may be in a modern play.

QUESTION: *How's the book you were writing?*

ULLMANN: It's finished, but I'm rewriting. I finished it while I was on tour in Norway. I read it over, and because I know I will have to stand up for it much more than I do for being an actress, I decided to keep working. I was trying to make a book for women, and I wanted to talk about what is common to us all. I had felt if there was a hint of my work, that I wouldn't be as sympathetic as I should be, that it would make barriers to talking directly. But that's silly. You can't talk from out of your own experience if you keep out a very important part of it. It's like lying. And people who read it would wonder what I'm trying to pull.

QUESTION: *You were trying to give wisdom without your own experience?*

ULLMANN: Yes, and then I don't really have any wisdom. I'm just try-ing to make essays about a woman's life. I found you can't deny some of the subjects, like work.

QUESTION: *You're in a great position to do it. You've had an interesting life.*

ULLMANN: Yes, and I feel like now I can sell my book so someone will buy and read it. Maybe in a year they won't, but I don't want to miss the opportunity. I'm part of a middle generation. We're really in between. I mean when I was young, women's liberation never came to my town. We had dreams about freedom, but we didn't know what to do. We are kind of a lost generation. We were never finding anything real, and we wanted to. Nobody has really written personally about how it feels to be thirty-five years old today and a woman. And the bewilderment. I'd like to try.

QUESTION: *Were you hurt by the reaction to* Pope Joan*?*

ULLMANN: I wasn't surprised because I'd seen the final cut, which had nothing to do with the director's cut. And I'd heard what happened to the music. Maurice Jarre had put a big crescendo at one point in the music, and the producer had taken it and put it in every time the char-acter had a thought. I mean it's such a touchy thing, a pope who gets pregnant. If you mess around with that, then it gets to be what it was. I was terribly hurt, because again it was a story I believed in. That's one of the professional things that has been most sad. Maybe the only really sad thing because it was something good that was destroyed.

QUESTION: *40 Carats wasn't well received, either. But I liked it.*

ULLMANN: It wasn't what people thought I should do. It's unfair with actors. The critics and public always say "bad judgment" and "why don't they quit?" You can't only do good things. You must do below and over. With actors suddenly it's "bad taste, no judgment, idiots!" Ten bad pic-tures in a row, maybe that's an indication, but they're quick to judge.

There aren't that many offers. And after a certain age, there are even fewer. Bergman is good because he's interested in women, which most directors aren't. And he's not interested only in very young women. We are lucky. The older his actresses become, he starts making pictures about more mature women. Fellini did it for awhile. Joanne Woodward has people who write for her. But who else? There aren't that many things to do.

QUESTION: *You'll be doing* A Doll's House *at the Vivian Beaumont in Lincoln Center next spring, won't you?*
ULLMANN: I've been in Norway since November doing *A Doll's House.* When we finished in Oslo, we went on tour all over Norway. It's fascinating to see one's country that way. I didn't know I would be doing it here when I started there. But it has always been one of my favorite plays. I did it on the radio some years ago. Nora is a part very near to some of the things I'd like to express. There's also a lot of comedy in it, I feel, depending on the way you do it.

Joseph Papp gave me a choice between *Hedda Gabler* and *A Doll's House*, and because I was already doing it, I felt that's what I would like to do here. Besides Hedda is a neurotic and I've done so many neurotics here already.

Liv Ullmann:
The Goddess as Ordinary Woman

MOLLY HASKELL/1974

IT IS NOT JUST the publicity releases that are comparing Liv Ullmann to Greta Garbo. Ingrid Bergman, and Jeanne Moreau. Along the length of Bloomingdale's Belt, where *Scenes from a Marriage* is playing at Cinema I, men can be found wandering in a daze. And some of them haven't even gotten inside to see it. Women are more guarded in their admiration, but most admit that Ullmann is "together" in a way that seems to elude many of us at this transitional moment of history.

What is it about the Norwegian-born Ullmann, aside from the Titian hair, and the blue eyes that one must resist translating into purple prose. If I hadn't been shamed by the interviewer from the woman's magazine in *Scenes from a Marriage*, who does just that, I would say they have the color and the astonishing pale brightness of a gray sky just turning blue. The color—as it happens—of the telephone she uses several times in the film. The color of the floor-length knit dress she wore the first time I saw her, when she came to Sardi's in 1972 to pick up a Best Actress award (for *Cries and Whispers*) from the New York Film Critics Circle. Not only the color, but the slight angora-fuzziness of the dress, emphasized her soft contours and ultra femininity, and suggested the awareness of a woman in perfect harmony with her exterior—and not above displaying it a bit.

I think the popularity of *Scenes from a Marriage*—if it turns out to be a popular as well as a critical hit—is largely explainable by her presence,

From the *Village Voice*, October 3, 1974, p. 5+. © 1974 by the *Village Voice*. Reprinted by permission.

and an audience's gratitude for what is not just the first real woman in months of drought, but a particular kind of woman—a radiant, soothing Earth Mother who appears to heal the wounds wrought by sexual enmity. I am not sure that the reconciliation isn't as illusory as President Ford's great healing act, but the fact that we grasp so desperately at something that is more than a straw but less than a sexual life-boat suggests that perhaps our needs have been given too short a shrift in American movies.

In the simplest terms, there is, underlying *Scenes from a Marriage*, an assumption that we are in this together, that both sexes are plunked on this planet without a guidebook, and if we join our heads and hearts and the rest of our bodies we will probably do better than if we spend all our time and energy trying to prove we don't need each other. If in Bergman's films, men need and revere women too much—thus imprisoning them in their "superior," traditional roles as mothers and nurturers, in American movies the reverse is true. Men, fleeing their own mortality and the love and knowledge that might redeem the pain of growing old, take refuge in greater and greater displays of violence, opting for the short physical spurt of the professional athlete rather than the long imaginative span of the man of wisdom. As has happened so often in the past, a European actress has come to fill a gap in our own culture.

Ullmann is that anomaly, an international star—the only one in Bergman's repertory to make the cover of *Time* Magazine—who has yet to make a good film outside Scandinavia. The uncharitable might attribute this to the famous *Time* cover jinx on movie stars, but I think it is rather that Bergman has probed, penetrated, and allowed her to reveal and extend herself in ways that no other director, including Jan Troell, has dared to do.

It is probably true, as she pointed out in our interview at the Pierre—the eventual subject of this piece—that critics have been unwilling to accept her in non-Bergman pictures. "If it's not Bergman," their thinking goes, "it's no good." But it's a little like taking a poor city kid for a few days on the Atlantic Ocean, and then sending him back to play in the fire hydrants of the ghetto. Once we have seen Liv Ullmann speak worlds just by narrowing her eyes or barely parting her lips in a Bergman close-up, how can we tolerate the distance she places between us and a fustian, posing Queen Christina (in *The Abdication*) who makes a mockery of woman's "search for fulfillment."

Having lived with Ullmann for some five or six years, Bergman knows her moods and contradictions and what it is like to watch television with her and sleep with her and help her wash the dishes, and it is this knowledge that seeps through the cracks of Johan and Marianne's crumbling marriage, filling the narrative frame with feelings and perceptions that are sometimes at variance with the middle-class stereotypes with which it is concerned. Although Bergman gives Ullmann a looser rein than heretofore to "become her own person," the film is ultimately not about Ullmann/Marianne's growth in understanding herself, so much as with Bergman's understanding of Ullmann—her strengths, her vanities, her evasions, her shuffling drabness, her sudden, dazzling beauty. Her gestures towards the women's movement are not particularly convincing, nor does her career seem to play any great role in her life. But her vibrations and metamorphoses as that classical creature, a woman "made for love," have an uncanny aura of truth: the way she becomes more alluring when she has "gotten over" him and is no longer emotionally dependent; her increased sexual desire, and abandon, when she no longer feels possessive towards him, or anxious about what he feels for her.

Ullmann, who once "exchanged identities" with Bibi Andersson in *Persona*, radiates a poise and self-possession that is strikingly unlike Andersson's more tenuously cerebral grasp of herself. The differences between the two, as they have evolved since 1966, are fascinating. Andersson suggests the insecurity of the more complex, intellectual woman, harboring an unresolved conflict between her sensual and spiritual selves. It is Ullmann's self-containment bordering on complacency, that drives her crazy in *Persona*, and that in *Scenes from a Marriage* galvanizes her into a momentary alliance with her despised husband. In Andersson, we think we glimpse the kind of woman who is constantly in search of something, who is tormented by doubts and driven by spiritual needs. Whereas Ullmann, even when she withdraws from the world in *Persona*, is responding simply, with a peasant sense of survival, by rejecting the world and its unanswerable questions.

As a woman who fulfills herself in love, she demands paradoxically less of men than Andersson, who requires that they engage her mind.

Andersson, the challenge, the mind, has sharp edges; Ullmann, the mother, the solace, has none. But in her soft sufficiency, she is invulnerable. The other side of her pliancy is what Johan/Bergman calls her "white, hard resistance." Perhaps she gives everything . . . and nothing. Only a great artist or a long relationship could uncover such cruel ironies, and with Bergman, Ullmann had both.

Certainly, when you meet her in person, you are likely to decide that even such failings as the screenplay attributes to her are unthinkable. There is nothing hard or resistant in this woman in red pants and top who, when I meet her, is cheerful, voluble, curious, frank, self-critical, and betrays no weariness at having to confront yet another interviewer except to confess that she is sick to death of talking about herself.

When I arrive at their suite in the Pierre, she and her companion Cecillia Drott, who did the make-up for *Scenes* and *Cries and Whispers*, are watching *The Mating Game* with that mixture of amusement and disbelief and dismay that makes American daytime television such a mind-blowing experience for Europeans.

Ullmann is still trying to recover from a show in which the wife, in the presence of the husband, was asked to tell the worst secret of her marriage, and she revealed, to her husband's horrified humiliation, that they had a lousy sex life.

"Yesterday I saw the Merv Griffin show," she said, "where Burt Reynolds and another he-man and a (laughing) he-girl were talking about what they would do to all the bad critics of their movie. I couldn't take them seriously—they are not like real people. If anyone ever came on a show and acted sincere and normal, he would look fake," she said with amazement. And I remembered all over again that European actors and actresses *are* different, that they are allowed to play their profession with more dignity and less psychic dislocation—probably because they are treated like artists rather than trained seals.

Ullmann speaks beautiful English, having lived in New York briefly as a child and studied it in school. There is only a slight accent—she also has a Norwegian accent in Swedish—and an occasional marvelous neologism (or transposition of a Norwegian word into English), as when she told me that some poor plagiarist whose book on Harlem had been much praised, had the "unluck" for somebody to discover the original.

I told her I had seen the two-hour, forty-eight minute version of *Scenes from a Marriage*, as well as the four-hour version (itself cut from the original six-part, five hour tv special), and asked her what she thought had been gained or lost.

ULLMANN: The four-hour version was a compromise of the television version. There were many of the same kinds of scenes, only slightly different. There were moments of relaxation which you need in a tv show but not in a movie. The film shows all the important things that happen, but some of the emotional scenes are cut because you can't watch everything in that short a time.

MH: *I found myself liking it much better the second time around. It was like watching it on television, getting to know and accept the people. In particular, I found the husband (played by Erland Josephson) more sympathetic.*
ULLMANN: This happened in Sweden, too. The first time around, people had enormous discussions the whole week. Then the next time around (the whole cycle was shown three times), what you said happened. They had seen more of the husband, and they understood his attitude in the first scene, his arrogance. They came to pity him, and they realized he was acting that way to hide his insecurity.

MH: *My male companion (as we say) didn't understand why Johan would leave Marianne. "She's so beautiful and extraordinary," he said. But I think women understand it.*
ULLMANN: Why he leaves her is that he suddenly feels afraid. He's trying to grab life while it's still there.

MH: *It's something we've begun referring to (apologetically) as "male menopause."*
    Ullmann appreciates the term and she and Cecillia Drott nod vigorously.
ULLMANN: Yes, men have it harder than we do. We can call it something physical, can get pills, go to the doctor, get pity. But men do all these crazy things—they get divorces, they suddenly turn homosexual, they walk through red lights. They feel lost but they have nothing to prove what's wrong. It is much more difficult.

We are very lucky if we have a relationship where we feel fulfilled, but if we are unfulfilled, the warning lights keep flashing that age is coming on.

MH: *In one of the film's most extraordinary scenes, you are interviewed by an elderly woman (actually Barbro Hiort Af Ornas who was the nurse in* The Brink of Life *who wants a divorce. Suddenly in the calmest possible manner, she confesses not only that she doesn't love her husband, but that she doesn't love her children, has never loved them; and that she feels her senses failing her—when she hears, sees, touches something it is remote, the "sensation is thin and dry." You start to say something, but then are silent. What was it?*
ULLMANN: Bergman never told me, but I think it is that the woman touches a nerve in me, something that I am used to hiding.

MH: *In the first scene, you and Josephson (the reader will forgive me for not always distinguishing between the actor, the character, and the person, particularly in Ullmann's case. The ambiguity, I think, belongs.) are being interviewed by a reporter, Mrs. Palm, from a woman's magazine. Some of the scene has been cut for the theatrical version.*
ULLMANN: Yes, she runs and snoops around when they've left the room, she even peeks in the bedroom. It's a very funny moment, but you know she is that kind of woman without showing that scene.

MH: *She reminds me of so many interviewers, when she pushes her glasses back on her head, and opens that enormous, all-purpose sack, the way she intimidates you with her clickety-click professionalism.*
ULLMANN: All the interviewers for the gossip magazines in Sweden are like that, with their little skirts and big belts, always snooping.

MH: *And you feel stupid because you can't respond in their terms, can't think of something cute and quick and "profound" about love and marriage. Having just endured a similar experience, I really appreciated that part, and the whole notion of the Happy Couple feature, which is predicated on the assumption that each partner was a cipher or a half-person until the marriage which miraculously completed and transformed them.*

But there are other things that have been cut, like our discovery that Mrs. Palm was an old schoolmate of yours. To me, it seemed an allusion to *A Doll's House*, and the scene when Christine comes to see Nora.

ULLMANN (thoughtful, then delighted):   Yes, you're right. I never thought of that. I don't have anything to say to the interviewer, I don't feel friendly. I try to move away, and yet I never quite got the bit of business when we were shooting the film. But then, when I was doing *A Doll's House*. I suddenly remembered this feeling and I used it, I moved away from Christine more decisively. I believe I felt at the time (of *Scenes*) that if I ever have the opportunity, I will use this gesture. And with *A Doll's House*, I remembered it and used it.

It's like when I was watching a production of *A Doll's House* a long time ago. It was a bad production, but a friend of mine, a good friend, was playing Nora. In the scene when she is decorating the Christmas tree, before Torvald is coming home, she suddenly starts decorating herself! At the time, most of us didn't understand, but when I came to do the scene, I started doing it, I started decorating myself. This is a woman who is always putting on masks for her husband.

MH: *Another interesting, and related, factor is that Mrs. Palm is addressing most of her questions to Johan. When she asks you one that you* can *respond to, and you finally open up, she immediately interrupts and calls for a photograph! This becomes especially ironic when you know that she is an old friend of yours, and seems to confirm something that Johan says later, in a semi-facetious diatribe against "Women's Lib," when he claims that all women are out to get each other.*

ULLMANN: Yes, but interviewers do that to men, too. With Bergman, they always interrupt him just when he is going to say something interesting, because they can't handle it. It doesn't fit, like a person suddenly acting natural on your tv game show. The interviewers come to get what they want to give their readers, so it is fake to begin with. It's like a bad director. When you at last find the right action or motivation, he will talk it out so much that you'll never find it again.

MH: *Why do Johan and Marianne, consent to the interview?*

ULLMANN: Why does anybody? Because they think it will be fun. They've never done it before.

MH: *What is Bergman's attitude toward the Bibi Andersson character? The scene seemed rather harsh on her.*

ULLMANN: He likes her. I think he likes her. He feels sorry for the man, but sympathy for her. He finds a kind of hope in the woman. Women are stronger than men.

MH: *I think the fact that Marianne blossoms after the separation is proof of that.*

ULLMANN: It's funny. One woman critic wrote that it was unbelievable—the man got more and more wrinkled and sad while she was lovelier than ever, but that's the point of the story. This is always happening in real life, women becoming more attractive after their husbands divorce them, or die.

MH: *I think it's partly just discovering that they* can *make it alone that gives them strength. I also love the scene when, after they are separated, he comes for dinner. She brings out the journal that, at the encouragement of her psychiatrist, she has started to keep. (With that wonderful insight into her female vanity, Bergman has her wishing she hadn't stayed up till three on that* night writing in it, as it has made her look tired.) She begins reading it to Johan, and he falls asleep.

ULLMANN: I've heard men say, heard Bergman say, they just want to leave when women go on and on about emotional things. This is a difference between women and men—men are tired, but women are always ready to go on about emotional things. That can be exhausting for a man. They are on another level where everything is not that important, and when you start up they say, "Oh, there you go again." He sees her like that.

MH: *Yes, but she never does go on and on. Johan is always criticizing her for faults you never show.*

ULLMANN: I agree, they say it about her, like when at the end he is surprised that she is jealous. He thinks she is not jealous. I don't know where he got that idea. It's not written in the character, but so what, let them say it about her.

Everybody has his own interpretation. It's like your friend saying, how could he leave her? I identify so closely with the woman, I felt it very natural that he should leave her. She's wearing those glasses and that night dress, she looks terrible. She takes the marriage for granted and he wants somebody who doesn't. She's plain and very uninteresting. It's all in what you see at the time.

MH: *There's a scene in the published screenplay that is one of my favorites, that has been cut out of the shorter version. It's when he's leaving her and they are discussing the details over breakfast. She mentions she'll have to tell the old housekeeper and he stutters and finally says, you don't need to—she already knows. Marianne looks surprised, and shamefacedly he explains that there had been a change of her schedule that he didn't know about, and he had brought his mistress home—the only time—and the housekeeper walked into the bedroom the next morning. On her face there's this incredible pain mingled with an attempt to see the absurdity of it.*

ULLMANN: Yes, to me that's one of the most horrible things that happens to her, maybe the most horrible—more than the humiliation of finding that all of her friends know. The fact that the cleaning woman is such an old friend, and that the husband brought his girl to her home. But men don't feel it that way. Bergman had to choose between the two scenes, and he kept the one with her on the phone, where rage comes for the first time. The other one is actually worse. But the way the man is talking about it, he doesn't know how terrible it is. If a woman had written that scene, she would have made the lines more cruel, to bring out the horror of it. But the way Johan is talking, neither the man who acted it nor Bergman understood the impact of it. That's what makes the whole thing so interesting.

MH: *How much freedom does Bergman give you?*
ULLMANN: A lot. He gives you a direction: you pass through a room. But the freedom of expression is yours.

MH: *I liked it when you just pulled the covers over your head, to make the whole thing go away. Did you think of that. It seemed such a reflex?*
ULLMANN: I don't remember. It was probably something I had done or would do.

MH: *And packing the husband's suitcase?*

ULLMANN: I wouldn't have done that. But I have a friend (she says a name and turns to Cecillia Drott, who nods) who always helps her husband pack when he goes on his affairs.

MH: *In the very last scene, there's a sequence in which you confess to Johan that early in your marriage you had affairs. That's been cut.*

ULLMANN: I'm glad. I never saw her as having affairs. I guess Bergman wanted to think she was more exciting and open to adventure than she was, that she had been exciting all the time. I didn't want to say the line, so I asked Bergman if I could say it as if I were lying. That's what I'm trying to do. Now afterwards, Bergman has been very nice about it in interviews—he admitted I didn't want to say it.

MH: *The abortion scene has been cut, but frankly I don't miss it.*

ULLMANN: There's a lot of life left out.

MH: *I would have liked to see the scene, cut from both versions, between you and your mother.*

ULLMANN: So would the woman who played my mother. I feel very sad about that. At first I didn't have the heart to tell her it had been cut, but I guess I will have to now.

MH: *I miss, too, the scene in which Johan admits to hating the children.*

ULLMANN: Well, there are always things cut from every picture that disappoint you. As a matter of fact, I miss more in *The Abdication* than in *Scenes from a Marriage*. If you really care for a picture, there will always be those scenes on the cutting room floor about which you say, "There's where I really show this other side of my character." (Having now seen *The Abdication*, she may be right. I'd like to think there were some footage somewhere that would show Ullmann as something other than a neurotic, posturing soap opera queen who makes decisions of state on whim, and religious conversions out of displaced sexual longing.)

MH: *What was it like doing* Persona, *your first film with Bergman?*

ULLMANN: At first I was terrified. I blushed whenever Bergman said a word. If I had not had Bibi there—I lived with her and her then-husband—I wouldn't have gotten through. Slowly I understood that he was kind and nice. Then he got excited about the rushes and I got confidence. Bibi was nervous, too, at the beginning, and broke out in nervous spots. Bergman knew very little about me, he had only seen me on the stage. And there I was this young girl who was always blushing, playing a mature woman. Bibi and I heard later that there was a lot of talk during the first week about cancelling the whole project.

We went to the island of Faro and redid all the scenes done in Stockholm. We had a wonderful time, always joking. We just thought we were making this small film on an island and nobody would ever see it, and then it became a classic. Bergman experimented a lot and let us be a part of it. The scene with the faces coming together, we didn't even know what was up until we went to the rushes. Bibi said, "Liv, you're marvelous." I said, "Bibi, you're fantastic." Then we saw the faces merging—it was the most frightening thing I ever saw in my life. Everybody has one good side and one bad side, or at least two different sides, one not as good as the other. Bergman had taken the worse side of each of us. To see this woman, moving her lips, and half of her is you! It's what schizophrenic people must feel. There were things like that all the time.

With *Cries and Whispers* you never had a somber atmosphere. Harriet Andersson was running around and making jokes in this little nightgown, and I was really getting worried, but when the camera said go, she looked dead.

MH: *What about the character you play?*
ULLMANN: She isn't really a sympathetic character. Someone says she's the kind of woman who goes through a room and never shuts the door after her, very selfish. When her sister needs her she can't give. And yet everybody still thinks she's sweet and nice—the audience, too. That's why she's dangerous.

Some people criticized and said Bergman is so bad what he does to me. I'm so stupid, I just thought it was the part's bad character, not mine. There is this streak of selfishness in me, though, that I wish weren't there.

MH: *Although you were highly praised for your role as the pioneer woman in the Troell epics, I always think of you as contemporary, as belonging to a world of people and particularly, men.*

ULLMANN: Actually, I've done mostly period things, except for Bergman. Classical movies like *The Abdication* also reflect modern people. I like that mixture, although I guess I'd like to do more modern stuff.

MH: *What about your American movies? One I haven't seen is* Zandy's Bride.

ULLMANN: I loved Gene Hackman. He is fantastic, very inventive. He played an unsympathetic, character but he did wonderful things with him.

MH: *One male critic told me he found you at your most attractive and most womanly in* Zandy's Bride.

ULLMANN: Then he must be a misogynist, because I was asked to look thin and haggard. I was a mail order bride, after all, and no great catch. The first thing he says to me is you lied about your age.

MH: Forty Carats?

ULLMANN: I'd do it again, willingly. Only with a little more control.

MH: *I didn't quite see you as the "older woman."*

ULLMANN: If I'd only had Cecillia to help me. What happened is they were so afraid I wouldn't look old enough, that they made me look ugly instead of older. The boy would have easily gone off with someone forty but more attractive. Only in Greece did I look okay—I had a scarf on my head. I'd really like to do more comedy. I have a disadvantage of working in the Bergman pictures. All the critics think if it's not Bergman then it's wrong. It's unfair that I have to do seven American pictures that are as good as the Bergman pictures before they will accept me.

MH: *The difference between you and, say, Garbo and Ingrid Bergman, was that they came here first, and their myths grew out of their American movies, whereas you. . . .*

ULLMANN: If I'd come here first, then nobody would have *ever* heard of me. Bergman and Garbo came at a time when they still made pictures for women in America. Joanne Woodward is the only actress who has scripts written for her. All anybody wants to see is Paul Redford. (We yelp with delight at this slip.)

MH: *I'm afraid it's women as much as the men who go to see* The Sting. *They get two for the price of one.*

ULLMANN: I guess women don't want to look at other women over thirty with the same problems.

MH: *Why is the situation different in Europe, in European films?*

ULLMANN: In Sweden, in Europe, they make more movies about women because they feel more interest in women's inner soul. On commercials here, nobody talks about the inner side of woman. They only do things to their outside, to their smell, their hands, their hair, for the husband when he comes home. That's their idea of attractiveness in a woman, while a man reads newspapers, does other things. They've made a myth of the American woman everybody wants to get away from.

MH: *What about European commercials?*

ULLMANN: In Sweden they don't have them at all. In England there is not the same emphasis. You don't have the same theme that all women must be this way. Here, it is really effective propaganda. When I watch for a while I feel I have to go out and get that shampoo. They talk even in a certain kind of voice because they know it works. There is this image of the sophisticated woman which very few of us are. All of us have to face the problem of what to do with ourselves, and what we are.

MH: *What about the Women's Movement?*

ULLMANN: I don't like the real militants. Their idea of what a woman is just as rigid. They have a fixed image that is even more frightening than the commercials. Everyone is afraid to show woman to herself. They think nobody will love her if she grows for herself.

MH: *I was electrified at that point in* Scenes from a Marriage *when we see snapshots of you as a child and a teenager, just seeing what you looked like. Marianne's voice over says she has always lived for others. Is that true of you?*

ULLMANN: Very much. I have spent most of my life and still spend most of it living for other people, doing what is expected of me, being scared of doing my own thing. I've wasted oceans of time doing what other people didn't care about my doing for them, while they were doing the same thing for me.

In fact, Bergman got hold of these pictures without my knowing it, and his insights were a revelation to me. Like the one where I am all dressed up with the hat and the pocketbook and the big bosoms. That was taken when I was seventeen and I went to London to study acting. I lived at the Y.W.C.A. with older girls—only by about two years, but they seemed much older. All the time, I was trying to be grown up, wearing a hat, and padding my bust, all these things that had nothing to do with me, just to be accepted by the older girls.

Then there's a picture with me lying on the beach, and the speech says I was obsessed with sex. I certainly didn't think of myself that way, but I look at the picture and it proves it. After years of padding, I have finally started to get a bust, and I've crossed my arms to make the crease show. There again, I was preoccupied with sex so people will accept me, so early on we get into these things.

MH: *How much of* Scenes *is your story, the story of you and Bergman?*
ULLMANN: It's not my story. I was terrified everyone would think that, but everyone thinks it's *their* story. A producer here in America who had divorced his wife told Bergman that once she invited him home during the separation and that she started telling him she had gone to sleep with her psychiatrist, and about her soul searching, and he fell asleep, exactly like in the movie.

Men have a facade. One part of women's nature is to be open to these emotional things, so they can see a film like this and fit it in, face it, but men aren't able to deal with it as easily. A man, a journalist, came here, he was very stiff and formal, but in talking about the movie he suddenly broke down. He had a similar situation, and was shattered by the film. He was so attractive when he broke down.

One reason a lot of women relate to it, is that I've drawn from so many women, from this friend and that one, I steal bits and pieces like a drawing. Things I've kept and collected I've used in this picture.

MH: *The divorce scene becomes extraordinarily violent although Johan's actual hitting you occurs below the frame.*
ULLMANN: Erland didn't want to do it, he didn't want to hit a woman. He just felt he couldn't do it and he felt sick beforehand, but when he got into the scene he lost himself. It wasn't that he lost control but

suddenly he felt it was right for his character. It took a long time to get to that part, twelve minutes. But we start with hating, so we are already at a high level. He will be able to do a lot more now. That's why it's important to have a director like Bergman who will allow you to do anything. (I don't know. I remember the story of Gregory Peck not being able to bring himself to hit Lauren Bacall when they were doing *Designing Woman*. She told Bogey and the boys when she got home and they were supposed to have gotten a big laugh out of it, but I always thought Peck was the hero of that story. Of course, American violence and Swedish violence are two different things.)

MH: *The jobs seem unreal, subordinated to the relationship.*

ULLMANN: Because love is more important than the job. You throw yourself into a job when you can't do other things, but deep down we want to talk about the human condition. Their story is really their marriage story, and that's also the reason the children—who wouldn't have changed what was between them one way or the other—are left out. It's *their* particular story. Some other couple, the children might have come between them.

MH: *Isn't it really about a relationship rather than a marriage?*

ULLMANN: Yes, it's very important that it's a relationship. Homosexuals also think it's their story. It's about a relationship and a longing for it, so even people who have never had one understand it.

MH: *How long did it take to shoot?*

ULLMANN: A very short time—eight weeks shooting. It was very hard, because there was a lot of dialogue to learn. We shot it in sequence, rehearsed for one week, then shot for a week. We couldn't have gone on like that much longer. There was no improvisation, for almost the first time with Bergman, who lately is very free. We were not allowed to depart one word from the script. This was important because there was a lot of silly, banal talk. If we had been let loose we would just swim out into sheer banality.

It was an extraordinary experience, fighting and crying. We got to know each other so well, we skipped all kinds of shyness with each other and with everybody on the crew. We worked intimately and discussed the scenes. Working on the island was so much fun, very relaxed. You had to walk for miles to a toilet and there is only cold water. We would meet in the evenings by the fire and drink and talk.

MH: *Bergman, too?*
ULLMANN: No, without him; he's a recluse in the evenings.

MH: *And how is it now since you have broken up?*
ULLMANN: Much easier. Before, if we had an argument at breakfast, I would be upset all day in my womanly way. Now we have the best part of a relationship. (She hesitates.) Or almost. The best thing you can have with somebody you lived with—friendship and working together.

Liv Ullmann:
Norway's Glittering Gift to World Film

DAVID STERRITT/1974

ONCE UPON A TIME it was Greta Garbo. And once upon a time it was Ingrid Bergman. But in the '70s it's indubitably Liv Ullmann—the latest leading lady to be hailed as the most gifted, most gorgeous Scandinavian actress of them all.

Nor is the Ullmann fame limited to her native realm. This veteran of six Ingmar Bergman films, plus scads of other Scandinavian movies and plays, has become a frequent visitor to the English-language cinema. Her pictures range from *Forty Carats* to *Zandy's Bride* to *Lost Horizon* (the recent remake, not the aged original). An international talent, indeed.

Miss Ullmann's trade secrets are no secret. For one thing, she's an enormously capable actress. For another, she has the knack of meshing so perfectly with a good movie that you hardly know it's still her you're watching—a quality Mr. Bergman keenly spotlighted in *Persona*. And for another, she has two of the most beautiful blue eyes in moviedom. It's a winning combination.

Oh yes—and she's a very hard worker. Just now, for example, she has two new movies in simultaneous United States release. One is *Scenes from a Marriage*, a nearly-three-hour condensation of Mr. Bergman's Swedish TV series of the same title. The other is *The Abdication*, at the opposite end of the movie spectrum. While *Scenes* is spare, modern, and talky, *The Abdication* is lush, historical, and costumey. And, critics agree, Miss Ullmann shines in them both.

Miss Ullmann started acting professionally at age eighteen, in her native Norway, after a year of theater school in England. But she always wanted to be an actress, "since I was eight or nine years . . . when we played theater at school. . . . At that time I did funny things, I saw all the children and the people laughing, it was so satisfactory. And all the excitement, and being on the stage, and dressing up."

The Ullmann career blossomed as a result of both long, hard work and the proverbial Big Break. Her first major role was in *The Diary of Anne Frank* with a small theater company. There she achieved the kind of local fame "any actress would get in that part." Later she went to Oslo and Norway's National Theater, and thence to films. One day, walking down the street with her friend Bibi Andersson—a major Bergman star—she met Bergman himself, who immediately asked her to appear in one of his movies. "I thought he was being polite, but he meant it," recalls the actress. The movie was *Persona*, and from then on it's been success all the way.

Bergman remains Miss Ullmann's favorite director. "I've worked more with him than with any other director," she reports. "He is one of the very best in the world. He works with a very little group where everybody knows each other, where they are all very professional. It's this professional feeling which I like very much. . . ."

Miss Ullmann feels she had certain advantages as a rising actress in Scandinavia. "In the United States I wouldn't have had such a good chance, I'm afraid," she muses. "Part of what went well for me was that I was able to keep to my own strengths, to what I had as an actress. If I had come to Hollywood when I was twenty-five, and not with the background I had—and then maybe done a musical or a light comedy, where they tried to make me into something else—I think I would have been finished. Because I'm not especially beautiful, I'm not especially sparkling [interviewer's note: Oh yes she is]. And I think it's easier in Sweden, that they take care of what is *you*."

What is that "you" in the actress's own eyes? "I think I have a—a reality. I think people can identify with me. I'm sort of—ordinary. . . . They don't mistake me for a Hollywood star. I think that might be my strength. I don't know."

Miss Ullman thinks long and hard about the balance between the two main roles in her life—as an actress, and as mother of a young daughter. At this point in her life she feels she needs both, and she is certain she could never be just a career woman, with no home life. "That is such a lonely thing, during a period when you're not working, to come home to a hotel room, to read words in a newspaper, and then just look at the wall. . . . But just to be a housewife, that would make many women happy, but me it wouldn't. Because I'm not creative as a housewife, and I want to be creative—to do something with my life besides loving two or three people. . . ."

Miss Ullmann speaks admiringly of *Scenes from a Marriage* because it realistically depicts problems and crises that many women (and men) face. And she finds the same meaningfulness in *The Abdication* despite its theatrical and historical framework. She tried to play the odd protagonist—Queen Christina of Sweden, once played by Garbo—as something of an "ordinary woman," not as "the great queen who had problems nobody else has had." But then, Miss Ullmann has had plenty of experience with unusual screen characters—beginning with *Persona,* wherein she played a deeply disturbed actress.

"I was only twenty-five when I did *Persona,* she recalls, "and obviously I didn't know everything about this woman. I was playing a woman at the height of her career, and all the emotional troubles of the career and the home and everything. And a lot of those problems I maybe didn't know that much about. So I had to go from my instinct and my feeling.

"And then you don't do it again, with small things, like in *Scenes from a Marriage,* which is very documentary. Then you have to really try and make it your own feeling. . . . It's a different way of acting, but it's also the same because it should be real, it should be recognizable. . . . Queen Christina's problems have never been mine. But her human condition—being afraid in a situation, lonely—that has to be mine. And everybody's."

Miss Ullmann doesn't think her Queen Christina will be easily compared with Garbo's, because their conceptions of the character are so different. "Garbo's Christina was very romantic," she feels, while the Ullmann version shows her more as she really was. "Our picture is about a lonely, tormented creature who abdicated because she couldn't bear men, because she couldn't bear the thought of having children. Greta Garbo was a great beauty. Queen Christina was famous for not being very attractive. She was actually appalling to people."

How has the lovely Miss Ullmann pulled that one off—the trick of seeming "appalling"? That, she reports, is the magic of movies. "With cinema you can show people in appalling situations; you can show what other people don't like with them. . . . But then you have the camera, and the camera can come close to you. And the camera can show . . . what other people don't see, because they're never that close. And you can then show the beauty of somebody longing, dreaming, really wanting. . . . That's what's so great with films, and you can never do that in theater."

A strain of humanism, a genuine liking for people, shines through nearly everything Miss Ullmann says, especially when she is discussing the meaning of her own work. She welcomes the camera's probing gaze, because "I think we should dare to show what's inside us. I think the problem with the world today is that we are having masks, we are guarding ourselves, we are so afraid of being 'dumb' and everything with each other. . . . The camera lets me be honest, and come out with things that maybe I wouldn't do. . . ."

An Interview with Liv Ullmann

VIRGINIA WRIGHT WEXMAN/1976

*Ironically, my profession requires daily exhibition of body and face
and emotions. Now I feel that I am afraid of revealing myself.*
                                                    —*Liv Ullmann,* Changing

LIV ULLMANN was born on December 16, 1939, in Tokyo, Japan,
where her father, Viggo, a Norwegian aircraft engineer, was employed at
the time. Though her family soon returned to their homeland, they left
again for Canada after the Second World War began. There, in 1943,
Viggo Ullmann met with a fatal accident and, after a brief stay in New
York, his widow took their two daughters back to Norway.

During her adolescence, which she remembers as lonely and painful,
Ullmann discovered that by giving recitations she could gain social
approval. She decided to become an actress, originally imagining herself as specializing in comedy roles. Twice rejected as a student by
Sweden's National Theater School, she spent eight months studying
dramatics in London, then joined a repertory company in Norway.
After three years, during which her performances were repeatedly
acclaimed, she returned to Sweden as a member of the Swedish
National Theater and of the Norwegian Theater in Oslo.

In 1964 she met Ingmar Bergman, introduced on the street in
Stockholm by Bibi Andersson, a mutual friend. As a result of this meeting he created *Persona* for the two actresses, and Ullmann became the
first non-Swedish star to appear in one of Bergman's films. During

From *Cinema Journal*, v.20, #1 (Fall 1980), p.68–78. © 1980 by *Cinema Journal*. Reprinted by
permission.

filming she also began an affair with the director, which led her to divorce her husband of five years, Dr. Jappe Stang, a psychiatrist. She lived with Bergman five years, during which time she gave birth to a daughter, Linn, and starred in *Hour of the Wolf* (1968), *The Shame* (1968), and *The Passion of Anna* (1969). After her breakup with the director, she continued to work with him on film projects such as *Cries and Whispers* (1972), *Scenes From a Marriage* (1972/74), and *Face to Face* (1976). In comparison with her work for Bergman, the films she has starred in for other directors have been relatively undistinguished, with the exceptions of Jan Troell's *The Emigrants* (1972), *The New Land* (1973), and *Zandy's Bride* (1974). Her American roles, in films like *The Devil's Imposter* (1972), *Lost Horizon* (1973), and *The Abdication* (1974), have been particularly disappointing. Nonetheless, she has been honored by many American awards for her performances, including six best acting awards from the New York Film Critics and the National Society of Film Critics. Her autobiography, *Changing,* was published by Alfred A. Knopf in 1977.

The following interview was originally published in *The Chicago Reader* on August 6, 1976. *Face to Face* had just been released in the United States, and the actress was touring the country to publicize it. I met with her late one afternoon in an elegant, regency-style hotel suite where she was being housed during her stay in Chicago.

She was simply dressed in a white embroidered cotton caftan. Though she had already been interviewed several times that day, she remained extraordinarily attentive, responding with unaffected enthusiasm and sensitivity.

Months later, on reading Joan Didion's account of her own attempt to interview the actress, in which the roles of interviewer and interviewee were subtly switched, I was reminded of that afternoon. Ullmann's aura of sympathetic receptiveness to the personalities around her sets her apart from the stereotype of performers who are self-absorbed narcissists. It is tempting to believe that this quality has made a substantial contribution to her astonishing capacity to imagine herself living other lives, playing roles which are not simply versions of herself but empathic renderings of the world around her.

VIRGINIA WRIGHT WEXMAN: *How did you feel about the role in* Face to Face *when you first saw the screenplay?*

LIV ULLMANN: I realized when I first got the part that it was an extraordinary tour-de-force for an actress—if I could do it. But there were difficulties with it as well, besides being difficult to act. It's not a lovable part. So I was at the same time afraid that even if I did it right, people wouldn't like it. You don't like to see your own close friend have these dreams; why would you like to see somebody you don't even know? It's not beautiful, it's ugly. It's everything inside us we don't think about.

VWW: *I was especially struck by the ugliness that comes out during the scene in which the psychiatrist first breaks down. The emotional pitch you're at is so high there—does a scene like that take a lot out of you?*
LU: I was very afraid of it because I knew that it was so crucial for the picture. But actually it was fun to do, too. Most of us have our fits—maybe not as big as that, but something like it. And I think it's fun in acting to do what you do in writing—to show a person, a character. Like in this scene where she laughs and cries and stops, and pulls herself together and falls apart again. It's like a train that stops at so many stations. So I enjoy it.

VWW: *That scene was done in one take, wasn't it?*
LU: Yes. My heart was beating and I was nervous, and I thought I'd never manage it. Because it's difficult to laugh on the screen and it's difficult to cry, and to do both at the same time, you know. . . . I thought I would never manage. I wasn't happy after the first take—which is the one Bergman used. I had envisioned myself doing many more clever things. And he let me do it three more times. But he was right, because I started doing clever things. And it was like an actress, suddenly, doing it.

VWW: *That scene is marked by the character gaining and losing control of her emotions. How much in control are you during moments like that? Is there a point at which you just let the emotion carry you along?*
LU: Well, I like to think I'm in control all the time, that it's not the character doing it. But it's a mixture. That's a very long scene, and by the end of it, I've been doing it for five or six minutes. It's like, if you talk a lot you get inspired and you talk better. But you get caught up knowing what you're doing all the time. You're not carried away.

VWW: *How do you prepare for a scene like that?*
LU: Well, I'm always very well prepared when I come to the set. I know my lines. I don't come with hangovers. When I'm working, I go to bed early so I'm prepared in the morning.

Emotionally, I don't prepare. I think about what I would like to show, but I don't prepare, because I feel that most of the emotions I have to show I know about. By drawing on real experience, I can show them.

VWW: *What do you think of the American style of method acting?*
LU: I think it's bullshit. I don't believe in it. I've worked with some method actors, and they're very difficult to work with because you never know who's coming in on the stage. Every day somebody new comes in. They have been behind stage concentrating so much that they're spaced out when they come in. Or else they've suddenly got themselves into "It was such a cold day outside," so instead of doing what should happen between the two people, they are doing a big thing about a person who is getting warm after having been out during a cold day. And that's very interesting, you know, but it's not what the play is about.

But most good actors actually do the same. The fantasy thing they do is just about the same. Sam Waterston, for example, could just as well be acting in Norway. And Marlon Brando is a method actor, but he is also a great actor. I don't think any method will ruin a good actor, because a good actor will always use what he needs. It's for the bad actors that the method can be dangerous, because they don't know what to take and what to leave.

VWW: *Your own British training, then, didn't attempt to teach you how to conjure up emotions?*
LU: No. I don't think that can be taught. That's something you have to learn through the years: how to concentrate, how it works best for you to be clean and real for the moment when the action takes place. And that is a kind of concentration and not getting uptight. I really think it's a kind of relaxation.

VWW: *How does Bergman work with actors? Take the scene like the break-down scene we were discussing—how does Bergman guide you in a scene like that?*

LU: Well, what she says is in the script. And he blocks it out very loosely, you know: that she is lying there, and that she gets up and laughs, and gets down and cries, and at some moment she gets over to the chair and tries to pull herself together.

But he's wonderful that way, as all good directors are. He really wants to use the experience of the actors and the fantasy of that actor to add to what he himself has thought. So by saying as little as possible, he gets the benefit of what I might know about hysterics that he doesn't know. Because the moment he says too much to me, I do his thing and I have shut out my thing. And instead, now he gets to see my version, and if that's not enough, or that's not what he had thought, then he can feed a little bit in of his own thing. But mostly he uses the actors and doesn't try to push himself on them. Because he already has done a lot in the script, in the atmosphere, in the wonderful blocking—he says a lot simply by saying, "She gets up and goes to sit down on the chair." He says that instead of saying, "She wants to pull herself together." So the other people on the set don't need to feel, "Now she should be showing this," because nobody heard him saying this.

VWW: *So Bergman won't coach initially, but if the scene doesn't go right, then he will coach?*
LU: Yes. Then he will say something like, "Why don't you try to give it more of this?" or, "Why do you laugh so little?"

VWW: *Can you recall a scene in* Face to Face *in which he had to coach you to get the effect he wanted?*
LU: In a way—we work so very closely and I know him so well that sometimes, when I'm not working with him but with a bad director, I think, "What would Ingmar say?" and I let myself be directed by him even when he's not present.

So I would say that I know when I am false to him. And he knows that I know. He says, "Thank you" when a scene is taken, and I know that he's going to take another one. And he looks at me. We communicate very much without words, as he does with his photographer Sven Nykvist.

VWW: *How about your personal involvement with Bergman? You've been quoted as saying that since you've gone separate ways in your personal lives, you now have the best part of the relationship left.*

LU: Well, it is better. I mean, think to yourself: if you live with somebody and then you have to work with them all day, whatever pressures you have in the morning privately will affect the day working together. But let's say that you like each other and you've stopped living together. Then you only have the benefit of liking each other, and you meet in the studio with no personal pressure in the morning between you because you have different lives. So you can just meet in a very positive way.

And things that would distress me before, because I'd get angry at him for them, now touch me because I know that I will not have to have any part of them. If I think he is vain or says something stupid to somebody, I don't have to feel ashamed—"Oh my God, this is my man!"—you know. On the contrary, I can feel touched, because I can see behind it and know why he's doing it. But it's not threatening me any more. It's only part of him that I can look at with love. But I don't have to live with anything I don't choose to.

VWW: *So you have the benefit of knowing and understanding without the sense of being ego-involved with the other person.*

LU: Right. I mean, if you can't have it all, there are a lot of benefits to be gained by breaking up the thing if you can keep the friendship. I'm not saying that it's better than having the relationship. That's of course the best thing. But if you can't have that, it's a lovely thing to have a friendship with someone you've been close to. It's like a brother or sister—closer than a friend.

VWW: *Do you think you've been able to do better work as an actress under Bergman since you're no longer personally involved with him?*

LU: Yes, I think it's easier for me. Also, I'm getting older, and I know more about the work. But yes, I also think it's easier when I'm not personally involved.

VWW: *There's a story about Bergman's younger days that has him attending rehearsals with a hammer in his hand and throwing it occasionally at the actors.*

LU: Not true! On the contrary, he's a very popular employer. He always gets the best crew because they respect him so much. He sees what they all do, and he admires when they do it well. Of course he has tempers at times, but everybody knows what this is. And you can look at it with tenderness.

VWW: *How does working with Bergman compare to working with another good director, Jan Troell, for example?*
LU: Well, they are very different. Jan Troell is a very shy person, and he isn't really a director, he's a photographer—and a genius photographer. If he has good actors, he can get marvelous things. But he can never even give you a blocking because he's too shy. What he does is he lets the actors do what they think they should do, and then he wanders around with his camera, and he picks what is true, what you didn't know about the scene. If you are up there in your head, the camera will be there on your hands and it will get the feeling of the scene. And of course for an actor this is very inspiring: you have complete freedom, and you know that there is a painter there taking the best of you, and you will see the best.

He's very slow. He always wants to cover from every angle. He takes about twenty pictures for every one he uses. That can be tedious. And he forgets the time. For that I like Ingmar better, because he is always very punctual. When it's lunch hour, it's lunch hour. And we end at four thirty. It's orderly. With Jan Troell, it's disorder.

VWW: *Was* Face to Face *made originally for television?*
LU: No. *Scenes From a Marriage* was. This time it was made for film and then there was so much material that it is going to be shown on television in Scandinavia.

VWW: *The television version is longer?*
LU: Yes. Four hours.

VWW: *So all of that material was included in the original shooting schedule.*
LU: Yes. Then they cut it down. I miss one thing: a scene where she talks to her tape recorder and tells why she wants to take her life.

VWW: *This comes after the suicide attempt?*

LU: No, before. When she decides. It clarifies a lot of things that now it takes a lot of time to get into.

VWW: *What does she say?*

LU: She says she's beginning to lose contact more and more with the world. Her reactions are not so strong any more, her feelings are not so strong any more. She makes love but she doesn't feel anything. She hears music but it doesn't get to her. She's out in nature and everybody is saying, "Isn't it beautiful!" and she is saying it too, but inside she feels nothing. She says, "No one has hurt me, and I don't want to hurt anybody. But I'm just losing contact. I want to die."

VWW: *That speech makes the character seem more aware of what is happening to her than she appears to be in the two-hour movie version.*

LU: Yes, it is changed a little bit. But Bergman felt it didn't have to be there because during the film the audience can grasp that she is out of contact.

VWW: *In several of the films you've done with Bergman, you play professional women. Yet the characters you play don't seem to find their professional lives terribly meaningful.*

LU: He believes that we can never get away from ourselves, that what we are, our personal lives, our personal feelings will overshadow anything in our professional lives. And I think that's why a film like *Face to Face* shows early that the profession will be secondary. I think he's giving women a profession to show that they are able women; it's not like a neurotic going home drinking.

VWW: *The published screenplay of* Face to Face *begins differently than the movie itself does. Why is that?*

LU: It didn't work as it was written in the original script. The actress who plays the mental patient I visit in the first scene is actually a ballet dancer—and a very good actress, marvelous face—but it didn't work for her to say these lines to the psychiatrist.

And it was good to change because the original scene was too much of a finger-pointing. The picture would have started with a patient saying to the psychiatrist, "Look, you are the sick one."

VWW: *It seemed to me that the later scene with the patient that finally was included was very effective. Instead of talking, there is a motif of touching in the scene, which picks up on a recurrent image in Bergman's recent work. Have you noticed in his work a preoccupation with touching?*

LU: Yes. The idea is picked up again in the tape recorder scene that was cut. She says, "I'm losing my senses. When I touch I don't feel anything." Someone still says it in the picture: "I long to touch some lips and just have the feeling immediately of 'I'm touching a pair of lips.'" I think Bergman is longing for the ultimate feeling where your mind doesn't immediately reflect.

VWW: *This preoccupation with experiencing the moment fully seems to have supplanted Bergman's concern with religion in his films. It's as if he's given up on struggling with the problem of an afterlife and has decided to concentrate on exploring the ways to get everything possible out of this life.*

LU: That's very right. I think that's the big thing now. Also, because he is growing older, there's not that many tomorrows compared to the yesterdays, and he really feels: "Life must mean something; life must be touched. Let's do it right away, while we're still here." That marks the great artist in people, this anguish that they try to share.

VWW: *One thing that characterizes Bergman as an artist is how well he seems to understand women. So many things in his films have so much to do with uniquely feminine experiences that it's almost impossible to believe that a man could imagine them. For instance, the scene in* Face to Face *in which Jenny, the psychiatrist, rebuffs her would-be seducer by impatiently confronting him with all the steps he is about to follow to get her into bed.*

LU: Yes, I think that's incredible that a man wrote that. That's intuitive. I know his wife hated it and she didn't believe in it. But I understood it. I've never said that, but I've had that feeling at times with men: "My God, are we going to go through all this bullshit now. If we are, then say it and I can say 'no,' but not the whole rigmarole."

He's a great intuitionist when it comes to people. And he's interested in women: all kinds. I think he finds them more interesting than men.

That's why he's gone from using Max Von Sydow and men in his pictures to using women.

VWW: *Why do you think he prefers women?*
LU: He finds them more interesting than men. They're more emotionally open. Also I think he finds actresses easier to work with than actors. Many men actors are really ashamed of their profession. And they really take care of their image. Look on the screen: they are all so virile. What Jack Lemmon did in *Save the Tiger* was very unusual, or Erland Josephson in *Scenes From a Marriage*. Mostly they are all bigger than life. And that's not only because they're men but also because they're men actors.

VWW: *I wondered a little about the ending of* Face to Face. *The Erland Josephson character seems to leave rather abruptly for Jamaica.*
LU: I just think he wanted to put Jenny finally in a situation where she was all alone. So that if she decided to go on with life, she would understand that this is part of it: "I am alone. Nobody can help me except myself."
   You know, I didn't know this before I came here, but he's added this epilog as well [which has Jenny going off to America]. He's sending her off too because he knows that maybe this picture is about Ingmar, and he feels it personally. And he doesn't want anyone to know, so he has to situate her: this is Jenny and she is in America now.

VWW: *Yes, everyone is really put in their place at the end. Actually, this particular film was especially autobiographical, wasn't it?*
LU: Yes. I was very aware that there were many of Ingmar's anxieties and childhood experiences that he was using me to share.

VWW: *There's a famous story about how Bergman discovered you walking on the street with Bibi Andersson and cast you in* Persona *without even testing you. How true is that?*
LU: He had seen one picture I'd been in. And it wasn't like he picked me up off the street, because I'd been an actress for many years in Norway. But he did take a terrible chance because I was very young—I

was twenty-five—and I was to play a woman at the peak of her career and having a neurosis, which I knew nothing about. So he decided to use me on intuition, and I did the whole part completely by intuition, because I only understood what it was all about many years later. But there was a feeling in me for the part.

But I was so shy the first week that I scarcely talked, and every time Bergman spoke to me I blushed. He told me later that he thought then: "What have I done!" But he stuck with me from intuition, and then we moved the production from Stockholm to Faro, and reshot everything there.

VWW: *Since you began your career on the stage, did you run into a problem adjusting your technique for film roles?*
LU: I'm more comfortable in film now. With the close-ups I've been able to find an intimate technique that works very well for me: you think right and it will show in your eyes. Of course, you can't do this on the stage. So I have more trouble every time I go back to the stage. Movements and everything else have to be bigger than life, and I feel myself false because I want so much to be real when I act.

VWW: *How do you feel about your experiences in American films?*
LU: Well, I don't feel they've been catastrophic. I feel like I've made wrong choices, but then they weren't wrong either because I had great fun, and I can't see . . . well, I mean, it's not *that* serious.

VWW: *How did you go into a project like* Lost Horizon? *Did you more or less know what it would be or not?*
LU: No, I didn't really look through the whole thing. I came to Hollywood for ten days to promote *The Emigrants* and all these offers came pouring in. People were offering huge sums of money and saying, "This is the part everybody dreams about." And I read it and I didn't see how it could be exactly the part everybody dreams about. But I thought, "Maybe I can't see it, and the whole thing is fun." And instead of staying for ten days I stayed for several months. I very soon discovered that nobody was interested in my acting ability and that I would look ridiculous in this picture if I put on my arts. But I was sharing my experience with Charles Boyer and Peter Finch. So to me it was a pleasant

working experience. I wouldn't have it again, because I felt humiliated when the camera was on me and I was not able to do my thing, which is acting. On the contrary, I had to have a painted face and wear strange clothes and smile.

VWW: *When you mention make-up, it makes me think of the Bergman films in which you don't seem to wear any.*

LU: No. Never in his films, nor in the theater do I use make-up. There are so many benefits, because so much can come through that can't come through with make-up. And this is true on the stage too. You can be red in the face or you can be pale, and these things actually happen to you when you go through these emotions, on stage and in life.

Bergman actually denies make-up. Oh, we have tried to cheat. In *Passion of Anna* we sneaked off and curled up our lashes, and I know Bibi tried some false things. But no, he came and took them off. And it's a little unfair, because we all look a little more ugly than we are sometimes, and older. And he's the first one to admire a woman with lovely plucked eyebrows. He says, "Look at her; she's not made up." He can't see that she's made up. But he knows our faces so well that when we try to do it, he knows.

VWW: *There's a story about a scene you do in* Persona *with Bibi Andersson, in which she tells you of an erotic experience she had on the beach. Bergman is supposed to have told you to dramatize the emotions you felt on hearing this experience by concentrating all of your feelings in your lips. Is that true?*

LU: Yes. That was a technical and very intelligent way to say, "Don't strain yourself and try to look like you're getting excited." Instead he gave me just a little technical thing and took away the anxiety.

VWW: *In a way it surprises me to hear you talk about technical details because I think of your acting style as spontaneous and free of mannerisms and acting tricks. Are you concerned with the technical details of your performances ordinarily.*

LU: I'm trying to work so that the craft will not show. I mean, some actors are very good at making masks and they are different people all the time. But the way acting is for me is that people should not think, "This is an actress," but they will think, "This is a person."

The Good Liv

PENELOPE McMILLAN / 1977

IT IS TIME for another interview, and Liv Ullmann is very sweet about it. She has just come off stage from a matinee performance of *Anna Christie*. There is yoga class, then an evening performance. Another newspaper reporter will be coming later. And then another.

"And soon the next one will be knocking on the door. Most of them want to know the same things . . ."

—*Changing*

She puts on a blue robe which sets off her blue eyes and red-blond hair perfectly. She smiles.

"When I came here the condition was no interviews, but sneaking in is now," she says, in her imperfect English and Norwegian accent. She is accommodating, because she feels "you don't have the right not to participate."

"They are waiting there in the sitting room with their pencils and their tape recorders . . . Am I a good mother . . . Do I believe in marriage . . . What is it like working with Ingmar Bergman?"

—*Changing*

From *New York Daily News*, April 24, 1977, p. 9, 41. © 1977 by *New York Daily News*. Reprinted by permission.

"I should never have written that," Liv smiles. "I never meant it as criticism." Oh, no. She loves interviews. "It's a complete concentration. It's a kind of communication." She offers coffee.

Still, "too much written is too much written," she says. She remembers when she appeared in Ibsen's *A Doll's House* in New York two years ago, so many interviews appeared that the *New Yorker* ran a cartoon with a lady saying to her husband, "I'm sick and tired of reading how perfect Liv Ullmann is."

"I was sick and tired of it too," Liv says and laughs. There is a pause. "Well of course I can say no." But she doesn't. "It has been so impossible." She smiles.

This is her time, though, and this she knows. There was an Academy Award nomination, for her portrayal of a woman going through a nervous breakdown, in *Face to Face*. There is her first book, a semi-autobiography, called *Changing*, on the best seller list. There is a starring role on Broadway, in Eugene O'Neill's *Anna Christie*. A movie, *The Serpent's Egg*, made for her Swedish director-mentor Ingmar Bergman, father of her ten-year-old daughter, is just finished. Another movie for Bergman is scheduled for shooting in August.

She is more famous and successful than ever. She has always said she is insecure, lonely, fearful, and now she says fame and success don't help. "Insecurities can be bigger because suddenly so many new people turn up who didn't care for you before and you wonder why are they suddenly turning up now. So you get suspicious of everything."

When in doubt she smiles, and her clear blue eyes look out at the world with a well-learned poise and an illusion of fragility. Both anger and strength are masked. The *changing* she has done has mostly been to be able to see through her own disguises. In the past, she often did not know she was acting in real life, too.

"When I put up the nice girl at least now I can see it," she says. "Before I didn't know I was doing it. I felt it was my duty to be a nice girl and everyone could do what they wanted, and had a right to."

Now, sometimes it is different. "Today I know that is not so. I've seen sometimes when I do get angry people don't start hating me. And sometimes I even get respect by telling what I want and not just waiting eagerly for what would please them."

"I was brought up to be the person others wanted me to be, so that they would like me and not be bothered by my presence."

—*Changing*

She was born in Tokyo of Norwegian parents. After her father died, Liv was raised in Oslo. She was a good little girl.

She is thirty-seven now, and it has taken that long, the way it takes a lot of women so long, to find out what she wanted and even what she felt. It was not until she wrote her book, for example, that she found out, through much writing and rewriting, what she thought about her five-year relationship with Ingmar Bergman, whom she did not marry, and their life together on the island of Faro in the Baltic Sea.

"I didn't realize I was unhappy those five years," she says. "And Ingmar didn't either." She showed him drafts before the book went to press. "He didn't want me to change anything but he was very saddened to read how lonely I had felt. And I didn't even know when I was there. It was after writing I realized this [almost six years later]. That's when I understood."

She has not stopped trying to please. She is all concern that the reporter's coffee, which she poured with so much grace, has remained untouched. Her gut reaction is that she does not agree with the reporter that the disciplines of writing and acting make very different demands on the creator—they are "very connected," she says. But then she does not wish to disagree, and quickly adds they are "two really opposite disciplines." And she smiles.

She is too busy, her schedule is so jammed with the demands of others. "Suddenly it's all filled in. It gives me a panicky feeling. Like this play is going until August 1. I don't have a stand-in so I know I can't be sick. I get letters from my book, I was looking forward to having a wonderful contact with people who write to me." But there is no time now. "It's just bad conscience. The more that happens, the more guilty I feel, and the less I can have happiness." But she still smiles.

Sometimes the old Liv and the newer Liv come together and things work out very well for her. Like the yoga classes held in the theater every day—she requested them, they were instantly provided—all during rehearsals, in Toronto, Baltimore, Washington and now New York as the play traveled. A lot of the cast and crew join the classes, which delights her. "We are so different, and then one hour a day we are together."

But the yoga came about because the old Liv felt sorry for co-star David Carradine's kung fu teacher when *The Serpent's Egg* was being filmed in Germany earlier this year. "David brought a teacher and then he was so tired all the time he didn't use her. I started off feeling she didn't get to do anything. I said I would love to take some classes." She got into the habit, and switched to yoga when she came to the U.S. for the play.

Anna Christie, the role she plays in O'Neill's *Anna Christie*, is a departure for her; the character is a New York barge captain's tough, cheap daughter who had actually been a prostitute while her father thought she was living a proper life in the Midwest. The play, which concerns Anna's first visit to her father in over twenty years, has her disguising her past, then confessing it, then being "saved" by a sailor who marries her in the end.

"They say it's so old-fashioned, this play, with her swearing at the end 'you can change me,'" she says. "But I don't think the play is that simple. Because you can also say it is a woman who has found herself and is so secure she can sort of help the man, because this is the only way he can take her. I don't think it's against women's liberation that if someone needs it, you lie down and swear what they need."

Liv Ullmann might lie down and swear what someone needed, and she also might get up and laugh the next day. "I was leaving a man, you know," she recalls, "and I was crying and he was crying—at least it sounded like he was. I looked up and I saw in the mirror in front of the sofa, you know, and he was"—she makes sniffling noises—"and at the same time he was arranging his hair." She laughs, "At the moment it didn't help me. But it helped the day after when I thought about him."

There is a lot of self-irony in Liv; it's in her book, and you can hear it when she talks. Sometimes it comes very close to sounding like she's putting herself down. "It comes with older age, the self-irony," she says. "I have a girl friend, Bibi Andersson [actress]. We have been healthy for each other because we have been terribly open, very open about all the times we have been ridiculous with men and made fools of ourselves."

"We can talk the whole evening, you know, just finding new places where we were ridiculous and laughing about them. It's so wonderful, it takes away a lot of the hurt."

Women talking—that is a big thing to her. When she gives interviews she clearly tries to say something; in her book she tries to tell her feelings. And through the character she plays in *Anna Christie*, she also tries to speak—"All parts you can turn into something you believe in."

"Women have to talk, really be very open, don't be so grand all the time, intelligent and fantastic," she says. "If we were more open these things that are supposed to be petty, like guilt feelings, if we shared them, if we knew other women had them, they would disappear."

Guilt. Liv felt guilty when Bergman was jealous of her dog early in their relationship, and she "rushed from one to the other." When she had her daughter Linn, she felt the same guilt over Bergman, and rushed from one to the other. "Sparkle." That was advice she was taught early. And she felt guilty because underneath she was so angry.

> "It is astonishing that so much anger can be contained behind such a mild facade."
>
> *—Changing*

She feels guilty as a mother—does she spend enough time? Is it all right to be away so much? The child is with her now, tutored five hours a day by a Norwegian teacher, tended by a nanny, and busy with ballet classes. "She has, at the moment, a good life," Liv concludes. But she says, "Every mother in the world has guilt feelings."

She feels guilty about her mother. It's like a wheel, she says, "this always guilty feeling." Daughters grow up "and start feeling guilty about their mothers. You feel guilty about your mother? I do. Mothers seem to think they get love out of making their children guilty and they don't. They get aggression."

Her daughter, she hopes, will never have this guilt. "I feel by being her friend, showing her that I am not only a mother," she says, but also a person, she has a better relationship than hers with her mother, who runs a bookstore in Oslo and feels very hurt Liv hardly mentioned her in the best seller. "I show Linn my insecurities, not those that would burden her, but my lack of knowledge. I show her I can cry and tell her why I am crying. So it's not fearful. And I give her a chance to feel responsibility for the family—she and me. She has been part of it when we decide whether I should take a job or not. She still is a child and all that, but she has had a chance to make decisions."

When she was a child, "I could feel they did me wrong but I thought they had a right to because they were grown up." It is not like that with her and her daughter, she says, and feels that is a good thing.

What does Liv Ullmann want of the future? To work. "But not this pace," she laughs, "which I say every year. But I really feel more and more a need for some tranquility, some months ahead where I feel free to plan travel, feel free to plan staying at home, feel free to improvise and suddenly follow a lust or something."

But right now there is no time for that. Liv Ullmann smiles.

"I had become an established film star, with photographs and interviews in the press. I smiled from pictures taken in capitals most of my family only knew from the atlas. Smiling, arm-in-arm with famous and stupid and wise and kind and rich people."

—Liv Ullmann, *Changing*

Liv Talks about Women's Role

TISH DACE / 1977

LIV ULLMANN'S DOOR is wide open.

She is speaking softly in Norwegian to her ten-year-old daughter Linn, who, her thin frame accentuated by faded pink leotard and tights, greets me shyly and slips out of the room to allow her mother to get to work.

"I feel very insecure as a parent," confides Linn's mother. "My success is used as proof I'm a bad mother. It's not like a man's career. Nobody asks President Carter 'Are you neglecting Amy?' But if I come to Linn with my guilt and ask 'Do you think I'm bad?' she tells me I'm wonderful. 'You have a lot to do,' she says, accepting that fact."

We ponder female guilt, fear of inadequacies at homemaking and such, as we look at photos of my sons. My ten-year-old looks like Linn, Liv observes.

We sip orange juice and tell the switchboard not to disturb us with phone calls. Linn's tutor for the tour is praised.

Liv Ullmann, international celebrity, wears no makeup and displays no pretensions as we speak of her interpretation of the title role in *Anna Christie*. O'Neill's heroine has attracted Lynn Fontanne, Pauline Lord, and Greta Garbo, but Liv hadn't thought of playing her til José Quintero suggested it. She accepted and only then took time to reread the play.

"I got a shock. I thought, oh, my God, it's so old-fashioned, I can't do this. Because in the third act she's free and in the fourth act, what is

From *The Soho Weekly News*, June 2, 1977, p. 31, 39. Reprinted by permission.

she doing! It took me a long time and a lot of thinking and feeling to see she doesn't regress at the end; on the contrary. Developing Anna is one of the most interesting experiences I've had in theater. O'Neill knew what he was about. The play has a very modern outlook on what a woman can be."

Anna Christie has been viewed as representing an essentially romantic apprehension of the world, a visionary dramatization of the redemption of a whore with a heart of gold which espouses mythic ideals and employs mythic symbols, such as the sailor Mat's baptism in the sea and Anna's cleansing by exposure to it. But the play clearly *criticizes* romantic illusions, particularly those about the pastoral idyll of country life and about the capacity of a young woman to survive economically without selling herself.

When we first meet Anna, she is, as a recent reviewer noted, "a woman who has literally been screwed by life." First exploited by her rural cousins—and raped by one of them—then, while she struggled as a nursemaid, pursued by men (and not for marriage), she has finally acceded to the demands of men exactly like her father who require access to some women's bodies so as to keep the rest pure on a pedestal. Anna shows up in New York ill, cynical, depressed, her spunk not dead but dormant until she revives it a bit with a shot of whiskey. Her only remaining vulnerability to passion is hatred of men. Prostitution is for her economic, but not sexual or psychic, liberation. For a short space she seems to be the prototype of the threatened male chauvinist's women's libber; the kind whose dogma is feared to be hostility towards men rather than efforts towards mutual respect.

When Chris sees his daughter for the first time in twenty years, he does respect her, which in turn enables her to begin respecting others as well as developing self respect and a sense of self. She moves onto her father's coal barge and rhapsodizes about the sea. Her appreciation of her own merits is increased by Mat Burke who, when rescued from shipwreck, blathers blarney about thinking her a mermaid. Burke brags of his strength in saving himself and his companions and indulges in considerable macho bravado about the men he can beat up—until Anna responds to his boasts by knocking him unconscious. The blow doesn't stop Burke from proposing to her or from pursuing her farther between acts two and three.

The third act opens with an argument between Anna and her father, who doesn't want her to marry a sailor. Chris thinks her too good for Burke, whereas Anna has resolved not to marry him because she's not good enough for him. Later Mat and Chris have their own argument in which both men act as though they own her and can force her to their wills. Neither man respects her autonomy. Each gives her, to use O'Neill's word, "orders." Anna awakens to her status as object, not person, finally protesting she's being treated like a piece of furniture and telling them both to go to hell. "Nobody owns me, see?—'cepting myself. I'll do what I please, and no man, I don't give a hoot who he is, can tell me what to do!"

She tells them, boyfriend and father, about her "going wrong" and why. When Chris won't listen, no doubt because of his own responsibility, she tears his hands away from his ears and insists "I was in a house, that's what!—yes, that kind of a house—the kind sailors like you and Mat goes to in port—and your nice inland men, too—and all men, God damn 'em! I hate 'em! Hate 'em!" and we can see why. She's no bitch. She hates the men who, whether cousin, customer, father, or would-be fiancé, have made her decisions for her instead of respecting her personhood.

With consummate disregard for the unfairness of the double standard he uses to judge her actions and his own sex life, Mat curses her and shoves her to the deck. He is worried about her having made a fool of him, for his male ego sees the incident in terms of the indignity, shame, and sorrow *he* is suffering. What *she* has endured worries neither him nor her father.

Spectators in 1922 didn't respond to the men's chauvinism as they do today. Now when Burke calls Anna a slut, people gasp. When he and Chris boast, people laugh. And when Anna comes into her own, they cheer, applaud, and even yell their approval. When Anna asks Mat, "How are you any better than I was?" a woman in the audience screams "Good for you!"

How does Liv feel about the vociferous audience responses?

"They react very strongly. I like the laughter. The laughter indicates awareness. It shows what women's liberation really has done. People are now taking notice, as they wouldn't have just five years ago, when things are said that shouldn't be. I'm sure O'Neill was aware of it as he wrote, but it has taken many years for people to listen. We've had spectators calling out things in other places too. Comments like 'yeah' when Anna objects to being treated like furniture. It's wonderful that theater can awaken this in people. That's what it's for. If this play is so old-fashioned, how can it create reactions like that?"

The old fashioned values in the play are held not just by the men but by Anna herself, who fears she shouldn't marry because she's no longer pure. A woman's worth is measured solely in terms of chastity and motherhood, concepts irrelevant to evaluating men's sentiments. Burke agrees, in the fourth act, to marry Anna only when assured and reassured that he is the only man she's ever loved, because this validates not only his manhood in general but his unique sex appeal in particular. He asks her to kneel with him and swear on the cross. And he "forgives" her. In 1922 people were shocked that she was forgiven.

"And today," muses Liv, "look how it has changed. Today they are just as angry that forgiveness is a consideration. The sympathy now is on her side. But what Mat does is difficult. Mat does what Helmer in *A Doll's House* doesn't do. Even though she's not a Catholic and she's been a whore, against his belief, against everything, he is still wanting her and is willing, let's not say to forgive, but to . . ."

She is pensive, knees pressed tightly together, a hand at her face, quiet, searching for the right word.

To accept?

"To accept. He is not forgiving, he is accepting."

You played the last scene with a smile which conveys the notion Mat really needs Anna more than she needs him.

"Yeah. That's the only way I can explain why she takes him. If she does it because *she accepts* what he is, what he needs, it works. We must be able to accept in other people that kind of weakness or fear. Give people reassurance if they need it, if you love them."

Is that one of your disagreements with radical feminists? Your willingness to make concessions to another's weakness?

"Yes. Not to *give in*, but to *give*."

We talk of her best seller *Changing*, and I speculate that another appropriate title would be "Giving." She smiles agreement—and surprise.

"I did think at one time of calling it 'Gifts.' Gifts you receive all the time, not only happiness but sorrow too. They change you, mature you.

Gifts such as sorrow are the ones you grow on because you can't be passive to them, they're challenging. With happiness you can just float."

We are interrupted by Linn for a moment and then return to *Changing*, to a passage where she admits to disguising her strength and her success for fear of threatening men and of losing their love.

"I was on a television show with Gloria Steinem, and she wondered whether those men with whom you have to hide your strength are worth knowing. I think they are, because they are still on their way also. Even though they may not have reached the point where they can take a woman's success in stride if it's bigger than theirs, they might be wonderful people. If I can diminish my success and make them feel better, I am willing to do it, though I sit beside myself at the same time and say 'Why is it like this? Why do you do this?' "

"Men's liberation will change this. It will be difficult for them, but they will get so much more pleasure. Demands on men will be fewer and on us greater. They won't have to protect us. They can be the weak ones and be protected themselves."

At the end, when Anna is willing to set up a household for her father and Mat, how does this differ from dependency, from desiring protection, from "lodging in someone's pocket," to use your phrase from *Changing*?

"That still troubles me. Then again, maybe one doesn't have to look on it as having someone support her, maybe she feels keeping house is supporting too. Is giving."

How do you motivate the extraordinary change in Anna, from hating men to such giving?

"In the first scene Chris speaks nicely to her. She says people don't usually talk to her that way. Then Mat doesn't treat her like a whore. He sees the cleanness in her and the beauty and that makes her clean and beautiful and opens up everything in her that is able to love. If you have only been met by hostility and brutality, of course you react with hostility and brutality, but if somebody touches you sweetly, you may be able to touch them sweetly back again. Because Mat thinks Anna is wonderful, she becomes wonderful. Nothing was asked of her before. Nothing except hard work and selling her body for a dollar. Nobody saw her before. Now two people do."

They see beauty and goodness, but do they, until she explodes and insists upon it, see her as a human being?

"No. No, they don't. That she has to see for herself. But she isn't able to until she is perceived as worth loving. She acquires a sense of self-worth and then we see what she does with it. We never see how Nora uses her new awareness. Ibsen ended his play, not with a solution, but with an opportunity, which Nora grasps. Whereas we see Anna wake up, we see her feeling of self, and we see her use it—in love, in acceptance of herself and her father and Mat. Nora leaves while still nearly a little girl almost. But we can watch Anna's developing awareness and maturity."

"One thing which helped me to show her development was something José did, without explaining why, and I'm not sure he knew why. Back in the third act where Anna's met Mat, I had a beautiful white blouse and a beautiful blue long skirt. Anna looked clean and able and strong. And when she had her big scene and told him the whole story, she looked like she could really get herself a job as a governess or anything. By using the same old dress, instead, it's not the dress that changes, it's the woman inside. Jose and I never put that into words to each other. And he has never commented on the smiling. Never. I wonder if that might be something only women recognize."

We turn to the subject of marriage and whether Anna or any woman can sustain the freedom of will to choose for herself, to be an integral human being within the context of marriage.

"It is possible, but very difficult. The reasons for marrying are so false for most people. Fear of loneliness. Fear of what other people will think if you're not married. Needing to be protected. Or to protect, to show how strong you are. Wanting a family because everybody else has one. When people divorce, there are discussions and discussions and discussions. That's when all the things are talked about that should have been said before marriage. If marrying were as difficult as divorcing, fewer people would be married. I have seen marriages in which it looks as though two people are growing together, free independent people who still confess to a need of each other. But it's very seldom."

I ask what valid reasons there might be for marrying, and she ponders for a long time, chin on hand, perplexed.

"Religious reasons maybe. Or a legitimate need to show the world that the two of us believe in growing together. For people who love each other, who really believe this will last and will nourish them, it is still very understandable for them to get married, and I might get married for those reasons too. Although I don't think so. There are times you get tired of always being confronted with 'Why are you alone?' Who said I was alone! One has days when one is very vulnerable on those questions and thinks it would be better to be married so one could meet people and talk about something else. I'm not putting down marriage. It's wonderful if you really love."

You certainly give the impression Anna marries out of strength and not weakness.

"Yeah, And if you can do that, it's beautiful."

I change the subject radically, and Liv is astonished at the similarity of our thoughts.

"I was just thinking of that. Oh, strange. I just thought of it also and was going to ask you about it. That was *very* strange."

I don't imagine people find ESP experiences rare with Liv Ullmann. She is open, completely open, like the door to her suite.

A Celebrity Is Not Me

ERNEST SCHIER/1979

LIV ULLMANN walks from the rehearsal room looking quietly spectacular in a loose-fitting rehearsal outfit consisting of a red pullover and wide-bottomed floor length slacks to match. Estee Lauder would commit suicide at the sight of Liv. There is not a trace of makeup on the face of one of the most beautiful women in the world.

The famous deep-set eyes recognize an old acquaintance and she offers a smile and a firm handshake. She is tall and, as always, serene. She munches from a carton of instant noodles and vegetables. "They say it gives energy, no?" she says, spooning doubtfully into the container.

Her secretary, an assistant stage manager and a press agent quietly withdraw, suggesting courtiers leaving the throne room. There follows a brief kabuki about who should sit where, the actress insisting that the caller should take the most comfortable chair. As all the chairs are the folding variety it doesn't really matter but Scandinavian courtesy to visitors does.

"I'm doing this," she answers with a standard response to a standard opening question, "because it is a challenge. It is something very new for me. I'm in a way, maybe, tired of seeking the darker side of human beings. Because I feel there is so much love and warmth, also, that one can express on the stage." Her speech is sprinkled with "maybe" and "you know".

"And the experience is a wonderful opportunity. Even the idea that they were asking me to do the lead in a musical, I thought was so extraordinary that it was enough for me."

From the *Bulletin* [Philadelphia], March 18, 1979, p. EA1, EA9.

The star of a dozen brooding Swedish movies directed by Ingmar Bergman, and the survivor of a couple of Hollywood bombs, will be making her debut in a stage musical when *Mama*, by composer Richard Rodgers and Martin Charnin (lyrics and direction) begins a tryout engagement Monday night at the Shubert Theater. The show is based on the 1944 family comedy, later a movie, and still later a TV series, by John van Druten. It deals with a Scandinavian family in San Francisco around the turn-of-the-century.

The actress has recovered from her experience in the one movie musical she has made, the disastrous 1973 remake of *Lost Horizons*.

"That I was intimidated by because it wasn't a musical about people. It was papier-mache and my part was"—she reached for the word—"nothing. Here in *Mama* it is about people you care for, y' know, and the people are much closer to what I want to be like."

Because the family in *Mama* is Swedish (Miss Ullmann herself is Norwegian) she feels she can personally relate to the musical. This is important to her.

She is not sure what register she sings in but the singing hasn't tired her. "Actually," she said, "you can get more tired on the stage from talking. Singing is only an extension of talking. At least, the way I sing is."

She rejects the notion that she is following in the talk-sing style made famous by Rex Harrison in *My Fair Lady*.

"I prefer not to comment on that. When I sing it is Mama singing and the show should be accepted that way. Mama is not, after all, a professional singer."

She admits preparations for the musical have been demanding. The actress has taken a one-hour vocal lesson every day and then gone on to rehearsals.

"There is more dance than I thought. And I enjoy it because I never in my life danced since I was very young. I have these complexes. I thought people would laugh when I tried."

Miss Ullmann is known for her unflagging energy but the rehearsals sent her home ready for bed.

"We start early in the morning and I come home at 9 in the evening. I've lost all my friends. I don't even return their telephone calls. I don't mind too much as long as I am doing what I like to do."

She has signed a contract to remain in the show through next June. If *Mama* is a hit it will mark the first time she has been obliged to repeat the same performance night after night for so long a period.

"But I trust it will be fun and when the show is running I will be able to settle down and do the things I haven't had time for."

Money, she says, was not a consideration in her decision to do *Mama*, but she hopes she will earn enough to repay her for the time she gave last year to working in the theater in Norway, where she receives the same pay as everyone else.

Producer Alexander Cohen gallantly refused to talk about financial arrangements for the woman he regards as a friend as well as his star, an affection Liv Ullman returns. "I'm an oldfashioned manager," he said, "and will not talk about her money."

From other sources it was learned that the star of *Mama* receives 7½ percent of the gross until the investment has been returned to the show's backers. Therafter, she will earn 10 percent of the gross. The theater in New York, the Broadway, will be scaled to earn $250,000 per week. A sell-out means she could earn up to $1.5 million for the year's engagement. A flop, means she could be out-of-pocket for many of her expenses.

It isn't quite the fortune it sounds like. "I pay double taxes, to the United States and to Norway." In Norway, the tax rate for her is 90 percent.

"I suppose it is stupid that I don't become an American citizen. I like it here. I like a lot of people here. But I always want to feel that I have my home, my roots, in Norway."

As a fledgling writer, the actress experienced great success with her first book, *Changing*, an autobiographical collection of events, philosophy and viewpoints.

"I am very proud that it was published in twenty languages. I get letters in all of them from readers. Not always complimentary. They write 'This is how I feel about life.' For me it has been a wonderful shared experience."

"I didn't realize at the time I was writing so open, so vulnerable. I see that now and if I was writing today I could not be so open."

She hopes for a future as a writer. "But mainly because there are not so many parts for a woman in the theater and not many parts as a woman grows older." It was an odd-sounding comment from an actress who is in the prime of her physical and intellectual maturity.

"I want to be more in direct contact with what I want to say. It is more creative and, also, I have some things that I want to put on paper. I would like to write about a woman in her forties entering middleage, and the things that are terrifying her. And her daughter, the little woman, who is entering into *her* world and how they will have to cut the cord. Y'know, most mothers and daughters enter these periods of life at the same time and the impact makes them pull apart."

Her daughter Linn—to whom she dedicated *Changing*—and books are the most important things in Liv Ullmann's life.

"There are people who never read books," she said, with a note of astonishment in her voice. "I can't understand that. On the plane maybe for ten hours and they are drinking and sleeping. Maybe a newspaper. But they don't bring books."

As she has grown older, she has developed an acute awareness of the passage of time. She has less patience now for wasting time.

"I think this is good. It is like Ingrid Bergman told me, she goes to a movie and she finds out in ten minutes if she likes it. If she doesn't she leaves. That shocked me. I always feel if you have gone in, maybe something good will happen. Not with Ingrid. 'Well I don't have the time,' she says. It is the same when we are working. Ingrid says, 'Let's not talk so much. Let's get going and do it.'"

"I think that is how she survived. Her life has been extraordinary with some sad things in it. But there is nothing in Ingrid that is looking back. She is an incredible woman. She is always on her way."

Liv supports the feminist movement but subscribes to no dogma. "I think it was easier in Norway for a woman to say. 'This is what I am,' 'This is what I want to be.' In America, there is so much competition and always the idea of success has been harder for women."

"I like women. Women respond to me more as a woman than as an actress or writer."

Returning briefly to her role in the musical she said, "Mama is a kind of basic woman. She is the kind of Mama we want or the kind we dream that we would be if we were Mama. She is strong. She is a little weak. She is a little inefficient. She is warm and loving. She is the center of the family. The family is her life.

"That is the not the way I could be but it is the way Mama is."

She often exchanges ideas with the women who write to her. "They encourage me about my insecurities, too."

Her problems with men, though it is inconceivable that she should have any at all, comes from the competition between the sexes.

"American men don't take pride in what a woman has achieved. There is a kind of jealousy. They have to be dominant. It is difficult because a woman has to underplay herself not to hurt the man. They shouldn't have to do that. When an American man believes the woman is stronger, he is afraid."

She laughed, "I'm not a very strong woman. I'm ready to be completely captured." She giggled an almost girlish giggle. "But I can't help how I am." She laughed at herself this time.

That means, she added, that she only knows men who have achieved so much they don't feel threatened.

"That makes it difficult for me. I don't always meet the people I would like to meet. The men who are more like me. People don't relate to me as they did before, because to them I am some kind of celebrity. A celebrity is not me. I am me. So maybe someone I would like to meet, some Mr. Smith, is afraid to approach me at a party."

"I think this is the most important limitation success imposes on women."

Artists and Their Inspiration:
Part I—"Life Without Barriers"

DAVID BROOKS ANDREWS / 1979

LIV ULLMANN is one of those rare actresses whose reputation mysteriously transcends the availability of her work. In Scandinavia she is considered a great actress; she has appeared in many of the films of Ingmar Bergman, but Broadway has seen her only occasionally, in plays like *A Doll's House* or *Anna Christie*; London and continental theaters not at all. It wasn't until the television production of *Scenes from a Marriage* that her work began to reach a large audience in the United States. And yet everywhere her name is synonymous with an artist of integrity, whose uncanny instinct portrays the depths and heights of the human spirit.

On film, her face becomes a mirror of the deepest sensibilities. On stage, her warmth fills the theater. Part of her growing reputation may be explained by her autobiography *Changing*—originally written in Norwegian but subsequently translated into several languages. It is the revealing of a woman—herself—who lives a life with few walls or barriers, who hopes "to find peace, so that I can sit and listen to what is inside me without influence."

She is at present appearing on Broadway in *I Remember Mama* and she gave this interview to David Andrews of the Home Forum page.

This article first appeared in *The Christian Science Monitor* on August 20, 1979 and is reproduced with permission. © 1979 *The Christian Science Monitor* (www.csmonitor.com). All rights reserved.

DA: *How do one's personal values and unique vision emerge through the art of acting—when so much is already established by playwright and director?*

LU: The values of any performing artist will shine through, because there comes a time when it's not the lines or the music but who *you* are which flows to the surface. Not just in the way you interpret the written word—or the music—but in the way you glow or don't glow, the way you listen or don't listen, the way words are dead in your mouth or alive. You can see two equally good actors play Hamlet, but one will be completely different, not just because he acts differently but because the human being is a very different man. It's true some actors are wonderful in disguises; then it's difficult to find the person. But very many actors, like me, use the same face and body all the time as the instrument, and that instrument will always reflect you as well as the character.

DA: *Isn't it difficult in today's theater to insist that your values shine through?*

LU: In the first years of my career, I took any part and didn't look for what was true for me. I'd look only for what was true for the character. But the older I get, the only value for me in acting—apart from being able to express wonderfully written drama—is to try and put forth what I believe in. I know that there are a lot of plays and films I would not act in because there's no way I could be part of them. More and more the choice is what do I want to communicate? What do I believe in? What is my conversation with people?

DA: *What can an actress do for our troubled world that no other artist can do?*

LU: She can hold up a mirror and say, "Look, this is how it is." Sometimes you can see it more clearly if the anguish is not in a newspaper headline or in your everyday life which you may shy away from. If you are sitting in the theater you can tell yourself it's only make-believe. But then if suddenly the make-believe helps you see what and why the anguish is, this can lift you, it can show you other possibilities. It can show you warmth where there is no warmth. It can show you faith where there is no faith. Theater is, apart from the church and the concert hall, one of the few places where people still can meet around an event—an event which tells them something, opens their eyes. And it's an experience shared with a lot of other people. It's not sitting alone in front of a television or with a newspaper. And I think this shared experience, which happens less and less in our world today, is something we as actors can give people. The audience can share our experience, our interpretation of words, of life—what it is to be alive.

DA: *How do those shared moments help to bring about healing and rebirth?*

LU: Everything that is shared is basically what the human person is longing for and where he grows the most. Love is shared. It's more real if it's shared, even in solitude. It's almost like a mass of positive energy that floats out because many people release it together. And that is what happens with an audience when you start to breathe together, laugh together, cry together. This makes more laughter and more breathing, although you are not aware of it because you are doing it with somebody else. If you had been sitting alone in the audience, you wouldn't have laughed so easily, maybe your tears would have been more silent. It *enables*; sharing enables people to come out with their feelings. But the trouble with us today is that we don't come out with feelings anymore; we are more and more suppressed, withdrawn, frightened because anguish is big. What's happening around us—because we know about it today—is inconceivable. In the theater you are not alone any more.

DA: *Fantasy is obviously an important element in your life. In your book* Changing *you have two bicycles talk to each other. Does fantasy have rejuvenating possibilities?*

LU: I think there's good fantasy and bad fantasy. The bad fantasy is what you see on television here—the commercials that tell you if you use this hair spray, a fantasy life will follow—your husband will come home on a white horse. That is a dangerous fantasy because that is not how life is. Good fantasy is to have bicycles talk to each other, the wonder of a flower, of a season when the trees get their leaves, and you make it alive. And the right you have to paint them the way you want to, to look a them the way you want to, to see a picture, a painting, the way you want to. That is a wonderful fantasy because it enriches what is already there with what is already in you. Even in reality there are lots of beautiful dreams. The other fantasy is dangerous and frustrating, very much a part of why people live in anguish because they've based their whole lives on unreality. On stage I'm aware of many things my character is thinking and showing which nobody in the audience or on the stage sees. It's only my fantasy filling in what's not in the script. And in life I certainly fill in a lot of things that are not there. Sometimes it's necessary to fill in empty spots. If it doesn't deceive us, if it makes the picture we're seeing nicer, why not add a little? If you see two eyes that look kind, it doesn't matter if they are not really that kind. If you read into them beauty because you need it at that moment, I think it is allowed. We all do it, because we all need to.

DA: *When we read into a couple of eyes a little more than is there, are we inviting something better?*
LU: When you read into a pair of eyes that they are beautiful it might also be that your eyes are open and beautiful, that you are actually look-ing at a mirror. Suddenly you think this person is wonderful—we talk the same language—but it is really *you* who are open, inviting the same openness in the other person. It's similar in the theater. If, for example, you hear smiles in the audience it's because there are smiles on the stage.

DA: *You conclude* Changing *with a wonderful line: "It may be the lost kingdom of childhood I'm in constant search for." How is that an integral part of your art?*
LU: It's the innocence of childhood—when we were still open, when we could paint a tree and let it look anyway we liked. It was the time before somebody came and said a tree looks like this and you must paint it so. The innocence which allows every kind of dreaming, that is what I long for. When I was in Australia I met a priest who said, "Your book is very religious." I didn't understand this because I hardly men-tioned God. He said, "Do you know what you are really saying when you look back? You're longing for the lost kingdom of childhood. That is an expression from the Bible, and that is also where we all are, in a Biblical sense." And that is true. I think it is not only looking back to your childhood, it is looking for a world where it is possible for all of us to be innocent. I want to use this in my work by showing simple, basic

feelings—an open hand, a touch of the cheek, two open eyes that have no barriers, a life without barriers. I want to show the innocence of life, even when I'm portraying a woman of great neurosis and inner difficulties. In the middle of all this I want the audience to see that behind her anguish two eyes are staring out, begging "understand me, see me, feel for me." People may not hear the cry if it doesn't echo their own cry, but suddenly, they can recognize the eyes that look through the anguish, and from that recognize the character behind the façade. It's the innocence behind all of us, behind all of our covers. Maybe it is a desire to talk about God—a belief, something really strong, unchanged for hundreds and hundreds and hundreds of years that we can all share. A lost kingdom of childhood—childhood which was a kingdom.

DA: *In* Changing *you quote a Danish author, Tove Ditlevson: "There's a young girl in me who refuses to die." What does it take to keep her alive and nourished?*
LU: Not to deny her. Not to say, "Listen, now you've grown up and you must get rid of this girl." To admit that much of me is still this girl. There are many things that I deny in myself, but not that girl because she is as much a part of me as I can ever be. I once rehearsed with a musician who was very shy and never spoke. Then he read my book and suddenly he said to me one day, "I have a little boy inside me too." From then on our conversation was like a joke, my little girl and his little boy, and we are today writing each other. We are very close. When we share the vulnerability or insecurity or longing that we all have, it makes for much better friendship, because after that we can be grown-up together, admitting deep down inside we are still surprised, that there is still a child waiting to be grown-up, who is wondering—when will my dreams happen?

DA: *Now that you are grown-up and have to struggle to find your way back to the kingdom of childhood, is there something richer about it?*
LU: Oh yes, because now both the past and the present are part of me. I can mature and find values that have to do with this world. But as a child a lot of the dreams or choices had nothing to do with this world; they were fantasy only. Now I can use what I want of my fantasy, incorporate it into living. My choices—of who I want to be—are bigger in some ways today. At the same time of course there are much fewer

tomorrows than there were twenty years ago, when all of tomorrow was ahead. Now there are a lot of yesterdays, but if I use yesterdays wisely all the tomorrows can be more enriched. That is, if I don't give up and say I'm too old.

DA: *You mentioned in a recent interview that your innocence works both for you and against you as an actress. Could you explain that?*
LU: It works for me because I'm open, not as open as I was before, but I'm still open enough for good things to happen to me, because I allow bad things to happen to me, also.

DA: *What do you mean by allowing bad things to happen?*
LU: If you are open, if you trust, if you believe in tomorrow, then you also allow a lot of disappointments because you believe so much in tomorrow. But if tomorrow turns out wonderfully, it's because you've allowed tomorrow to be completely open and full of faith. To me that is the positive aspect of innocence. And maybe the negative is when you take the wrong train because you believe too much in people who say this train goes to some wonderful place. You know you have a lot to learn, so you take the train and you get off the tracks for a long time, and you have to walk back home. It happens in everything we do, because every day is a choice of living.

DA: *You make use of the bad train trips or the bad experiences?*
LU: Yes. Actually what I've found, and I don't think it's an act of rationalization, is that I've learned more on that train ride and the walking back than I have with the happy moments, though they were wonderful and I wouldn't do without them. But you didn't have to struggle in them, you didn't have to think or wonder. They filled you with joy, but in the other experiences you had to struggle, overcome, cry, fight, and that is very positive. You understand I'm talking about troubles you've brought on yourself. The boat people who are struggling at sea, I don't think those troubles are necessary for people. That's something different and terrible. We need our everyday troubles and disappointments to grow. But nobody deserves or should have what is going on there; and it's terrible that we are sitting here and they are there, and there's little one can do.

Artists and Their Inspiration:
Part II—"Allowing a Little Quietness"

DAVID BROOKS ANDREWS/1979

DA: *You said In the recent book* Without Makeup *that you must work for what you believe is true and what other people in the audience will recognize. Do you ever have any difficulty coordinating your truth with what others will recognize?*

LU: It's very difficult to be truthful all the time on the stage and it's impossible for it always to be recognized, because the audience's experience may be different. It needs someone to receive it. The performing artist should be able to overstep this difficulty, but I know no actor who can always do so. You're lucky if you reach one receptive person.

DA: *How do you step over this barrier if you feel the audience is not responding?*

LU: Often you do all the wrong things. You try to do more, which of course makes it less truthful. You give up and do less, which makes it even less truthful. Sometimes you make a third try—start to be glib and do things that you know are safe. All actors do that at times because we're a little vain, we don't want to go down the drain. At those times you try to look very pretty or you try to be funny with lines that are really sweet and charming. You try to make the audience fall a little in love with you. A lot of actors do that, including myself when I really

---

get insecure. You aim for surface things. But if you can't reach an audience, it's best to do nothing. It's like a conversation or being with somebody—if you don't reach each other, you'd better take a pause. Maybe the pause is the very thing, but in the theater you seldom have time. Though maybe you can make a little quietness around you.

DA: *There's a line in* Changing *where you describe a dedicated audience—people who've bicycled long distances to the theater in Norway and sat on the hard benches. What would you like the dedicated audience to bring to your performance, to the theater?*
LU: Openness, curiosity, need, warmth, because then, at least, they are receivers and they are givers, too.

DA: *How does an audience give?*
LU: They give as much as the people on stage. An audience is much more part of a production than they know. They can give in their silence because in the silence you can hear their listening. They can give in their laughter because you hear in their laughter that they're sharing the joke. They can give very much by just smiling because you can hear on stage when a smile goes through the whole theater. And they give through crying because you can hear if an audience has tears in their eyes—it's a kind of movement. An audience is very, very much a part, and night after night it is different because of the audience. It's the same as when you talk with somebody. If you feel that person really wants to listen—even if what you're saying is not very special—you say it with more heart. On the other hand, if what you have to say is profound, you may be so afraid that you come out with a kind of telegram. It's the same in the theater.

DA: *Do you feel the equivalent of an audience when you are filming?*
LU: The camera is what I feel. I use the camera. Here's fantasy again, but the camera is so quiet that you can read everything into it. If someone is watching intensely, that helps too. When I work with Ingmar Bergman, for example, he's a remarkable audience. You can feel him leaning forward, listening and watching; afterwards he's seen what you were trying to show even if it hasn't come out successfully. He will say "Do a little more or less," and you are willing to show him everything

because you know it will be recognized. That's what makes most people flourish—they need someone who recognizes them.

DA: *In* Changing *you talked about Bergman's letting you do and feel things that you'd never felt before. Can you as an actress help the audience discover emotions they've never felt before?*

LU: It's seldom that I can reveal anything on the stage that people don't already know about themselves, but I think I can help them recognize something they haven't thought about, which can move them. It's easier in a film to reveal something suddenly because in the close-ups you come right into the eyes and the skin. On the stage you can't forget the master who is the writer. If you play Shakespeare or Ibsen, you are the tool; they are the revealers. But in a film the actor can also be the revealer; you can go beyond what the script writer wrote. You can do that in a play, too, but with less ease.

DA: *You've said "I'm more in danger of doing too much than too little." Why is that restraint so important to you?*

LU: Sometimes if the part's not easy for me, I try too hard, I try to cram everything into it. When the words or the action are not there, I try to put them there by doing things instead of letting the part rest in peace. I did much more before in this play [*I Remember Mama*] because it didn't have all the words and scenes for what I wanted to show. It's not Shakespeare, this play, but I would like to show the spirit of motherhood, though I don't have the words, the scenes. If I allow some quietness around me, people can use their own fantasy. If I want to show the spirit of motherhood, and I don't find it in my material, the audience and I must create it together. If I'm a little more quiet and I allow you to interpret in me what has been silent, you will have a better experience than if you've had a very busy lady all over the stage trying to prove *I am Mother*. That is why less is always better than more. After a while in a play I relax a little more. In a film of course it's easier because it's one shot and you give it that chance of reality whereas on stage you rehearse every day and you can overdo it.

DA: *So the limit is really your text?*

LU: The limit is the text, and much more in the theater than in film. Because in film you can always add by a closeup. You may say a stupid line but your face can defy it and make the line inconsequential, for your face is telling what the feeling really is. On the stage you can't do this; you stand there with a line and that's your line. Sometimes in the theater you get scared—if you have done as many films as I have—for you think you'll reach no farther than the third row—you'll never reach the balcony. If my character's proud, I know what her expression would be and that's very simple. The third row can see it, but can they see it in the balcony? So I create an expression of pride that is too big. And something strange goes up to the balcony as well as to the third row. I give them no chance to see pride because I do too much. I don't trust that if this is real it will go to both the third row and the balcony. But if I trust, then the details won't matter because I'm not doing anything wrong.

DA: *Not getting in the way?*
LU: I'm not getting in the way, and that is very important for the actor. Don't get in the way for the audience; let them be creators, too. Let them come in with their fantasy.

DA: *What makes your approach to experience different from somebody who isn't an artist?*
LU: Because in doing this job I'm a people watcher. I'm very curious—if people are angry I like to know why. I love to look behind things. That can be very dangerous because you can start to watch yourself too much. But if you have this in charge, no creative artist or performer can be without it. You can't just float through life and not look to right and left because what are you then portraying? My material is the life I'm living and the life I'm seeing, the life I'm reading or listening to. That's why I'm happy I'm an actor because it has enabled me to experience a lot of things I otherwise wouldn't. I would probably still be in Trondheim, Norway, if I weren't an actor.

DA: *As an actress you have a remarkable ability to make yourself vulnerable to what is going on, to the other characters, to experience. How do you keep yourself both vulnerable and intact?*
LU: You never die, or rot, if you are vulnerable because you are always open. It can be painful, of course, and you can't go around like an open

wound all your life. But you have gained much more experience than if you'd decided you had all you need. At the same time if you are too vulnerable, you can end up very naive, not growing at all, because you are afraid of losing your sensitiveness. Part of maturing is actually allowing some innocence to go because you can't afford it, and it's not suitable any more.

DA: *Is there any danger that your art could become just vulnerability and not art?*

LU: That's a danger for a lot of actors—their work becomes too much feeling, they cry their own tears, and that isn't art. I think I'm aware of that; I'm trying on stage not to cry my own tears and shiver my own shivers. Actually the fun of acting is to use your openness in such a way that the character can come through you. And if the character needs to cry, it's the character and not you feeling all over the place. It's a kind of openness that allows you to stand beside and watch, like having an instrument so tuned that whatever you choose to play on it will come out right. The moment you feel too much private anger or private anguish, you aren't in tune anymore, and that is when you start making up things because you are not relaxed.

DA: *How have the other arts—literature, painting, music—fed you as an actress?*

LU: Books have—a lot. Books have been people talking to me. I can't understand people who don't read; I think it's the richest way of sharing even if you're sitting reading alone. It's a mass impact of thought so it's really very shared. Paintings less. When I was very young I went to museums all the time looking at paintings, but paintings I know very little about. I wish I knew more because I'm sure it's a wonderful world. Music a lot again. Maybe music in some ways is the highest art, because it's almost religious—bigger than being human, it's out of the body—it's really freed emotion. I feel pity for young people today who only know disco music. As wonderful music influences you and becomes part of you, just so people who grow up on cartoons and disco are influenced by that, and this is a cover-up for who they are. It might ease some superficial kind of anxiety, but it certainly doesn't reach down where one should be reached. Depending on when you grew up establishes a lot of who you are. And later you have to fight to forget or to come through those years when you were influenced the most.

DA: *Did that happen in your own experience?*

LU: Like a lot of women of forty I grew up under authority—a nice girl who was quiet with grown-ups, expected to become a housewife forever. And suddenly when I was thirteen or fourteen, women's liberation started coming. We were told a real woman is a free woman who follows her own feelings and is independent, who goes out and is creative. I was told everything I had just learned was wrong. So whenever I'm out there being liberated, one voice is always telling me "this is wrong for nice girls." Yet when I'm a nice girl this other voice says "Listen, a liberated woman doesn't do that." I have to fight this every day in order to find out what I really want. Every five years there's something new. Sometimes it's wonderful, but even when it's wonderful it is still mod—everybody has to do it, and that's dangerous. Your thoughts are not your own and your feelings are not there; you are just saying what everybody else is saying. You're reading what everybody else is reading, and it never becomes part of you.

Liv Ullmann

LOUISE SWEENEY/1981

WHEN LIV ULLMANN begins to tell stories about the plight of
refugees she has met, the theaterful of wriggly children hushes up.

She tells them about the hungry boy in the Cambodian refugee camp
who told her, "Sometimes I cry, but only when it rains, so the other
children will not see."

Then she says, "You and I can help wipe his tears away."

She tells about an African refugee camp where water is so scarce that
"the women dig in the brown mud, and that's what they drink."

And she tells of visiting another camp where a little girl who owned
nothing in life but a tiny ring with a red glass stone took it off and gave
it to her for some child who needed it more.

Liv Ullmann tells the children these stories for a reason.

The Norwegian actress who became internationally famous through
Ingmar Bergman's films is touring the world this year as a goodwill
ambassador for the United Nations Children's Fund, UNICEF.

It's as an ambassador, not an actress, that she appears on stage one
Saturday morning at the National Theater here in Washington in a pro-
gram for and by children. It includes the Suzuki violinists, Irish dancers,
Nigerian dancers, and the National Children's Choir.

Her stories move the young audience.

When the program is over, and children are crowding into her dressing room, one little girl, perhaps remembering the story of the refugee

From *Christian Science Monitor,* April 21, 1981, p. B2+. © 1981 by the *Christian Science
Monitor.* Reprinted by permission.

child, steps forward and takes off a small silver ring with a heart at the center. "When you meet a little girl in one of those countries, who needs a ring, please give this to her," she tells the actress.

"They hear about refugees," Miss Ullmann points out later. "They hear about aid. But they don't even know" what the words mean, she says.

So she's explaining to them in a way they can understand.

"It's important to teach them the key words, because they are going to be the future. And their conscience and their ability to understand and feel compassion is sometimes much greater than ours." Maybe these children will speak to friends, will learn from the UNICEF booklets they've received what they can do, and will send a contribution to help the UNICEF aid effort, she adds.

"Their lives can take on a new activity . . . a good one, a giving one. . . . For many . . . it will not last, but it is . . . a good impulse."

After the performance and a press conference, Miss Ullmann goes on to a luncheon in her honor at a private home, where she talks some more about UNICEF between bites of *boeuf bourguignonne* in aspic, followed by cheese-cake with strawberries.

Today she looks very much like Alice in Wonderland among the grown-ups, with her long, golden hair flowing straight down her back, her open face, and wide, fjord-blue eyes. The dress she wears reinforces the image of Alice. Cut full like a nineteenth-century child's smock, it is of blue cotton patterned with small red and yellow flowers. With her cream-colored leather high heels, she is a tall Alice, but she still looks like someone a child could identify with. And she still sees childlike qualities surfacing in her grown-up world, as she explains in her 1977 best-selling autobiography, *Changing*, which opens with a quotation from a Danish woman, author Tove Ditlevsen: " 'There's a young girl in me who refuses to die.' "

Miss Ullmann then writes, "I live, rejoice, grieve, and I am always struggling to become grown up. Yet every day, because something I do affects her, I hear that young girl within me. She who many years ago was I. Or who I thought was. . . . Some mornings I decide to live *her* life, be something other than what ordinarily is my daily role. I snuggle close to my daughter before she is awake, feel her warm, peaceful breathing, and hope that through her I may become what I wished to be."

As she tells children with upturned faces at the theater, "I wanted to do something else than acting that was more important," so she accepted the UNICEF ambassador's role that Danny Kaye and Peter Ustinov had filled before her.

Asked what she considers the single area of greatest need in her travels around the world for UNICEF, she answers, "At the moment it is obviously Somalia . . . together Somalia, Ethiopia, Uganda, and a little country called Djibouti," all on the Horn of Africa.

"Although the need is enormous still . . . for the refugees from Cambodia, the world community has looked that way; aid has been given. I was there one and a half years ago, and I saw a terrible situation. . . . I went back half a year later, and I saw . . . that situation had turned into one of hope, because . . . aid had been given."

"But, even at the worst there, it was never as bad as the absolute starvation and lack of water I saw in Africa. . . ."

"The two biggest rivers in Somalia, around which the two biggest camps are built, have now dried. . . . Since there are 70,000 to 80,000 people in each camp, and there are several such camps, you can imagine—how do you transport water . . . ?"

"There are people there who go without water now for a week. That's like horror stories from the desert. And on top of it, they don't have any food. They have nothing."

Yet the world community is not responding to the plight of the Africans "the way they did with the Cambodian refugees and the boat people from Vietnam." Miss Ullmann adds. "We [residents of the West] are going to be responsible for mass murder, because we are going to see that millions of people are going to die on the Horn of Africa."

"And, you know, your newspaper had such a wonderful article on what happened in Thailand with the Cambodian refugees, a really wonderful article. I wish the same article of hope would be [published] for the people of Africa. The numbers are so much greater. . . ."

"It's hard for people to identify in the same way. . . . There were a lot of feelings of responsibility about the lives of the Vietnamese and Cambodians. . . . There is less a feeling of responsibility when it comes to the African refugees."

"So that is another thing we have to overcome."

"And the only way, really, is to present the people, who can give, with faces . . . so that they know they're not giving to somebody foreign, somebody different—so that they know misery has no color."

As she talks about the tragic conditions in refugee camps, Liv Ullmann's face mirrors the shock and horror and compassion she feels at what she saw there. She has projected those emotions before, on film, in one of Ingmar Bergman's most devastating pictures, *The Shame*. In it Eva, the young wife she plays, survives a savage war that leaves the country desolate and its people refugees.

This time, though, the emotions are real. The anguish on her face as she talks about the refugee plight is of a different dimension from even her most celebrated film achievements: her long collaboration with Bergman in such films as *The Shame*, and *Hour of the Wolf*; the best-actress awards from three American critics' groups for *Face to Face*; two more American best-actress awards for *Scenes from a Marriage*; best-actress citations from Sweden, Italy, France, and Germany for various films; and acclaim for roles in Bergman's later movies *The Serpent's Egg* and *Autumn Sonata*, in which she appeared with Ingrid Bergman.

Although she's had an occasional fluffy role, like that of the divorcée in the Hollywood romance *Forty Carats*, many of the heroines she's played have been complex, strong women like the earth-mother in Jan Troell's two-part saga of Swedish immigrants in America, *The Emigrants* and *The New Land*. Miss Ullmann received three citations for those Troell films, including an Academy Award nomination, to add to her slew of prizes.

In her native Norway she has received the Order of St. Olav from the Norwegian King. She was the first woman to receive the Peer Gynt Award, given by the government for outstanding work in Norway and abroad.

Liv Ullmann, whose face is eloquent in any language, speaks English fluently with the faintly rocking rhythms of her native land. Her voice rings out clear as a girl's at a brief press conference following the UNICEF performance. Someone asks her rather snittily what a mere actress can do, even with the help of media exposure, for such a cause.

"I think it's very important that people who do reach the media," she responds, "use the media for other things than talking about their measurements and future plans. And I think that more and more are doing this. I believe there are people who have more box-office appeal that could do [still] more in this way. . . ."

As for results, she says, they are impressive. "With the help of the media we raised $75,000 in San Francisco [in] one evening. One article in one newspaper in Chicago . . . gave us $60,000" in contributions.

"The media are enormously important. When we do talk shows, UNICEF gets so many checks. . . . The tendency is for 10,000 people to give $1 each," rather than one person to give $10,000, she adds, "because those who give first and most willingly are those who have very little, those who themselves are on welfare or social security, who write and excuse themselves and say, 'I don't have any more, but I promise I will write and give when I have more.' "

"There are others. I even had a man who had a Rembrandt and said, 'I will be happy to sell that and give the money [to UNICEF]'; and a plastic surgeon who said, 'I will operate for free on all the [refugee] victims you tell me about.' "

The children's ambassador smiles as she adds, "I go to a restaurant, and people come to the table and leave $5 and say, 'Please give it to UNICEF.' Or they stand outside where you are, and they have their checks ready to give.

"There is such a willingness to give, but they have to be motivated, and the media is the only way they can know."

Miss Ullmann, who is also vice-president of the International Rescue Committee, has worked actively for several Cambodian and East African relief efforts in the United States, Europe, and Asia. She adds quietly toward the end of her press conference, "Why is it always [to solicit] aid for people, to help them stay alive, that we are . . . having fund raising? Why is there not fund raising, instead, for submarines and war planes that are used to kill people? There is something really wrong there. One day the opposite will happen: . . . people will have money to live, and the others will have to raise money for submarines and war planes."

The actress writes evocatively in *Changing* of her own childhood, her father's early death, her girlhood in Trondheim, her stage debut at eighteen as star in *The Dairy of Anne Frank*, her early marriage to a doctor, which ended in divorce, and her stormy years with Bergman. Running like a leitmotif through her autobiography are her constant thoughts about her daughter, Linn, now fourteen, who is spending the year in the U.S. with her mother. What is the most important thing Liv Ullmann can teach Linn?

"Well, I've found there are very few things you can teach children. Being with them is your way of trying to show them values, because very early now they want to find their own right and wrong. . . ."

"They don't listen, don't trust authority the way we did. . . . I think the best thing I could hope for her—and that I try to encourage—is to trust her own integrity, to trust her own values. . . ."

"What I'm scared of—and the only place I set rules—is where it comes to drugs. . . . alcohol, . . . things [that] might endanger her life, being places I feel are not safe."

"I wish I could teach her compassion, understanding, love for other people. But, you know, that has to come from within yourself. . . ."

We sit in a sunny dormer room splashed with blue and yellow flowered wallpaper. "It's like a room from childhood," she says with pleasure. We talk about a film she admires, *Summer Paradise*, directed by another Bergman disciple and actress, Gunnel Lindblom. In it there's a line to the effect that there are no more children, that society has taken childhood away from children. Miss Ullmann agrees:

"I think today children are losing their innocence much too early, very much because of violence and other things on TV and in films. Very much because society has turned toward—and I'm talking about the rich part of the world—commercializing [childhood] . . . by fashions, by special toys . . . taking away the fantasy world of the child, the inner world."

"They don't play with swings. They don't make [doll's] clothes. They don't see fairies any more, because everything has become so realistic. Everything has become so frightening, because they know they are surrounded by war. And worst of all is the commercialism. . . ."

"If Mozart had been a child today, he wouldn't have had a chance. No one would have respected him as the talent he was. He would have been put on a shelf which was that of a child. . . ."

"The children of the third world find something that the others have lost, because at least they are still allowed to be children—to show enthusiasm and laughter, although they have so very little to be enthusiastic about and to laugh about. But you can see when you reach for them, when you play with them. Their smiles . . . are still unguarded. They are still trusting. They are still allowed to be children."

"We are in many ways the underdeveloped ones, and you learn that when you come to the so-called underdeveloped countries. . . . Although they have little to live on, they have a lot to give. . . . I'm not romanticizing being poor; I'm just saying that we are losing—the industrial world has taken away—the innocence of childhood. . . ."

In addition to her unpaid job as children's ambassador, Miss Ullmann is dandling several other roles on her lap. Earlier this year she was one of four women to direct a short film, part of a longer Canadian feature, *Acts of Love*. The various sections of the film are written and directed by celebrated women, including directors Mai Zetterling and Suzanne Cohen, writers Nancy Dowd, Edna O'Brien, and Penelope Gilliatt, and singer/songwriter Joni Mitchell.

In addition, Miss Ullmann is working on her second book, *Tides*, which will recount some of her UNICEF experiences. *Changing*, her first book, was like an impressionist painting, full of light and interior images, but not at all a photograph of her life. It has been printed in twenty-five languages.

Tides will have a quite different form, Miss Ullmann suggests, and part of the difference is in the nature of her subject. "The difficulty is that when you write about the third world you mustn't be preachy or critical. You mustn't make statements as if no one knew about it before. That is the difficulty: to find a form that is not offensive to anybody and at the same time is true to your experience. "And I know so many people have been there before, so many people have done so enormous much," says the woman who has done so "enormous much" herself. She raised $195,000, for example, from theater lovers for the International Rescue Committee, after her trip to Cambodian refugee camps, over a year ago, traveling to Thailand on a "March for Survival" with a group of women who took twenty truckloads of food and medicine there to aid refugees.

In the last two months Liv Ullmann has also appeared several times on Capitol Hill, testifying before members of the House Foreign Affairs and other committees, urging them to support the Reagan administration's $77 million African aid proposal to assist victims of the famine there. "I have no understanding of budgeting or diplomacy or whatever," she told the congressmen. "I can only tell you that the suffering is enormous. If you met these people there is no way you could say it is not your business."

In addition to her work as ambassador, director, and author, Miss Ullmann is also planning to act this summer on a Norwegian-German film, *Jenny*, to be directed by Per Bronken (whom she calls "the best director in Norway"), and later this year to act in another Bergman film. "He promised me a comedy," she says, but indicates with a roll of her eyes that it's anything but.

How does this woman who has played so many different parts see herself?

"I'm hopeful . . . impatient . . . vulnerable. I'm lacking in a lot of things I would like to be."

The film role that's most like herself, she says, is that of the wife in Bergman's *Scenes From a Marriage*—"but not the end of it. I didn't like the end of it."

Flicking back through a list of theater roles that includes O'Neill's *Anna Christie* and the Richard Rodgers musical version of *I Remember Mama*, she concludes that the role most like her is Nora in Ibsen's *A Doll's House*. Why? "Because—very much—that was my life," says the actress who slammed the door on her early marriage years ago.

But her all-time favorite role is that of the radiant wife in *The Emigrants*. "I loved her," Ullmann says. "I can't say that's like me, because she stayed home and with all those children. Maybe deep down inside me that's what I picture, what I would have or should have done if things had been different. But I just loved that woman."

But hasn't she had it all?

"No, I'm not staying home and having many children and taking care of them. No. I'm not. But I liked her, and I liked some of her purity and sternness. I liked her a lot."

Liv Ullmann: Actress Extraordinaire, Writer, and Director

GARY LIPTON/1982

LIV ULLMANN POURS steaming coffee, as a Bach concerto filters through her spacious apartment. The actress radiates warmth, and her lips break into a delightful smile. She feels safe and snug in Manhattan. "Coming home," says Liv, "it's so nice to have my doorman ask, 'did you have a nice day?' Of course, I enjoy a privilege, but I also want to help those who are less fortunate."

Liv lives close to her feelings, and dislikes actors who hide behind their roles. "Onstage and off, the worst mistake is being theatrical, rather than being yourself," says Ullmann. "I integrate theater and reality, and don't switch off my personality."

The actress plays women who relentlessly explore life. Under director Ingmar Bergman's guidance, Ullmann bared her soul in such film masterpieces as *Persona*, *Cries and Whispers*, *Scenes from a Marriage*, and *Autumn Sonata*. She made her Norwegian stage debut as another seeker of truth in *The Diary of Anne Frank*. "I identified with Anne," Ullmann remembers, "and as a young girl, shared her sweet belief that all human beings are good."

What changed her mind? "Visiting refugee camps in the last few years, I saw much distress and suffering," Ullmann explains. "A five year-old Somalian boy, his body wrinkled like an old man, took hold of my finger and aimlessly led me through the camp. He had nothing but an

From *West Side TV Shopper*, December 11–17, 1982, p. 17.

empty plate. Two days before Christmas, I returned to my nice hotel and heard 'Jingle Bells.' I cried. If people truly cared, why did this child suffer? At that moment, I exchanged Anne Frank's words for Martin Luther King's message: 'We shall overcome!' "

As a good will ambassador for Unicef, and as an active member of the International Rescue Committee, Ullmann aims to galvanize public awareness. "We can't sit back and expect results," she says. "These starving children are too weak to tell their story. Being in the media, I speak for them, encouraging people to end human misery.

"It's so easy to be grouchy, to send out blackness," she continues. "You don't have to be an actor to communicate positive feelings. Every job is important, because through work we touch people, and give happiness."

Stretching her talents in new directions, Ullmann is currently learning the joys, and agonies, of writing. "Writers must acquire self-discipline," Ullmann concludes. "An actor does what he's told. You come to the set on time, follow the director's instructions, and get permission to leave. The writer sets his own hours, and must push himself to get the job done. Communication is the core of both professions, how an artist expresses feelings, experiences, inner knowledge.

"I would never give up acting if I could always play an O'Neill character, or speak Ibsen's lines." A girlish laugh. "But sometimes, you have to interpret Mr. Klutz! My writing is becoming more enjoyable, because I draw upon personal experience, and use my own words."

Of course, actors don't wage war with editors. Now Liv Ullmann does. "They snip a word here, knock out a transitional sentence, eliminate the emotional colors, and otherwise chop your article to bits," she reports. "It's frustrating. That doesn't happen to actors. The worst director may not help you, but at least he lets you say your words."

What sets the great director apart?

"True understanding. He sees everything you do, and says, 'This is your objective in this scene.' He never says, 'you missed it!' In his rehearsals, you feel free to experiment, to try new things. The actor and director read each other's thoughts, and experience the play together."

Ullmann's description fits Ingmar Bergman, who shared an intense personal and creative relationship with the actress. "He taught me to respect my work," says Ullmann. "Ingmar explained my strengths, my limitations, and showed me how to be truthful onscreen. We had many discussions about our goals, and perhaps because he was older, Ingmar won most of the arguments. But he helped me win my most important battle, realizing what I wanted from life." The couple's daughter, Linn, is a sixteen-year-old beauty who models and may pursue an acting career.

An artist takes the bitter with the sweet. Ullmann recently returned to Broadway in Ibsen's *Ghosts*, which received biting reviews and a quick closing notice. "Critics insisted we were playing scenes for laughs," she says evenly. "But we weren't going for humor—the playwright *put* it there! Ibsen looked at life with ironic detachment. I, too, put bad experiences in a humorous perspective, and say, 'that was really ridiculous!' Life is, after all, a mixture of tragedy and comedy."

Given her unaffected warmth, why isn't Liv a busy comedienne? "No one asks me!," she sighs. "Directors expect me to play intense women. *Forty Carats* was my only comic film, and I didn't get many laughs. I broke the first rule of comedy: Never try to be funny."

Without trying to be busy, Ullmann's creative life is thriving. She directed "Parting," one segment of the feature film that will be released later this winter. In 1983, she appears onscreen in *Jenny*, and films *The Wild Duck* in Australia. Liv enthusiastically promotes her first teleplay, soon to be produced by English television. "It's about a contemporary woman, who discusses love and reason. Her blue eyes twinkle. "Perhaps the two are incompatible!"

Liv won't lean back and be a celebrity. "The moment you stop working, you're dead." A thoughtful smile. "It's good to struggle, to overcome obstacles. Nobody's got it made!"

Liv Ullmann: An Actress Listens to Her Conscience

KRISTIN HELMORE / 1985

ONE DAY IN 1980, a celebrated Norwegian woman with light blue eyes and reddish-blond hair walked down a dusty road to a Kampuchean refugee camp and was changed forever. It was the first of many journeys Liv Ullmann was to make throughout Asia, Africa, and Latin America—journeys that have since become the central focus of her life.

In a talk with one of the world's most acclaimed film and stage actresses, who has in recent years almost abandoned her career to combat world hunger and poverty, an interesting question arose: Did her theatrical training in going deep inside another person's feelings sharpen her ability to feel empathy for the people in the troubled and impoverished countries she now visits? When she answers, Liv Ullmann turns the cause and effect in this question upside down.

"I think the reason for the choice of being an actress is interest in people: Who are they? What are they about?" Miss Ullmann leans forward in her chair, her eyes searching her visitor's face, as if to illustrate the interest she is referring to. "That's the reason to be an actress, and I think it's the same reason why one would sit with a woman from another country and be curious and want to communicate who she is or what I understand of what she is."

From *Christian Science Monitor*, January 31, 1985, p. 33+. © 1985 by *Christian Science Monitor*. Reprinted by permission.

Since she began this work for the hungry of the world, and in addition to starring in an occasional film or play, Liv Ullmann has written her second book, *Choices*, a sequel to her best-selling autobiographical work, *Changing*, published in 1976.

The choices she examines in her second book involve listening to her conscience—instead of to what others may expect of her—as the directive for her actions. She writes in *Choices*: "I am learning that if I just go on accepting the framework for life that others have given me, if I fail to make my own choices, the reason for my life will be missing. I will be unable to recognize that which I have the power to change.

"I refuse to spend my life regretting the things I failed to do."

It was while she was starring in the 1980 Broadway musical *I Remember Mama* that Liv Ullmann asked herself the question, "What am I doing with my life?" And it was as a result of the caring of many in the Broadway community that her answer to that question began to change.

"The crisis of the Kampuchean refugees had been highlighted (in the news media), and then it wasn't highlighted anymore," Miss Ullmann recalls. "Some Broadway artists came together and decided, 'We want to collect money for them,' because there were great needs in the camps, we had heard. We got $200,000 by having collections in our theaters, and I was the one who was to give a check to the International Rescue Committee. And, well brought up as I am, I said to the chairman, Leo Cherne—actually, I've dedicated this last book to him—'If you ever need me, please call upon me.'"

Miss Ullmann looks amused. "I didn't mean anything with that, you know," she confides with a chuckle. "That's what you say in Hollywood. But you don't say those things to Leo Cherne. He called me just after that and he said, 'I read that your play is closing. We are doing a journey to Thailand, to the border of Kampuchea, to do a demonstration. We would like to go inside there with food and medicine, and I think you should come along.' So I went along, and to me it was a revelation.

"Not that I didn't know there were refugees and poverty and hunger, but I hadn't been close to it. I came from a world which was so confined and protected and the contrast was so enormous, and there was no way I could then go home and pretend it hadn't happened. So I started to do a lot of speaking engagements for the International Rescue Committee."

The International Rescue Committee, with headquarters in New York City, was established to resettle, rehabilitate, and assist refugee victims of totalitarian oppression and war.

"Somewhere in there UNICEF phoned me out of the blue," Miss Ullmann continues. "They said they needed a woman spokesperson. They said, 'We'd like you to travel to a few developing countries. You can see our aid programs and learn about them and then maybe when you come back you will know whether you can talk about it or not, or (whether you) want to.' Again I was thrown out into an education and meeting with things I had never seen close before, and coming back I was ready to really start to be a social worker—to stop completely with what had been my life before, because I found this much more important. I felt I could be useful. I'd learned so much—I wanted to tell all the people about what I'd seen."

What tangible evidence has Miss Ullmann seen in her travels through poverty-stricken areas to indicate that the work of these relief organizations is effective?

"Every place you go you will see miracle stories," she says. "You will see the water pumps, and you will hear about the drought around that village before, and you will hear the mothers tell what they are doing with their day, now that they don't have to walk for four or five hours to find polluted water. You will see the women who have a workday maybe of thirteen, fourteen hours, and when there is a kind of educational meeting in their community after the long workday they will come, they will sit, they will ask questions.

"And you will see the health workers. You will see how much three months' education can do when one is elected from the community and gets education in the very common health work. You'll see a doctor in Colombia at the poorest hospital in Bogota, San Jose, where the poorest mothers all had premature babies, some as small as 800 grams (28 ounces). This doctor, Dr. E. Rey Sanabria is his name, used to have only one incubator. He always had to make a choice, whom to put in there. And one day he said, 'No more.'

"He devised this very simple method which is now part of UNICEF's program, to take the naked premature baby, strap it to the naked body of the mother, put the clothes over the mother, and send them both home. The baby would still then be with the warmth of the body, with the heartbeat, the movement, everything it was used to, (with) free access to the milk. I came to this hospital, I saw these little, tiny babies and one just grabbed my finger—it's a strong grip. That baby would have been dead earlier. And now, miraculously, in this hospital within one year the mortality rate went from 75 percent to 5 percent. Now doctors from developing countries all over the world are coming to study Dr. Rey's method. All the time you see these miracles. It's not big scientific things, but who said scientific things are what save lives?"

Obviously Liv Ullmann feels that the work of such organizations as UNICEF is effective in a long-term sense.

"Absolutely. The interesting programs are the long-term ones like health care; like education; like women getting job opportunities by (having) a sewing machine that enables them to create things of cloth and then sell them on the market; like fish ponds so you can start having your own place of finding food. Because it's not like we are talking about lazy people who don't want to work, and they're just sitting there waiting to get food. Give the tool, don't give the fish. Give the net, and the first fish, and that will just prosper. It's very fun and interesting to see what aid programs really are and how much thought is behind them. It's so much more than the simple feeding.

"It's also very important to say that if we cut down the mortality rate, statistically, we immediately cut down the birthrate. So the cold question people ask—isn't it better to let them die, the population is so high?—it's not true. These people will not have more children if the children they have survive. They have children because they have no trust in life."

While it's clear that Miss Ullmann's work for the hungry is very rewarding to her, one wonders how she feels about her interrupted career as an actress. As it turns out, she is now using this career to serve her new activities.

"My profession is acting. That's where I earn my money, and that's where UNICEF can use me. Because I'm still working, I still have media interest, and that's when UNICEF needs me—because in my media interest time I can talk about the programs of UNICEF and motivate people to give, not necessarily to UNICEF but to give to those who have the need."

"I'm Trying to Show My Solidarity"

MICKI MOORE / 1988

LIV ULLMANN, THE WORLD-RENOWNED Scandinavian
actress of the stage, cinema, and television is also the best-selling
author of two books, *Changing* and *Choices*; and she's a goodwill ambassador for UNICEF.

Born to Norwegian parents in Japan, she lived her early years in
Canada and New York and then returned to the family home in
Norway when World War II ended.

Ullmann studied drama in England and made her theatrical debut in
Norway in the title role of *The Diary of Anne Frank*. She became world
famous for her roles in *Cries and Whispers*, *Scenes from a Marriage*, *The
Shame*, and *The Passion of Anna*, all films of Swedish director Ingmar
Bergman, who was also her mentor and lover. Although she has won
numerous acting awards, it was her role in *Scenes from a Marriage* that
captured the Best Actress Award from both the New York Film Critics
and the National Society of Film Critics.

More important to her than her career at this time is her work for
social causes. In 1980, Ullmann was appointed UNICEF Ambassador of
Goodwill and has since toured the corners of the Third World and the
industrialized countries to increase public awareness of the critical
problems mothers and children faced in developing regions.

Ullmann has been honored by the king of Norway with the Order of
St. Olav, the youngest person ever to receive this honor. She also has

From *Toronto Star*, August 16, 1988, p. D1+.

been given several honorary degrees in the arts and humanities and awards for her humanitarian role.

Her two soon-to-be-released films are *Moscow Adieu* and *La Amiga*. Ullmann has been married twice, once briefly in her early twenties to an Oslo physician, and in 1984 to a Boston businessman, where she now makes her home. From her close relationship with Ingmar Bergman, Ullmann has one daughter, Linn.

MM: *You have made a personal crusade of assisting mothers and children in need throughout the world. What is that connection, that bond you feel with them?*

LU: I feel an identity with every mother because I suspect I cannot be the only mother who has worries about her child, who wants her child to be happy and have a possibility of a future. I'm trying to show my solidarity for women and children by talking for mothers who don't have my opportunities.

MM: *I know you feel that world hunger is inextricably linked to the politicians in power. If you could speak directly to world leaders, what would you want to say to them?*

LU: It is time to look into world priorities. It is time we stopped talking about it being naive to say that all the money that goes into the machinery of war is taking away from health care and educational possibilities for children. It is not naive. And when they say, "What about defense against invasion?" I say, "Okay, one needs the defense for the unknown threat; I accept that. But why is that such a priority in terms of money." My answer is, "What about defense against illnesses that kill children. Isn't that as important a defense as any defense?"

MM: *Describe the transformation of Liv Ullmann, a shy, quiet person, isolated in the world of film and theatre, into a political person with an important message. What happened to you?*

LU: I was suddenly touched by reality. For me, the most important thing is to be human, but my everyday reality was in a really wonderful, privileged life. And then one day, by some circumstances, I was in a refugee camp in Thailand and there was another reality.

I knew what was going on, but I had not been close to it to really experience that here were people not very different from me with such a different life, with such a meagre chance of having anything that my family and I had. I think being touched by that made it impossible for me to continue my life on the same path it was before.

MM: *In the two autobiographical books you wrote,* Changing *and* Choices, *you talk about those profound changes that have happened to you during your life. How would you describe the woman you are today compared to Liv Ullmann in her twenties and thirties?*

LU: Tolerance has crept into my life. I don't believe anymore that everyone has to think and act the way I do. My choices in life are not the only right choices. Because I no longer believe there is one wonderful, passionate love waiting for me around the corner, I now have much more love in my life. That is because I'm touching more aspects of my life and love than I did when I was twenty and thirty. I also think I'm quieter as a person and in my aspirations. I don't think I can change the world, or be the best at everything. I have an easier time fulfilling every day as a day, which I feel is very much worth living.

MM: *In your twenties, you lived what was, perhaps at one time, every woman's romantic fantasy. Your lover, Ingmar Bergman, was also your teacher and director, the man who helped you reach international stardom. What was good and bad about linking your professional and personal life so closely together?*

LU: The most important thing that I learned from Ingmar was recognition and trust. He has a great ability, both as a professional man, director, and as a private man to really listen, to really watch. As you know, when you are with somebody, sitting and talking, and you see they are listening to you, suddenly you want to give because they are interested in what you're saying. Once that trust is established, you kind of bloom much more. This is what Ingmar did for me. He made me think that I could do more than I thought I could do. As a person, I could love more and as a professional, I had more to give. This he taught me, not by saying the words, but by being this listener and this watcher. Then, obviously, the negative side was that we did all this listening and watching very much isolated on an island for five years and my need of expressing went beyond the island and beyond what was our private love. I had a need to be connected with other people; a much greater need than he has.

MM: *There was a tremendous age difference between the two of you. You were twenty-five and he was forty-six when you met. I had the sense that the freedom he gave you in the studio was the freedom he denied you at home.*

LU: That's probably true because in the studio he gave me every trust in the world because he made me think I could do anything and he allowed me to try everything. But privately, his limitations, or the way he chose to live his life, were different than mine and what I wanted was threatening to him.

MM: *I know that even today, you and Ingmar Bergman have a very strong friendship and love. Why is it possible for the two of you to be friends and not lovers and not have it the other way around?*

LU: It's much easier to be friends because lovers have so many needs, daydreams, and cravings they think have to be fulfilled. Friends allow much more. They allow weaknesses. Ingmar and I became much closer when we became friends, but again this was something that we allowed because once we stopped living together, we both continued to connect by fighting. We didn't hang up the phone, we didn't cut the cord and I'm so happy for that because at the end of that terrible time came a wonderful time, which is still here.

MM: *You also have a daughter together. Because you were not married at the time there was tremendous societal and media censure of your pregnancy. When you look back, how did it affect you?*

LU: When Linn was born, it was very difficult because this was twenty-one years ago and society looked upon it in a very different way. There were write-ups; it became so public. Actually, it was against everything I thought my life would be because I was brought up to think you would marry young and live together happily ever after, and have small children who grew up and looked like mommy and daddy. Of course, this isn't what happened and I had to face some realities both about what society is and what I was. Actually, I would have done it all again with all the knowledge I have now because it gave me tolerance, which I didn't have then. I was a very intolerant young woman . . . very ready to criticize people who lived differently than I.

MM: *How have you wrestled with the issue of being a good mother and a great actress, fulfilling both your professional and private life?*

LU: I think the best way to survive is to live with your guilt and know that that's inherent probably in women, in mothers and that you continue on, in spite of the guilt. I think my daughter said something very important when she was recently moving out to live on her own. She said: "You'll stand there in the door and you'll be crying. I will not feel guilty because I know that you chose to have your own life, you chose to have your career, you chose to have your friends, and do all these other things. So when you're standing there crying, I don't have to feel guilty because I know I'm not taking your whole life away from you because I'm not your whole life."

Children, in one way, are our life, but they shouldn't be the only thing that gives us reason to live. That, I think, is the ultimate burden and pressure on children. I think women of my generation have felt that a lot because we had mothers who stayed home. A lot of these mothers are still giving us guilt because we feel that we are all they have. We are still children at fifty years of age. We are our mother's children and I think maybe that's not healthy. This consummate love is saying, "You are all I have and all I am."

MM: *I think your most consummate love affair has been with the camera. More than any other actress, it x-rays your soul and emotions. Can you explain?*

LU: It's probably that I feel good about being open. I'm not ashamed of what the camera might see. That's very much what I learned from Ingmar, to not feel ashamed, by either what my emotions are, or what my face might tell in terms of age or distress. So I feel very comfortable with what might come out of my face. I'm very sorry for our times now when people are so scared of what their face might tell in terms of age and life. We are hiding life by stretching and changing our faces and bodies with cosmetic surgery just because we are scared of that camera, or that person coming close to us and seeing who we are.

MM: *Does that mean you feel comfortable about aging?*

LU: Yes, I'll be fifty soon, and honest to God people were talking about being forty as the ultimate catastrophe and probably I was scared of it too. But the richest years of my life were between forty and fifty when so many things happened. I am very confident that between fifty and sixty the possibilities are there. Maybe different things will happen and maybe they won't be earthquake things, but life will be there. Obviously I'm not happy that I don't look at times like my daughter when she dresses up, and clothes don't naturally just flow on me and look great every time and that my face, at certain times, is not flawless. I'm only scared of aging in terms of health, not being able to read, hear, or able to move as easily as I do today. And maybe worst of all, to suddenly find myself, as too many old people do, alone in a room with the telephone that never rings. I just think it is sad for all of us that wrinkles have become the ultimate threat. Instead of reaching a certain age, with all the fantastic possibilities to learn and change your careers, or do something absolutely new, we are pouring all this money, time and concern into trying to change the surface. And nothing is there. I never met anyone who suddenly became more loved or more happy once her stomach became smaller.

MM: *Are you suffering from cinematic fatigue? You don't seem to do as many films as you used to. Is that your choice?*
LU: I did three films last year and one film this year, but yes, the fatigue is there. I'm not as challenged anymore and I'm perfectly happy by the thought that I might never do a film again, although I know I will. I'm perfectly happy if I would never be on the stage again, at this moment, because there are many other things I want to do.

MM: *What has this mission to help end world hunger and disease given you that a life devoted to film and theatre cannot?*
LU: The chance to live more fully. The opportunity to do something that will make a better life for another person. I'm learning a lot. I never went to university, but now I have a university education in foreign aid.

MM: *You have had homes all over the world, you can slip in and out of five different languages. What are your roots, what gives you that inner sense of who you are?*
LU: I do travel a lot, but it has always been very important to me to say my roots are in Norway because that's my passport and that's where I grew up. But today I think my roots are simply by being, who I am, and doing what I choose to do. I travel a lot; I'm all over the place, so now I feel my roots are inside of me, wherever I am.

Liv Ullmann Seeks Truth, Not Disguises

MARIAN CHRISTY/1989

HITTING THE BIG 5-0 has not been without incident for Liv Ullmann.

When the Norwegian actress was in Germany recently filming *The Rose Garden,* the director told her to look up and hold her head high in a scene where she was pouring coffee.

"The camera revealed neck wrinkles that I didn't even know I had!" she laughs. "Later the makeup girl started talking to me about cosmetic tricks, disguises."

In this interview in her Boston office, shortly after undergoing an appendectomy at Massachusetts General Hospital, Ullmann talks about the positive side of maturing.

She tells how the events of her life, including failures, have helped her develop interpersonal skills she didn't have in her youth. She says her strong sense of self has "particularly impacted" on her four-year marriage to Bostonian Donald L. Saunders, president and chief executive officer of Saunders & Associates, a real estate firm.

Ullmann was divorced from Dr. Gappe Stang, a psychiatrist, in 1965. She has a daughter, Linn, twenty-two, from a five-year liaison with the Swedish film director Ingmar Bergman.

She was born in Tokyo, where her father, a Norwegian aircraft engineer, was working. When she was five, he died of injuries he received when he was struck by the moving propeller of an airplane.

From *Boston Globe,* April 5, 1989, p. 35+. © 1989 by the *Boston Globe.* Reprinted by permission.

Ullmann is a 1956 graduate of a private girls' school, Trondheim Borgelige Real School in Trondheim, Norway. On April 25 she will receive an honorary doctor of arts degree from Pine Manor College in Chestnut Hill and deliver the Founder's Day address. Her husband will receive an honorary doctor of laws degree.

"I used to think a husband was there to look after you. Now I realize that I'm not in a relationship in which I'm 'the little woman.' I'm not a housewife. And I don't feel guilty about that. Before, it troubled me."

"Marriage is companionship and friendship with love. You feel somebody is on your side, somebody dependable. I'm also there for my husband, someone equally dependable."

"I'm more tolerant now. I no longer expect my husband to have the same interests as I have. My new attitudes are born of past experiences. I have learned from my mistakes."

"I didn't have this kind of relationship at twenty, thirty, or forty. This marriage has no illusions. It is based on reality. I'm me. And I don't have to give up 'me' to make my husband happy."

"My husband gave me a fiftieth birthday present that I'll never forget. It was the best present I ever received. He said only this: 'Have a suitcase packed for a warm climate.' We went to St. Thomas and there, on a boat, were all my sewing-circle friends and their husbands from Norway. We sailed the Caribbean together, reminiscing. My friends call Donald 'St. Donald.'"

"We are good for each other, my husband and me. I'm not into the idea of passion. He is full of humor and kindness. The word I most often hear is: 'Sure!' The men I knew before never said 'sure.' Decisions were a life-or-death matter."

"I'm a feminist. I bring my feminism to my marriage. I made a compromise to my marriage last year. I didn't do theatrical things."

"It was appreciated. But I felt I wasn't being me. I felt as if I was in summer camp. I thought I had nothing to show for a year of my life. So in January I went to Germany and made a film."

"Both of us are happy again."

"I was five years old when my father died. My mother romanticized his death. She said: 'Daddy is sitting in heaven looking down at you.' I wrote him letters, begging him to come back."

"My mother's way of dealing with death was wrong. She didn't face death, look it in the eye. She rewrote it. She didn't allow us to grieve. I think tears and suffering are a way of self-healing."

"I also know the grief of leaving someone you love. Someone alive. Someone who is there but won't be there for you."

"You can't always be strong and brave. You have to cope. But you can cope only when you question things. When you learn to live with difficulty, that's coping. When you go on despite the difficulty, that's coping. Sometimes as you cope, you cry."

"When I parted from Bergman I was in despair. But he left his phone open for me. We talked ten times a day. I went to Rome. Then, one day, sitting in the sun, I wrote him a goodbye letter. I said: 'It's over between us.' "

"Later, how we laughed about that. He had recognized it was over for us five months earlier. He just let me go through my sorrow until I came to my own realization."

"We are friends. It was my relationship with him that advanced my sense of confidence. He said I was a good actress. He never told me what to do in a scene. He made me feel he trusted me, my judgment. He recognized my talent and he liked me as a person and a woman. That gave me my first deep sense of esteem."

"I was self-conscious before that. I didn't think I was pretty. But I had mastered a craft. I became a mother and mastered that. The friends I made in my youth are still around. These things made me feel that important areas of my life weren't disasters."

"Even lost love turned out good. Loves that didn't last became friendships."

"I know I've failed in some things. I failed to pass the audition for Oslo's government-subsidized National Theatre School."

"The moment of failing is painful. You think people don't recognize your abilities. It hurts because you think you're not living up to your expectations. It's feeling that you're less than you really are."

"But failure is temporary. It lasts only if it makes you better. The way to get over failure is to try again. If you fail again, then you have to try again and again. I never give up. I have failures only I know about. I'm always trying to correct them."

"The other day I sat with a friend and told her the things that trouble my life. She told me the things that trouble her life. We burst out laughing. They were the same troubles."

"I wish people would talk more to each other about their alikeness."

"We look at other people and think they're better off, more attractive, more secure. In reality, they aren't. What all people have in common is their wondering, their questioning, their curiosity, their fearfulness. If people would indulge in the art of conversation, they'd realize their commonalities."

"I've never believed much in psychological therapy. I'm my best guide. I confront myself. I question what I do. I talk with myself. I trust my own instincts."

"If you're not an evil person, you should trust your gut reaction. This is the truth of you."

Ullmann Quietly Gets Noticed

GERALD PEARY/1992

INDEED, THAT IS LIV ULLMANN, the best-selling author of *Changing* and *Choices* and international star of Ingmar Bergman classics (*Persona, Scenes from a Marriage*), walking down the streets of Boston.

In recent years, the Norwegian-born actress has settled quietly in the United States. She's married to realtor Donald Saunders, co-owner (with his brother, Roger) of the Copley Plaza, Copley Square, and Boston Park Plaza hotels.

"Nobody knows who I am in Boston," Ullmann says in an interview this week at the sixteenth Montreal World Film Festival. She and Saunders live near the Boston Common, and, she says, "I rent videos at Videosmith. It's a wonderful way to start the day, to watch an old classic movie at six in the morning. Maybe a Bette Davis, who's so great, or my own little festival of movie stars."

There are less tranquil times, when Ullmann is deeply involved with humanitarian work for UNICEF, or filmmaking in Europe. "When I come home to Boston, people ask if I've had a good vacation," Ullmann says with a laugh.

Last year, Ullmann left Massachusetts for a long, arduous stay in Copenhagen, Denmark. There, she co-wrote, directed, and helped edit an ambitious feature film, *Sofie*, which premiered this week in competition at the Montreal Fest.

Sofie, which will be shown here November 18 at the Museum of Fine Arts to conclude the Boston Jewish Film Festival (with Ullmann in attendance), proved a smash hit in its Montreal screening, both with the Quebec audience and critics. Ullmann's directorial debut is an early favorite to capture Montreal's Grand Prize, to be announced Monday.

"I didn't choose *Sofie*. Somehow, it chose me," Ullmann says.

The producers sent her the Henri Nathansen novel, asking if she'd write the screenplay, and then asked her if she'd direct it.

Sofie tells of a Jewish woman at the end of the nineteenth century who rejects the great love of her life, a Christian painter with a burning soul, for marriage to a likable dullard, who placates her religious family because he is an Orthodox Jew.

As an American critic succinctly described the narrative, it's "a Jewish *Madame Bovary.*"

Ullmann says, "The story is very important to me. I am a Christian but, for many years, I've had many Jewish friends. I'm married to a Jewish man, and writer Elie Weisel is one of my closest friends."

Because "as a Christian, I didn't want to slip up," Ullmann enlisted much of the Copenhagen Jewish community and also a Danish rabbi as advisors for scenes of Jewish ritual, including Kosher meals and a full-scale Bar Mitzvah.

"The rabbi was as interested in making a Jewish film as I was. Sometimes I had to fight him for writing and directing."

In the first weeks of the shoot, Ullmann found her directorial abilities being tested by the overwhelmingly male crew. She says, "Sometimes when they want you to be insecure, they put names on things. A technical language. I wasn't going to let that happen. I think it's important for women's voices to be heard on the set, feminine voices.

"We must be allowed to talk a language descriptive of feelings. We don't have to be so clever always, conquer everything. We can even say, 'I don't know.' "

But one thing Ullmann is adamant about is the final edit of her film. *Sofie* is almost two and a half hours long, and that's where it will stay.

"This is my cut of *Sofie*. From the heart, for the heart," Ullmann says. "When people finally go out today, why not spend two or three hours in the cinema? You don't want the dream to end."

Jewish-Themed Drama *Sofie*
Ullmann's Choice

JUDY STONE/1993

FOR LIV ULLMANN, *Sofie*, her first film as a director, is a way of honoring her grandfather's memory and saying something about the relationship between mothers and daughters.

Set in the late nineteenth century, it is the drama of a young Norwegian Jewish woman who falls passionately in love with a Gentile artist, but dutifully gives in to her parents' insistence that she marry within her own faith. Erland Josephson, Ullmann's frequent co-star, and Ghita Norby play the devoted parents.

Ullmann, author of two memoirs, *Changing* and *Choices*, also wrote the script. It is freely based on the novel *Mendel Philipsen and Son* by Henri Nathansen, who committed suicide before World War II.

"Making the film was an incredible experience," Ullmann said at the Montreal World Festival, where *Sofie* premiered. "Everything I have learned professionally, both in writing and acting, I felt I could put into *Sofie*. I was scared at first that personal ambition might come in. I was afraid I'd envy the actors. But it never happened. I loved Karen-Lise Mynster, who played Sofie, and her character. Never once was I the actress. It was a new thing. I was grown up!"

She's a grandmother now but still as pretty as a girl, looking natural and unaffected in a deep-violet cotton jacket over a black blouse and slacks. She wore a small gold clown pendant, its tummy filled with two

From *San Francisco Chronicle*, June 6, 1993, p. 25. © 1993 by *San Francisco Chronicle*. Reprinted by permission.

tiny movable diamonds, two emeralds, and a ruby, a gift from her husband. Pinned to her jacket was a gift from a Jewish woman director who had wept when she saw *Sofie* and told Ullmann, "You are a director!" The woman had removed the gold mask of drama she always wore for sentimental reasons and gave it to Ullmann. "I knew what it cost her to give it away," Ullmann said, "so I always wear it."

Ullmann's association with Jewish themes began when she was eighteen and made her theatrical debut as Anne Frank. Years later, she was thrilled to play Ida Nudel, a feisty Russian Jewish dissident who was exiled to Siberia before being allowed to emigrate to Israel. In a sense, Ullmann was carrying on in the tradition of her paternal grandfather, who died at Dachau concentration camp after he was taken hostage by the Nazis for helping Jews escape from Norway.

Ullmann traces her commitment to Jewish causes to her meeting with Elie Wiesel, the author who survived the concentration camps to become a voice of conscience in the world.

In 1978, she and Wiesel met in Thailand, where they were trying to send food, doctors, and medicine to the Cambodians. Wiesel told her that he was there because of his wartime experiences, when the Jewish people were "closed off from the world and nobody listened or saw what was happening." It was the beginning of a close friendship.

Two years later, Hadassah, a Jewish women's organization, invited Ullmann to visit its hospital in Jerusalem because of her interest in children. "Elie told them I was a 'closet Jewish Christian,'" she recalled with a laugh. "So I saw Israel and it changed my life."

Since then, she has spoken often under Jewish auspices. At one talk in Boston, she met Donald Saunders, a Jewish realtor and hotel owner. They were married eight years ago.

Sofie, Ullmann said, is a "declaration of love" for the Jewish people she knows—especially Wiesel. But she has been perplexed by the reaction of some Jews. "First they say yes and then they say no to the film—particularly to a synagogue scene. Christian friends love it, but one Jewish friend, a producer, suggested I cut that scene. Why?" she asked rhetorically, sadly. "Do they think it's none of my business? Is it because I'm not Jewish? I'm not one of them?"

She said she has never considered converting. "First of all, I'm a Christian. I believe in Jesus," she said. "It's hard to convert because there are very strong things you have to do as a woman (in the Jewish faith), which I couldn't do because I don't believe in them."

As for Sofie's parents' insistence that she "not marry a goy," Ullmann said, "It's so foreign and difficult for me to accept that, but I do understand it: that it was important for Jews who have been persecuted—at least, to stick together. It's some kind of shelter. But personally, I wish Sofie had followed her heart."

Josephson, playing Sofie's father, was the only Jewish actor in the cast. "But he is completely assimilated," Ullmann said. "He never kept traditions or talked about it, but during the film he found his roots. When he was a little boy, his Orthodox grandfather took him to synagogue and he suddenly remembered the Hebrew words for 'you must love your neighbor.' It was incredible to see the look in his eyes (in the synagogue scene)."

Ullmann and Josephson have acted together in more than six films and co-starred in *Pygmalion* on the stage. They are the best of friends, "almost like girlfriends," in the way they confide in each other. "He is so funny, so playful. From the moment he comes into the studio until he leaves, he is a bundle of laughter," Ullmann said. "But after *Sofie*, we were almost a little shy because something happened to both of us. We can't talk about the film, but he is a brilliant writer and I'm sure he will write about this experience."

The two women stars and Ullmann did a lot of talking—about their very strong mothers. "We all wanted to get at our mothers, who forced us to do certain things," said Ullmann, whose air force pilot father died in World War II. "That's why I wrote the confrontation scene between Sofie and her mother. But when I started writing, I suddenly remembered that I'm a mother, too, and in the middle of the scene, I went over to the side of mothers. I wanted to say that sometimes we fail, but our intentions are good."

Her daughter Linn, by Ingmar Bergman, is a journalist, married to a lawyer and a "fantastic mother" of a three-year-old boy. "She tells me some of the wrong things I did," Ullmann said. "I wanted to say to her—and I did it in the film—be careful you don't do to him for something you feel you didn't get. We don't want to repeat our mothers' mistakes, but we do lots of new ones."

How does Linn, twenty-seven, feel about her father, who was married four times and has eight children? Ullmann lived with him for five years but made most of her films with him after they separated. (Her favorite is *Scenes from a Marriage*.)

"Linn admires Ingmar tremendously. She likes him," Ullmann said. A very long pause followed and there was a tear in her eye. "I think she worships him. Sometimes it was tough because I had to do a lot of things that he could have helped me with. She went on vacations with him and I was the bad guy then and he was wonderful. But pretty wonderful.

"He made an extraordinary speech at Linn's marriage and I thought, 'So, OK, he didn't do diapers but still to have a father who can send you out in life with such words is great, too.' Also, Linn's tough. She sees what he isn't. She's not blind."

Ullmann has a different kind of motherly feeling for *Sofie*. "I feel very proud of it," she said. "I don't expect everybody to like it, but I had something in my heart I wanted to tell to other hearts—and there it is!"

The Other Side of the Camera

DAVID BROOKS ANDREWS/1993

LIV ULLMANN talks of three enormous handicaps she had to overcome when directing *Sofie*—being middle-aged, a woman and an actress.

Describing her first week as a director, she says, "To the crew I was invisible, not because they were cruel or bad but because it was the only way to do the little power games."

The crisis came to a climax when crew members walked away from her while she was talking to them. "I knew either I act very 'womanly,' and emotional, and start to cry," she recalls, "or I follow the group and say, 'I'm sorry, maybe you didn't hear me out, but this is where the camera is going to be. And this is what the scene is going to be about."

To see the film is to realize that she chose the latter course, and convinced those involved in the production that Liv Ullmann is a director worthy of their skills and commitment.

She comes to the role of director with considerable experience, including thirty-five years of acting and fifteen years of human-rights activities. Having visited refugees in more than forty countries for the International Rescue Committee and UNICEF, Ullmann remains profoundly involved with the world that lies beyond the glare of arc lights and applause. She works to raise funds and public awareness by speaking about the refugees she has met—telling their stories, often in their own words. These days she makes her home in the Boston area with Donald Saunders, a commercial real-estate developer to whom she has

From *Boston Globe*, July 4, 1993, p. A5, A7. © 1993 by *Boston Globe*. Reprinted by permission.

been married since 1985. For the last several years, *Sofie* has been at the center of her professional life.

In adapting a decades-old Danish novel about a tight-knit Copenhagen family sounds like a fairly restrictive vehicle for the directorial debut of a woman best known for her devastating performances in Ingmar Bergman films (including *Persona, Scenes from a Marriage* and *Autumn Sonata*), Ullmann had similar concerns at first. She feared there would be little room for what she had to say, particularly because there seemed such a gulf between Sofie's experience and her own.

"Sofie's Jewish; I'm Christian," Ullmann says. "She's turn-of-the-century; I'm very much a century later. I have so-called freedom; her whole dilemma is she doesn't have freedom of choice or feels she doesn't have. But all these differences made the likenesses—the more I worked on it—so much more apparent."

It soon became clear to her that "deep down we have the same fantasy. Basically deep down there's no difference between Sofie and Liv and you. To be alive, and to breathe, and fall asleep, and write a diary, and hope for love, and feel bad because you are not seen—that hasn't changed. You still feel that. And that's what's basic."

The film does keep its eye on what is most basic to human beings, those small moments that in the end are what give life its profound joy and unutterable sadness. Moments such as a young woman allowing a shawl to slip off her shoulders at a ball in hope of being noticed, the opening of a letter that announces an elderly relative's death, and the little conversations that take place in bed as the lights are turned off.

In showing us what we so often fail to notice, Ullmann keeps the camera trained undistractedly on the actors, particularly their faces, watching for evidence of what goes on inside the soul. This is hardly a surprising choice for a director whose own face provided some of the more memorable close-ups in film. It's a choice that created a kind of actors' paradise, say the performers who contributed.

Torben Zeller, who plays Sofie's husband, Jonas, found that during his screen test Ullmann placed her face very close to the lens, making it possible to play directly to her rather than merely to the cameraman or thin air. It made a "fantastic difference" for Zeller, who says many Danish actors so dislike screen tests that they often refuse to take them. Ullmann's close involvement with the actors continued throughout the eleven weeks of shooting, in which she let them know they were doing brilliant work but that they could always take it a step further.

"You can put yourself in a position as a director that you don't really suffer with your actors," says Zeller. "If you do that, then you have no risk. It's not so risky to sit far away from your actors while working with them. . . . But to go *in* the work, and to be part of their feeling, and to try to feel the way they have to feel to solve the role, as Liv did, that is a risk. She took a risk, and that made us eager to take a risk, too."

Rehearsals were usually half-speed, and the actors were asked to save what they had for the camera. Unless there were technical problems, Ullmann would shoot only one take. She believes that in doing numerous takes, actors will "start doing those little extra things . . . so it becomes willed, not clean and restrained anymore."

After filming a scene, she was careful not to use too many words because she didn't want to violate the actors' sense of the moment. "Sometimes you just smile to each other when the scene is taken," Ullmann says. "The actors know when they are good, and the director just smiles. That's the best praise, because then it's this secret understanding, which is the most lovely thing anyway between people." Following the shooting of one scene—in which a troubling realization flickers across the face of Karen-Lise Mynster, who plays the title role—Ullmann was so moved that she cried.

The actors in *Sofie* described working under Ullmann as the experience of a lifetime, setting standards and creating a working atmosphere that they wistfully acknowledge they may never experience again. "Liv, she generates love," said Jesper Christensen (who says that before working with Ullmann he was cynical about anybody being "*that good*"). "She must love people. At least she loves actors, I'm sure. And she makes them feel brilliant, and beautiful, and wanted, at the peak of their abilities—and who doesn't want life to be like that? She creates such a concentration and attention around what you do. And she believes that you are the best in the world. If you work with a director who thinks like that, your performance doesn't necessarily end like that, but it really helps you to be nearly what she thinks you are."

Like any other, the production did have its challenges. At one point the tension on the set was so thick that Torben Zeller, whose training includes improvisational comedy, decided that a few stupid faces might help. Ullmann began to laugh, relates Zeller, and to make "wonderful stupid faces back."

When talking with Erland Josephson, a Bergman stalwart who plays Sofie's father, an inevitable question arises: What is the difference between acting under Ullmann and Bergman? He responds, "Liv is very brave with the sentimental feelings, with the good feelings, with the positive feelings. She doesn't need to tell stories about desperation and destruction to be brave. She can be brave in the positive things." He adds, "I don't know if you understand what I mean. I don't know if I understand it myself."

Part of Ullmann's bravery lies in the fact that she has made her film her way. It is in fact so much her own that while introducing it at a film festival last fall she could say it contains "everything I know about being a woman, being human, about life." If those words sounded like eloquent hyperbole, by the end of the film it was clear they were merely a statement of fact—so much so that later Ullmann wonders aloud whether she has left herself anything to do.

"But when you start to think about it," she continues, "there's so much left. That's what's so wonderful about doing something. While you're doing it, you can't think of anything else. And then you sit down, and suddenly something new just pours upon you.

"I want to do a film about old people," she starts to muse.

Liv Ullmann: Out of Bergman's Shadow

DAVID BROOKS ANDREWS/1996

THIRTY-FIVE YEARS of acting and ten films with Ingmar Bergman make her a director actors love to work for.

"You can feel him leaning forward, listening and watching. Afterwards he's seen what you were trying to show even if it hasn't come out successfully," Norwegian actress Liv Ullmann said of being directed by Ingmar Bergman, never dreaming that one day she herself would be directing films. "He will say, 'Do a little more or less,' and you are willing to show him everything because you know it will be recognized. That's what makes most people flourish—they need to be recognized."

A decade and a half later, Ullman is the first woman to direct a Bergman screenplay, *Private Confessions*. Filming was completed in late December. Her first two films as director and scriptwriter—*Sofie* (1993) and *Kristin Lavransdatter* (1995)—are based on historical novels with a strong female protagonist. In the first, *Sofie* surrenders her heart's desire to obey her parents' insistence that she marry a fellow Jew, while in the second, Kristin defies her parents' will in order to marry a dashing knight with a scandalous past. Ullmann admits that she has had a little of each woman in her, but "when I've been one of them, I should have been the other."

Thirty-five years of acting have prepared her—to an extent that few directors have been—for stepping behind the camera. Determined to "be the kind of director I would have wanted or needed myself as an actress," she sees her role as being a "receiver" and "listener in the deepest sense," much as Bergman was for her.

Actors describe her as profoundly involved in their work. Elisabeth Matheson, who plays the title role in *Kristin Lavransdatter*, says, "She must live with us to see so well. If she were just watching the monitor, she couldn't know all that she knows. Her method is like living in the situation. She's not leaned back at all."

"It's not so risky to sit far away from your actors while working with them," says Torben Zeller, the husband in *Sofie*. "But to try to feel the way they have to feel to solve the role, as Liv did, is a risk. She took risks, and that made us eager to take them, too."

Before actors work with her, they often are concerned that she is such a good actress herself that she will want to show them how to play their parts. Their fears are quickly quieted. Erland Josephson, who starred with her in *Scenes from a Marriage*, was delighted to discover that her approach as a director is "not to demonstrate but to give impulses to the fantasy and to the feeling and to the experience."

Ullmann is wary of not saying or doing too much, especially when first working with an actor. "I would never use a lot of words with the actors because I know how destroying that can be. They have their own fantasy around something. And if I say too many things it could destroy what they had created. You sense if they feel it right, and then you leave them with their feeling. You don't ask them to put words to their feelings. You allow them the complete privacy of their feelings and then to express that as the character when on camera."

Another concern evident in Ullmann's direction is that her actors not exaggerate. This grows out of her own experience as an actress, explains Josephson. "When she acts, she has such a vitality, and an imagination, and so many proposals to show. Her ambition is to show the possibilities of the part all the time. When she worked with Ingmar Bergman, he was so inspired by her and at the same time so aware that he must tell her that you have to make choices, not to give everything, in every moment, in every direction."

Ullmann vividly remembers learning this lesson on the set of *Persona*, her first film with Bergman. "I was to sit and listen to Bibi Andersson telling a very sexy story. It was just to be me smoking and listening. I thought I had to let the cigarette kind of shiver in my hand to show that I was getting upset or excited by her story and put my other hand at one time to my chest. Ingmar told me: 'Stop it. Don't do things. Just listen.' So the cigarette became quiet, and the hand didn't go to the throat. It was just the face listening. And then things happened in the face that I as an actress wasn't even aware of."

While I was visiting the set of *Kristin Lavransdatter* in Jar, Norway, I saw the lesson being passed along to an actress from the next generation. Elisabeth Matheson was asked simply to watch the hanging of a young man who had once accosted her and murdered her childhood friend. The performance she gave was impressive for its complexity but drew too much attention to itself. Over the next four or five takes—with Ullmann talking privately with her between each one—the acting became increasingly simple, more direct, and as a result, more powerful.

Ullmann explains: "It doesn't look good on film when you do three things instead of one—one thing which is clean and beautiful. The challenge is to show one really clean feeling because the camera sees immediately when you're false. You can do complexity; it doesn't mean doing two, three, four things. It means in one gesture show a complexity, too."

One doesn't have to understand the language Ullmann is filming in—whether Danish, Norwegian or Swedish—to sense the unique atmosphere on the set and what it makes possible in an actor's performance. Jesper Christensen, who appears in *Sofie*, says: "Liv, she generates love. She must love people. At least she loves actors, I'm sure. And she makes them feel brilliant, and beautiful, and wanted, and at the peak of their abilities, and who doesn't want life to be like that. She creates such a concentration and attention around what you do. And she believes that you are the best in the world. If you work with a director who thinks like that it helps you to be nearly what she thinks you are."

When I ask Ullmann for a final word of advice on working with actors, she responds: "The best thing is to listen. To be there as the one who will encourage. Not encourage by coming with all your words and your fantasy. It's to give them an atmosphere and then inspiration and within that they have to create; they have to grow. Everyone grows best from their own experiences. Leave them alone. And be there like a wonderful part of an audience who really listens, who really watches, and says 'Maybe it's too much or maybe too little,' but all the time gives a lot of trust. Some directors want to talk and talk, and never give trust away. The best directors, as in a love affair, give trust and honesty".

Trolling for Authenticity

JEFFREY GANTZ/1997

BEING IN THE PRESENCE of a great actress is intimidating
enough; having to talk to a great actress who's on her way to becoming
an outstanding director is far worse. Especially an actress/director who,
in her fifties, is still beautiful. But the Liv Ullmann who was so intelligently unpretentious in Ingmar Bergman's films is just as intelligently
unpretentious in real life, sitting in Boston's Park Plaza's tea room and
stealing bites from a piece of apple pie while explaining why it took
some seventy-five years to turn Sigrid Undset's classic into a film, and
how she came to direct it.

"For fifty years a lawyer had the rights, and he never would sell them
for some reason. All of Hollywood wanted the rights, but then they for-
got. But suddenly this man died, and then some Swedish producer
bought the rights, and for two years it was in preproduction with a man
director from Sweden who also wrote the script. After two years he said,
'I can't work with you guys,' which I understand now. And then he
jumped off and I got the offer almost by accident because I was in
Sweden at the time, I had just had a great success with *Sophie*, my first
film, and I was offered it.

"I wrote a completely new script because the other script had very little to do, I feel, with Sigrid Undset's world. The old script was also only
Kransen ["The Garland," the first of *Kristin*'s three volumes], but there
were a lot of poetic licenses. And you can do that, but they weren't

From *Boston Phoenix*, December 15, 1997. © 1997 by *Boston Phoenix*. Reprinted by
permission.

licenses that went to her fairytales. The *dvergmøy* [troll woman], the woman coming from the ground, was a young girl coming in naked and dancing for her and making Kristin naked—I mean, it was very strange. I wrote a new script, and then we started all over again with a new costume designer and a new cinematographer [the peerless Sven Nykvist]. Preproduction was three-quarters of a year and I wrote the script all the time, many drafts. And it turned out to be, no comparison, the greatest success Norway ever had in film.

"I love everything about directing and writing the script except that it does take two years of your life. And if you really want to do it, and believe in it, that *is* your life. I love it while it lasts. But then it's finished, and everybody wants your baby. The producers want to dress it differently; the distributors want to sell it differently, and it's very tough."

Ullmann's original version, as seen in Norway, ran three hours and twenty minutes—not excessive for a novel as packed with insight as *Kransen* is. But for international distribution the producers, being producers, insisted on a shorter version. "For a year I resisted cutting it, and then they cut it, which was a catastrophe, and I said, 'I'll take my name off that.' But then a year had gone by, and I thought, okay, I will walk into her life without showing her childhood so much—there was very much of the childhood, because in the childhood it's the forces, it's God, it's love. I cut a lot of the people who lived at Jørundgård [Kristin's farmstead], Bentein [the priest's son who tries to rape Kristin], and Arne [Kristin's childhood friend]. I had to say goodbye to them, and to some of the people working on the farm. The community had to go. But that's the world of cinema today."

Any chance Ullmann will make the other two parts of *Kristin Lavransdatter*, *Husfrue* ("Housewife") and *Korset* ("The Cross")? "No, because I will never work with them [the producers] again. And they still have the rights. But I don't think anybody will take over, because it was such a big success. I think they had somebody else on to continue but it didn't happen." Memo to *Kristin*'s unnamed producers: your director is a smart lady who played Kristin on stage back in 1957 and has this novel—a Norwegian national treasure—down cold. Already she's made a miraculous film that will go down in history. Let her do the rest of it. Then you can go down in history too.

Ullmann: *Private Confessions* Plumbs Hard Truths, Gentle Lies

DAVID BROOKS ANDREWS/1998

NORWEGIAN FILM DIRECTOR Liv Ullmann takes questions about truth, lies, and infidelity to a far deeper level than the ongoing national discussion in her latest movie, *Private Confessions*, starring Pernilla August and Max von Sydow.

The script is written by Ingmar Bergman, widely considered one of the world's greatest film directors. It first aired as a five-part TV series in Scandinavia in the fall of 1996. A somewhat shortened film version (in Swedish with English subtitles) receives its United States premiere engagement at the Museum of Fine Arts tomorrow and will run through February thirteen with some twenty-eight screenings.

In a rich Norwegian accent, Ullmann suggests in a recent telephone interview that telling the truth can be as damaging as telling a lie, or even more so, if it is told out of a desire to hurt or destroy someone. "It depends on who you are being honest to," says Ullmann. "How much can they bear? You can't come home and be completely honest to a person who is going to be in pain for the rest of their lives. It might be good for the person who wants to be honest. But maybe it isn't good for the person [receiving the news]."

Such levels of complexity and compassion seem to be missing from much of America's current dialogue. But they're very much on Ullmann's mind.

From *The [New Bedford, Massachusetts] Standard-Times*, December 31, 1998, pp. C1–C2.
© 1998 by *Standard-Times*. Reprinted by permission.

Especially since the protagonist of *Private Confessions*, Anna Bergman (Pernilla August), confesses to her Lutheran confirmation priest and longtime friend Uncle Jacob (Max von Sydow) that she has been having an illicit affair.

The film is set early in this century when such things were not so common.

Von Sydow strongly urges her to break with her lover and confess the affair to her husband. She does tell her husband, but out of anger and bitterness rather than genuine contrition. What follows is a scene—acted with extraordinary realism and subtlety—in which the couple at first is more emotionally intimate than they've been for years. Nevertheless, a slow fuse is lit inside the husband with life-altering consequences.

This is the third full-length feature film that Ullmann has directed (*Sofie* was her first, followed by *Kristin Lavransdatter*, which recently became available on video). Of all of them, this is the most like the many Bergman films that Ullmann starred in herself—in terms of its searing emotional honesty, its fearless exploration of the dark regions of personal relationships, and its unwavering focus on the human face and soul.

Cinematographer Sven Nykvist provides spare but exquisite shots, with interiors that seem like an early twentieth-century version of Vermeer's masterpieces.

The protagonist and the story as a whole are based on Bergman's own mother, whose experiences he mined by reading her diaries. He expressed concern to Ullmann that, although his mother is long dead, someday she would be upset about the secrets of her life being revealed in the film. Ullmann responded, "No, she's going to be very happy wherever she is."

"I've seen pictures of his mother," explains Ullmann, "and she didn't look understanding and happy. She became a little bitter and her mouth a little narrow. Yet I wanted to show him that his mother wasn't necessarily a bitter, disappointed woman, but that she was also a woman who went on with her life, and learned a lot of things in life."

It would be easy to draw parallels between Ullmann's *Private Confessions* and Bille August's *The Best Intentions*. In both cases, the scripts were written by Bergman about his parent's marital troubles, and both films feature Pernilla August, Max von Sydow, and Samuel Froler.

Pernilla August won the Cannes Film Festival's best actress prize in 1992 for her work in *The Best Intentions*, and the film picked up the festival's Golden Palm award.

But at the start of filming, Ullmann made it very clear to her cast that *Private Confessions* has nothing to do with *The Best Intentions*. She wanted them to think of her film as a story about an "everyday woman, an everyday man, and an everyday priest, not Ingmar's story."

Ullmann is tremendously pleased with the performances that her actors give.

"Pernilla is full of secrets," she says, "full of emotions and stories and experiences and a lot of dark sides. It's not something she would verbalize to anyone face to face. If you met her, you would just think what a beautiful, normal, sweet woman and mother, because as a person she gives so much warmth and energy—and no hostility, nothing like that. But you say 'camera,' and then all these secrets come tumbling out, and her eyes they change. That's what makes the best actors and actresses—it's the secrets. When the camera rolls, there the secrets are."

As for Max von Sydow, Ullmann at first found herself a little shy with him, because for years they had acted together (in films such as *The Shame*, *The Passion of Anna* and *The Emigrants*), and she didn't know how he would feel about taking direction from her. "But I think that's what so wonderful about good actors," she says. "They get their parts, and they do them, even if the part is 'Now I'm going to have a different relationship with somebody that I know very well in another way.' After the first or second day, I had always been his director, and he had always been my actor."

During a twelve-minute take—which is extraordinarily long by American standards—von Sydow suddenly became too emotionally choked up to say anything for a full minute. Ullmann thinks it may have had something to do with his personal life, rather than his character, since his marriage was breaking up.

"It was so right for the whole thing," says Ullmann. "He knew that I would not stop shooting. I knew that he would use the moment and translate it into the role of the priest. Because we knew each other so well from the acting point of view, we also knew deep down what was happening with each of us. We were both at peace. And it's one of the most stunning close-up scenes I've ever seen."

For all of the emotionally demanding scenes of the film, there are some delightful moments of humor as well. In one, Pernilla August's lover, played by Thomas Hanzon, sits uncomfortably naked, feeling very exposed, beneath an extremely formal portrait of a man from an earlier generation. The contrast provides a wonderful comic release. As does a shot of two little boys, in this case fully clothed, with their bottoms straight up in the air.

Ullmann's next film, *The Faithless*, also will use a script by Ingmar Bergman, this time based on an experience from his own life. It's a story about a director/writer and an actress who starts to assume the persona of a woman with whom the director once had a relationship. "I think it is something which I have a lot more freedom on than he," says Ullmann, "because he's tied to the real story, and I'm not. It had nothing to do with me."

Pre-production begins in March with plans to start filming in August.

When an observation is share about *Private Confessions* that hadn't occurred to Ullmann or an interpretation is offered different from her own, she is fascinated and generous. "That's what is so nice," she says, "because we all will find our own truth in things. If a film is well written or well done, these truths are there whether the actor, director, or script writer thought of them. The audiences are going to find truth that I won't necessarily have recognized myself. And that's what's so great about art, I think."

New York Film Festival 2000 Interviews:
Liv Ullmann on *Faithless*

STAN SCHWARTZ/2000

ONE OF THE HIGHLIGHTS of this year's New York Film Festival is Liv Ullmann's *Faithless* with a script written by Ingmar Bergman. A dark and uncompromising film of extraordinary intensity—not surprising, given its author—*Faithless* is primarily the story of an infidelity. Marianne, a successful actress (Bergman regular Lena Endre, in an extraordinary, shattering performance) jeopardizes a happy marriage to a world-renown conductor (Thomas Hanzon) by commencing an affair with David, a theater director (Krister Henriksson), who also happens to be a friend of the family. Suffice it to say the consequences are tragic.

But *Faithless* is much more than just the story of an affair, as evidenced by the very particular device Bergman uses to frame his film. The story of the affair is recounted in the form of memories summoned up many years later by an aging writer/director named Bergman (Erland Josephson) as he sits in his work room by the sea on the secluded island of Fårö. Sound familiar? And the ghost of Marianne is now Bergman's muse: as she recounts the story of the tortured affair long ago, Bergman makes notes in his notebooks, and the pain and suffering is presumably transcended as the writer/director transforms his past into a work of art for the future.

Director Ullmann's association with Bergman goes back over a quarter of a century when she first appeared in his 1966 masterpiece *Persona*,

From *IndieWIRE*, September 16–21, 2000. © 2000 by *IndieWIRE*. Reprinted by permission.

with other historic performances in Bergman films over the years including *Cries and Whispers* and *Scenes From a Marriage*. In more recent years, Ullmann has become a director in her own right, with *Faithless* being the second of Bergman's scripts she has directed (the first was *Private Confessions* in 1996). Warm, funny, articulate, and looking as luminous as ever, Ullmann was happy to chat about her film, Bergman, and her career during a recent visit to New York.

INDIEWIRE: *What attracted you to the script?*
LIV ULLMANN: As a matter of fact, Bergman wrote three scripts. The first script was incredible. It was very long and that attracted me tremendously because it was so multifaceted in many ways. And then he wrote a new script that wasn't attractive for the actors, because they were all gone. It was only a monologue of [the character Marianne]. And then he wrote the third script that had many of the elements of the first script. Since I was the director doing the shooting script, I could use my knowledge of the first script [to influence] my knowledge of the third script.

IW: *It was strictly Bergman's idea to rewrite it twice?*
ULLMANN: It was definitely his own decision, not mine. I just loved the first version. It was very much based on the talk between the two of them. To me, the most fascinating of the two stories is between the writer and the woman. She's an actress and you really see this back and forth [tension] between the writer/director and the woman/actress, the play of power, and all of that. So that is what attracted me.

IW: *Given your history with Bergman, there must have been some personal associations as well . . .*
ULLMANN: Yes. I saw myself as the woman who is asked to come into [Bergman's] work room and give images to his story. And he felt that these are images [he] cannot do himself, or [he didn't] want to do. [He] wanted a woman's images, her experiences. So he asked me to direct it. And I also know that work room of his so very well. So I completely copied that. So I've done it with tremendous love for him but also because it gave me a voice in someone else's script.

IW: *Is Bergman's script strictly dialogue or is there some indication of camerawork or blocking?*

ULLMANN: There is no indication of camera or blocking. If there was, I wouldn't have done it. And he wouldn't want that either. The exciting thing for him was what would I put them in. And I even said to him, "Should we discuss it?" And he said no, he thought it would be really exciting to see what images I would [come up with].

IW: *Was Bergman happy with the finished film?*

ULLMANN: I don't want to talk on behalf of him, but I know he showed it to many people. He showed it to all his children. And when he published the book of his first script, he dedicated it to Lena and me, which he wouldn't have done [if he didn't like the final film]. And I know that he was also very pleased that the child is now very much in the movie. You know, he said, "Now why didn't I think of that?"

IW: *Is there any extra pressure when you're directing a script with that name attached to it that you wouldn't feel if it was someone else's script?*

ULLMANN: Yes there is. Because [Bergman] is very strong and controlling. We didn't talk about the movie for two years [of production]. We talked about other things when we were on the phone or when we met or whatever. I knew that if we had talked about it, then, of course, he'd say "But why are you doing that? I think you should do this and this." So we didn't talk about it. And afterwards, it's tough because if it goes well, it's a Bergman movie, and if it goes bad, I ruined his script. But still, it's a great privilege that you work with someone like that. So if [the public] likes it and says it's a Bergman movie, that's okay with me.

IW: *You've done plenty of things completely outside the "Bergman galaxy," both on stage and film and other things outside show business completely— the political activism and refugee work. To what extent do you feel people still link you to Bergman and does that bother you?*

ULLMANN: For a while, people didn't. But of course now, with the two last films, certain film people start to link me again. But I did that knowingly. And it doesn't bother me, because the people who really know me and know what kind of life I've had also know how very different it is from the life Ingmar has on Fårö. And you know, I understand my daughter [**Linn**, whose father is Bergman] better now than I did before in terms of how difficult it is to have famous parents. I thought she'd be so proud of that, and you know it's a struggle because people don't talk to her like she is who she is. They talk about her father, or maybe even her mother. And now I understand it because yes, I do sometimes get tired of . . . you know, I am not me. I am the muse of Ingmar, or he is my mentor. And you know, he has never been my mentor. I don't even know what a mentor is in that way, because my life has been very rich outside of him. And now my daughter has become a writer in her own right—she has a book out now in the United States.

IW: *It got excellent reviews here . . .*
ULLMANN: Yes. And I think it is wonderful. You know, her dream was, when she was little, "One day, you're gonna see, you're gonna be my mother." And I've had that experience a few times: "Oh, Linn Ullmann is your daughter, is she?" And it gave me great pleasure. I would rather be the mother of Linn Ullmann than the muse of Ingmar Bergman. Although I am very, very proud of all the years we've been together. I think it is fantastic to have started when I was twenty-five and gone the full circle: all the movies as an actress, then the family life, then for many, many more years the friendship, and now, directing his scripts. It is a story that never ends, and that is a very, very privileged story.

IW: *What's next for you?*
ULLMANN: After this, I want some time for myself in the "now." I have some very good offers—projects to direct—and I will make a decision.

IW: *No acting?*
ULLMANN: No. I might change my mind tomorrow. But the way I feel now, I just want to be in the "now" and see what I really want to do with the talent that I have. You ask me if I want to act. You know, it gives me so much pleasure to see someone like Lena do what she's doing in the movie, and I don't think I would have felt such pleasure if I was trying to do that myself. Watching someone else do that gives you such pleasure. And that is a real privilege, to be around that and allow for that. Because there are so many directors who would trample on someone like that.

Through a Glass Darkly: Ullmann Analyzes Bergman

STEPHEN PIZZELLO/2001

DURING THEIR NINE FILM projects together, director Ingmar Bergman and actress Liv Ullmann explored the depth and breadth of the human psyche. Many of the characters in these great Swedish pictures, including the roles played by Ullmann, appeared to be splinters of Bergman's own personality, and the auteur often used the fictional guises to examine his own inner conflicts and neuroses.

With *Faithless*, the duo have taken this cinematic psychoanalysis one step further. Directing from a partially autobiographical script penned by Bergman, Ullmann puts the great film-maker under a microscope in a fascinating narrative that ultimately issues a stern moral critique. Well received at the 2000 Cannes Film Festival, the picture is slated for U.S. release this month.

The plot of *Faithless* focuses on the creative process of a nameless, elderly writer (Erland Josephson), whose true identity—"Bergman"—is only disclosed in the film's written script. Living in isolation on a remote island, where he's working on a screenplay about a past love affair, the writer dreams up an attractive muse, Marianne (Lena Endre), who plays the lead role in his imagination. In flashbacks, we observe Marianne's friendly interactions with David (Krister Henriksson), a playwright who's also close to her husband, Markus (Thomas Hanzon),

From *American Cinematographer*, v. 82, #1 (Jan. 2001), p. 24–28. © 2001 by *American Cinematographer*. Reprinted by permission.

an internationally celebrated orchestra conductor, and the couple's young daughter, Isabelle (Michelle Gylemo). The friendship between David and Marianne soon blossoms into longing, and the pair arrange to meet in Paris for a romantic rendezvous. However, their plans for a brief, discreet interlude are soon complicated by a passion that provokes disastrous consequences for all concerned.

According to Ullmann, the story is based on a real incident from Bergman's life, which made her feel initially that he should direct the film himself. "Ingmar sent the script to me when I was in Oslo about three years ago, and I thought it was wonderful—it was written more like a monologue than a traditional screenplay," Ullmann says during our interview, conducted in her suite at the Four Seasons Hotel in Los Angeles. Shifting a bit in the plush chair she's curled herself into, the actress adds that "the material was so personal that I told Ingmar, 'You really have to do this yourself.' He insisted that he didn't want to direct the film, though. I then suggested that I could do the studio work, and that he could do the preproduction and the editing, but he didn't want to do that either. I told him that my vision of the script would be very different from what he had imagined, but he thought that would be exciting. In a way, our situation was similar to what happens in the movie: a woman comes into the man's studio, and he wants to find out what she thinks. The story is really a dialogue between a screenwriter and a woman who knows him very well."

There are hints in Bergman's past work that the idea for *Faithless* had been germinating for some time. In the film, Marianne's surname is Vogler—a moniker that turns up in several other Bergman films, including *Hour of the Wolf* and *Persona*. Ullmann herself points out that in *Scenes from a Marriage* (in which she also appeared with Erland Josephson, as a woman named Marianne), a husband leaves his wife to go to Paris with another woman. "I've heard the true story from Ingmar's own life, and I'm sure he had it in his mind all these years," Ullmann agrees. "The way I see it, the David character is the writer in his younger years, and I said to Ingmar, 'The writer in the story must be you, because he's called Bergman. And he just replied. 'Well, I couldn't think of another name.'" She laughs, but quickly adds that after she agreed to direct the film, "Ingmar and I didn't discuss it again—I just went ahead with it. He and I had no consultations during the production, because that was the deal we struck. He's very creative and controlling, and if he'd been involved it would have been tough on both of us."

After signing on to direct the film, Ullmann spent nearly a year in preproduction, writing down her ideas and even drawing her own set of storyboards. She also screened many of Bergman's films for a very specific reason. "I wanted *Faithless* to be a bit of an homage," she says. "In writing the script, Ingmar was making an homage to himself, but not a flattering one. In the finished film, there are certain sequences and images that recall scenes from Ingmar's films. For example, some of the scenes in Paris, when David and Marianne are riding in a boat on a lake, recall the comedies that Ingmar made very early in his career."

In striving to realize her vision, Ullmann hired cinematographer Jörgen Persson, who had previously shot her 1992 directorial debut, *Sofie*. The cameraman, whose credits also include collaborations with renowned directors Lasse Hallström (*My Life as a Dog*) and Bille August (*Pelle the Conqueror, Best Intentions, Smilla's Sense of Snow* and *Les Misérables*), says his initial reading of the script convinced him that the film would require a very naturalistic look. "I tried to use as much natural light as I could," he relates. "For example, we used a lot of natural light on location at the villa where the conductor and his wife live, without adding a lot of big lights outside the windows. We had very good weather while we were filming those scenes, which really helped me to work that way. In situations where I was trying to simulate natural light, particularly during daytime interior setups I would generally position HMI lights outside the window and bounce the light off of polystyrene boards to create soft 'daylight' and also to separate direct units to create 'daylight.' I would then use Kino Flos to provide a bit of fill light on the actors.

"For night interiors, I used practicals with additional Kino Flo lighting, and for night exteriors, I mounted HMIs on skylifts. The Kinos were very useful, since I generally worked at a stop of T2.8 or T3.5 with Zeiss Variable Prime lenses. Other than that, though, I mainly love to work with available light as much as possible. In fact, several of the film's day scenes were shot solely with available light."

Ullmann notes that she sought to tell a good deal of the story via close-ups of the characters' faces, as Bergman had done in *Scenes from a Marriage*. "I believe the landscape of faces is most important, and I also felt that it was very important to show the effect of the landscape in which this writer is living," she offers. "When we shot the exteriors of the island where he lives, I specifically wanted to show that this landscape, and the isolation of it, is reflected in his face. If I want to know something about someone, or understand them, I study their face, the way they sit, and other small details. Face-to-face connections between people are important, and in all of Ingmar's other films, people come face to face with each other. In this one, however, it's as if the writer is face to face with himself; even when he's talking with the woman, she seems to be just another element of his personality."

In fact, the film's rocky beach exteriors were shot on Fårö, the island in the Baltic Sea where the real Bergman has lived since he shot *Persona* there in the mid-1960s. For interior scenes of the writer's studio, an exact replica of the great director's actual workspace was created on stage at the Swedish State Television Company (STV) in Stockholm, with a faux exterior built beyond the window. Persson says that one of his trickiest tasks on the show was making this background appear to be realistic. "To make scenery outside the window look natural, we built a big reflecting 'sky' and bounced 12 K HMIs into it," he explains. "To get a more directional light, we also bounced some 6 K HMIs into [reflectors]. The shore was carefully created with real trees and bushes. The sea and sky were painted backdrops, and some reflective material was applied to the surface of the 'water.' The studio was a bit too small to get the depth we needed, and balancing the interior and exterior was critical. In the end, though, it all worked out fairly well."

Realizing that he would be capturing many close-ups, Persson opted to shoot the picture with Fuji film stocks running through his Arri 535A camera. "I always choose a film that seems to fit the subject and the story, and in my opinion, Fuji's emulsions have a nice, soft look that provides very nice skin tones," he says. "We used Fuji's 500 ASA stock [8572] for all of the interiors, and Fuji's 125 ASA stock [8532] for all of our exteriors, since it matched very well with the 72. On the male actors I used lighting that was a bit harder; I softened things up a bit on the women, but I didn't use any diffusion on the camera. The look was achieved strictly through the lighting." Persson adds that he employed some color correction on his lamps, as well as Rosco frost on windows and occasionally the Kino Flos. From time to time, he also used grad filters to control certain parts of the frame.

In one of the film's most striking shots a distraught Marianne confronts her own reflection in a mirror as she considers the effect that her careless actions have had upon her daughter Isabelle. As Marianne gazes into the glass, which is rendered nearly invisible by the surrounding darkness, Isabelle's face appears in the background, where it seems to float between the twin images of Marianne's face. Reminiscent of the famous double images and merging faces in Persona, the sequence was achieved in a straightforward but elegant manner. "We hung some black material behind the little girl and brought the light up on her with a dimmer," Persson recalls. "To light Marianne's face, I simply used Kino Flos."

Kinos also proved handy during filming of an elaborate Steadicam shot that provides an introductory tour of the married couple's home. The sequence was shot on location at the villa, with operator Mike Tiverios guiding the camera around the interior, where it glides past pictures on the walls and other family mementos. "We shot that scene at dusk so we could match the light outside," Persson notes. "We used Kino Flos to bounce light around corners, using door opening and backlight from the ceiling. Kinos are very useful that way, because they're much easier to hide than larger lighting units."

Considering the film's moral message, Ullmann indicates that she was attempting to make a statement on two levels. In a more general sense, she says she wanted to make a film of substance, with a depth that's more common in films from the 1960s and '70s. "I think so-called art films should always be in vogue, because if we keep losing the ability to relate to people and what happens within them, we will lose our sense of those values," she maintains. "There are no values if you're just showing people shooting other people—you don't care about those types of characters. Children today are wrapped up in violent videogames and movies, in which the stories are all about killing and destroying people. That sort of thing just devalues human life, and I think filmmakers and everyone who's part of the media should take their responsibilities more seriously."

At the same time, she recognizes that the emotional violence in Faithless can be just as crushing, in the dramatic sense. "To me, there's one victim in this story, and it's not Marianne, who's a grownup making her own choices—it's the little girl, Isabelle. My hope is that when the girl grows up, maybe she will understand what happened to her family, and she'll be able to overcome it. In my mind, the little girl represents a part of Ingmar, just as all of the other characters do; there's certainly a lot of Ingmar in the woman's husband, who loves music so much. But that particular character—the child who was never loved or recognized—appears in many of Ingmar's films and always reflects his own painful memories. After *Faithless,* I don't think he will ever write about his life story again, because I think he's achieved a kind of closure. He's watched the film many times on his island, and he told me he cried when he saw the mirror scene."

Liv Ullmann at the Helm

LEWIS BEALE/2001

YOU CAN BE FORGIVEN a feeling of déjà vu when watching Swedish actress Lena Endre deliver a mesmerizing monologue about an intense sexual encounter in the new movie *Faithless*. The scene is eerily reminiscent of Bibi Andersson's tale of casual sex in the 1966 Ingmar Bergman classic *Persona*.

But then both films were written by Bergman, and in *Persona* Andersson was addressing an actress played by Liv Ullmann—who happens to be the director of *Faithless*.

"Yes, [the scene in *Faithless*] reminded me a lot of [*Persona*]," says Ullmann, a Norwegian born in Tokyo in 1939. She adds that she was even considering using two different takes in the scene, one of Endre, the other of the actor she is talking to—which would have made the sequence even more reminiscent of *Persona*. She didn't use the extra take in the end, because "the movie is long enough."

This is turning out to be Liv Ullmann month in New York. In addition to the Jan. 26 opening of *Faithless*, Film Forum will be showing a new print of *Persona* Jan. 19–25, and the American Museum of the Moving Image has programmed a Jan. 13–28 retrospective of Ullmann's work as an actress and director.

Most of these films in some way circle back to Bergman. The 82-year-old Swedish master starred Ullmann in nine of his films (including *Cries and Whispers. The Passion of Anna, Scenes from a Marriage* and *Autumn*

From *New York Daily News*, January 7, 2001, p. 5. © 2001 by *New York Daily News*. Reprinted by permission.

Sonata), was her lover and the father of her daughter, Linn, and he has long been her inspiration. Bergman also has written the screenplays for two of the four films Ullmann has directed.

And *Faithless* follows a familiar Bergman-like trajectory—it's a literate tale of a marriage destroyed by infidelity.

"He is not the greatest example of the state of marriage," says Ullmann of Bergman, who has had five wives. "But I think his wish would have been exactly what my wish is: That he had met someone he could have stayed with forever. What he is showing is not that the state of marriage is bad, [but] that it is too easy to break up, too easy to taste a little of something good in spite of hurting somebody."

Ullmann claims *Faithless* says a lot about the lack of values in today's world, where people believe they are accountable only to themselves. It's somber, almost metaphysical material. Ullmann defends its weightiness.

"If you see a movie and recognize something of yourself, if you connect to some feelings or something that is said, to me that is not heavy," she says. "To me, it's more heavy with the Farrelly brothers, where you make love to a chicken [a reference to *Me, Myself and Irene*]. Because what is life about then? About nothing? Going to the cinema and watching that? Talk about lack of values."

After an impressive career as a stage and screen actress, Ullmann began directing films eight years ago, when she was asked to make a Danish movie called *Sophie*, which she also wrote.

"The first week I directed that movie I knew this is where I should be," she says. "I was already very tired of acting. At my age, with a lot of bad directors and not so many good scripts, I wanted to do other things. I like to write, I like to travel, there were other things that fill my life. And suddenly there was this opportunity. I was more than fifty, and I got the opportunity to have a new adventure."

Directing came comparatively easily to her. She felt she had a strong visual sense and knew how to work with other actors. The toughest part was learning how to take control of a set.

"If I don't have a structured set, everybody will walk [on] me very easily," she says. "And the first movie I did a little of that—'Can I get you coffee?' and so on—and I learned very quickly. I'm a people pleaser. And it was tough to make decisions and stand by them, and know that not everybody's going to love you."

Surprisingly, Ullmann says watching Bergman direct was not that instructive. "You observe more from bad directors, what not to do," she says. "I was a good actress, and I knew what they did to really kill me and trample on my fantasy. They didn't know I was creative, hadn't done their homework, and were experimenting and—argh!"

Her commitment to serious, challenging cinema certainly echoes Bergman, however.

"It's wonderful to go to a movie to be entertained," she says. "And sometimes it's wonderful to maybe not be entertained so much, [to be] stirred inside, and come out and talk: 'What does *Faithless* mean? What are the values?' Or get angry, or get upset, or get really quiet, and say 'I'm not going to talk now for a while.' That is what an audience should also do in a movie—they should be creative and find things in the movie that the writer, director and actors never thought of. That is what a good movie should do."

Liv Ullmann, Part I

SHANE DANIELSEN/2001

INGMAR BERGMAN'S MUSE, collaborator and one-time lover, Liv Ullmann became the emblem of arthouse cinema throughout the sixties and seventies. In recent years she has moved behind the camera, directing the family saga *Sofie* and her current film, *Faithless*, from a script by Bergman. On stage at the NFT, the luminous star of *Persona* and *Cries and Whispers* revisited past triumphs and old disasters in conversation with Shane Danielson.

SHANE DANIELSON: Some of you might have heard that this event tonight is in some way a reprise of an interview in August at the Edinburgh Film Festival, and in the car on the way here both of us confessed that this is something like a second date for us.

But one of the things I found out that night was that she didn't particularly like the word icon, though it's been used many times to describe her. She didn't object to it violently, but she did point out that an icon is something that is a couple of centuries old and covered in dust and can usually be found hanging on the wall of an Orthodox church rather than in front of a camera making good films.

In place of icon I would like, therefore, to offer another word for Miss Ullmann, which is "emblematic." Because in the minds of cinema goers, particularly cinema goers of a certain generation, she is the personification of a certain kind of cinema, and identified too with a certain kind of director—in this case Ingmar Bergman. And it occurred to me that this was similar to the way another Scandinavian born actress, Anna Karina, was with another great director, Jean-Luc Godard.

But the differences couldn't be more profound. Karina exemplified capriciousness and everything that, for Godard, was about the unknowability about women. Whereas Ullmann was always known: she projected a woman who laid herself open on the screen for us to see and seemed comfortable projecting the most naked and raw emotional states, and that's, I think, what we recognise in her and what many of us love and admire in her as well.

Tonight, to start off, I've chosen two clips which I think highlight both sides of her career—both as a great screen actor and as a film-maker of international renown. The first clip is from the Bergman film *The Shame*—a single take framed almost entirely on her face—and the second clip is from her debut feature *Sofie*, in which she tried to retain the values in Bergman's films: the unflinching emotional honesty, the truth to characters and their motivations and the respect and compassion for everyone that is on the screen.

The other difference between her and Karina is that Godard and Karina burned brightly and briefly whereas Ingmar Bergman and Liv Ullmann have enjoyed a professional relationship which has varied between lover, muse, collaborator, actor for well over thirty years now, from *Persona* in 1966 to *Faithless* today. Here are the clips.

SD: *When we turned up here in the car tonight there was a big crowd standing outside the doors and Liv looked out of the car and said in typical Liv terror, "Ah! They hated the film! Everybody's walked out of the film. It's going to be a disaster. Why have you brought me here?" And they turned out to be the hoards of autograph hunters. But the point is that one of these people just held out something for her to sign and said over and over again, "You are lovely, you are lovely." And she certainly is, and one of the great film-makers of our day, Liv Ullmann.*

So, not an icon?

LIV ULLMANN: Not an icon. Actually, what Shane said about outside the theatre was nicer than what I heard in the airport not so long ago. A lady, she came very close to me and looked at me and said, "Didn't you use to be Liv Ullmann?" So that was nicer!

SD: *You've tried to preserve many of the lessons you learnt with Bergman.*
Bergman casts such a long shadow over your career, for better or for
worse. . .
LU: Well those are your words. . .

SD: *I go on the basis of the book you wrote,* Changing.
LU: Well I wrote it twenty-five years ago. . .

SD: *So it was fresh from the heat of it in a way.*
LU: Well, yes, but then I lived twenty-five more years. More than that.
After we split up as a loving couple—that's thirty-two years because we
have known each other for thirty-six years. I think it is. Yes, he is
absolutely the best director I've worked with, as an actress on, I think,
ten films and as a director on two scripts. But I think what you are as a
person is also part of what you reflect in your work, and so his shadow
is not what I'm walking under. It's my life I'm working with and it is
my life and my experience which I present.

   In terms of learning, what you learn the most from is—if it comes to
directing—it's really the bad directors you have, because it's through
the bad directors that you learn what you shouldn't do with actors and
the people you are working with. Those that trample on your fantasy
and do not respect your experience. You learn more from that if you
want to be a director yourself. I would say I work in the sunlight of so
much that Ingmar's given me. Actually, I don't work under anyone's
shadow.

SD: *I'm glad we cleared that one up.*
LU: That was the long answer.

SD: *You talked about bad directors, it seems to me that your biggest*
experience of those would have been when you went to work in America.
There's a game I like to play on stage with somebody which is bringing up
their worst film, and I have to say two words: Lost Horizon.
LU: Yeah, that was rather bad. There are a lot of critics who have that
on their list of the fifty worst films that were ever made, and it almost
tops them. But I had a fantastic time, and the cast—Charles Boyer, John
Gielgud, Peter Finch—it was a great cast.

SD: *That's what puzzles me. When you're on something like that and it turns out to be such a monumental turkey. . . I remember interviewing George Clooney about* Out Of Sight *and he'd just come off that Batman movie and he said that even when he was making it, he and the guy who played Robin were sitting there going, "This is going to suck." Did you know that at the time?*

LU: No! Well I knew that I couldn't dance and I couldn't sing. . .

SD: *Which for a musical is kind of an obstacle. . .*

LU: Yes, I know! I did say that to them and they said, "Oh, it doesn't matter, you're so sweet and so *charming*, we'll work around it." So somebody sang my voice and then I danced, and that looked kind of stiff and strange, but what I said was true. It was my first time in Hollywood and I believed everything they said, and they said every woman in Hollywood wants to do your part in *Lost Horizon*, and I believed that too. I lived in this incredible house with this swimming pool and my friends came over, and the bathroom in the house was like, like this whole room! It was fantastic! Give that to any thirty-one-year-old from Norway and they will think that it's the greatest time in their life.

I still feel that the film wasn't a success, but it was a fantastically good time. As a matter of fact, that first year I was in Hollywood—it was my last year too—I did four movies. As opposed to Greta Garbo, who just grew and grew, I managed to close down two studios. And this is true! And it's fun for me because the tragedy never reached me, because by the time I'd done my year—and none of the films were out yet, so I still thought, "Oh, what a success I am"—I went to Sweden and the film I did then was *Scenes from a Marriage,* so I wasn't really aware that I had closed the two studios.

SD: *At the time did you say in interviews in Sweden, "They love me in America"?*

LU: Yes I did that. And they said, "She's really got stuck up now." They didn't understand that it was a great time. I still think it was a great time. I took the best of it with me and I went on from there and that was, like, thirty years ago, so who cares?

SD: *Absolutely. You're associated with Bergman in so many films. You're also blurring the lines between collaboration and life partnership. . .*

LU: That was only for two films.

SD: *But even then, after that, you're still in his orbit, in his films. When you got out of that, how was he about you being in* The Emigrants *(directed by Jan Troell), for example? Many directors get possessive and don't allow people to play in other fields. . .*

LU: He's a little like that. I did it anyway. And by the time I did *The Emigrants* it was more or less over in terms of the love relationship. As a matter of fact it was not Ingmar who brought me to Hollywood but *The Emigrants. . .*

SD: *Because of the Golden Globe—you were nominated, yes?*

LU: I won. And I was nominated for an Oscar and that was when I went to Hollywood and got the four films. He kind of realised that I wanted to taste that world and when all that was over I went back and did a film for him, and he thought, "Well, she has learnt now and she'll do *Scenes from a Marriage*, and she'll be happy to be here."

SD: *How big a priority was it for you to be a success in America, in that after the European success you would have to start almost from the bottom. . .*

LU: You don't start from the bottom when you get a lead in a musical. . .

SD: *But* Lost Horizon. . .

LU: But it didn't seem like a tragedy. And what they couldn't do with me . . . because I was thirty-one years old, they couldn't do what they'd planned: create me into something different, because I was secure with the kind of person I was. And I had very good luggage because I had worked with Ingmar Bergman. I don't know if I had dreamt of being a success in Hollywood, I don't think I've ever been ambitious in that way. I just thought it was an incredible opportunity of life, and it came to me and I did it. And I don't regret it and for me, it gave me great pleasure. I think you should say "Yes," even if you do fall on your . . . behind.

SD: *If you say "No" all the time then I suppose you never live.*

LU: That's true, because I did another musical. That one was on Broadway. That was maybe more sad because that was Richard Rodgers, and that was the last musical he ever wrote, and again they said it doesn't matter because I was still sweet, and I said I couldn't sing and to look at *Lost Horizon*. They thought it would go anyway.

The musical was called I *Remember Mama*, it was newly written, and I was taken to Richard Rodgers and I told him I really don't sing and he said, "I'm used to that. I've had a lot of singers that don't sing. I just want to know your range." And I said, "This is really embarrassing because I really don't" and he said, "Don't fear". He was already sick and old and close to eighty at that time, and just sitting at his piano and he was so sweet and thin, and he said, "Just sing Happy Birthday." So I sang Happy Birthday and he aged ten years, just like that.

The incredible thing with him was, and this was his last musical, and he knew he was making it for me—seven songs that I mishandled, and he came each night to the theatre and he was loving and nice and just kind. It was eight months of a fantastic thing on Broadway. And because I was older I knew what I was doing. I thought that this was going to be fun to tell my grandchildren, you know: "I don't dance, I don't sing, and here I am a star in a musical."

SD: *Which killed Richard Rodgers. . .*
LU: No. It didn't kill him. Because he was already sick before he met me. . .

SD: *Moving swiftly along. You said you weren't particularly ambitious for success. You just wanted to make the films you wanted to make, and yet at the same time from an early age. . .*
LU: If life presents itself to you, you have to say "Yes". Or at least that was what I felt. Now I am more careful with my choices. Now I know it is more serious because I am older and everything. But you have to allow yourself, in my business, fiascos. Because that is what you really learn from. The other things you get so much praise from you can't learn anything from that. But when you do bad you have to think, why did I do badly, was it my choices, was it the way I did it, and you go on and have a better life because of that.

SD: *Did you believe the publicity you got, or were you always doubting yourself?*
LU: I would doubt myself after the reviews of the mistakes, but that doesn't live forever either. It's now many years since I read reviews in that way and it doesn't mean what it used to mean because life is so

much grander and more exceptional than to read reviews of what you do at work. Life is what you fill your day with, why you wake up in the morning and what you want to do in terms of being a human being. I'm not portrayed by what was bad and what was good in terms of my work, I'm portrayed by what I try to give in to my work.

SD: *Sure.*
LU: Was that too serious?

SD: *No, not at all. In the second clip, from Sofie, I thought it showed the difference between Bergman, say, and yourself, that you've just touched on. The fact that you draw this distinction between life and your work and that one doesn't necessarily consume the other. The portraitist in the clip will take any emotion he can get, it's all grist to the mill, and that's what Bergman does, clearly.*
LU: Yes, that's a kind of cannibal, but not necessarily in the wrong way. Some artists use every moment, how can I do this, how can I note this down, how can I use it. There are some people that do that, but also just live. I would rather be of that kind. When you die and God says, "What did you do in life?" you can't just say, "I did good work." You have to say a lot of other things as well.

SD: *You tried to live a good life.*
LU: Yeah. I hated and I loved and I sang and well, whatever. I came from the States this morning so if I say things like that it might be jet-lag too.

SD: *You said in Edinburgh that you had remained friends with Bibi Andersson. There was a community of women around Bergman, but it didn't seem to be competitive, or if it was, not in a way that destroyed the group from within. I don't mean because you were women, but a group of creative people around a director doesn't necessarily encourage good behaviour.*
LU: We were very close friends, the women who worked for and with Bergman. Bibi Andersson and I are the best of friends and we are like sisters. The first time that we worked together was in Norway many years before I worked with Ingmar in a film; it was a Danish film. There were no houses, it was on an island north of Norway, and we all lived in a school house and Bibi and I shared a classroom, there were beds in

there. We used to lie at night and dream of the future, both of us were newly married and we were twenty years old and we said if we ever get to be parents we'd be godparents to each other's children.

I think we bonded so strongly then that even though later I got to do more films with Ingmar than she did, she continued to be my sister and never faulted me. That says a lot about her strength and friendship is more important than work. I don't know if I would have reacted in the incredible way she did.

SD: *Was it hard having gone from being intimate with Ingmar to stepping back to a purely professional relationship?*

LU: Oh, that was a blessing, that really was. We did two films when we lived together, *The Shame* and *The Passion of Anna*, and the break-fasts were terrible. He would sit there thinking about what he was going to do, and if he had had nightmares he would tell me about that too, and I thought, "Oh, god. I'm going to do that nightmare on film." It wasn't really life affirming for me. Later, when those things were behind us, we each could go home to our own home, where the other one wasn't; it was incredible. We worked so much better when we were friends, and we are truly very close friends, than we did when we had other agendas in our relationship.

SD: *Was he supportive when you wanted to be a director?*

LU: Yes. He was very supportive. My first film, *Sofie*, I sent him the cut of the film when I was finished and asked him what he thought about it. And I thought a lot about what I had learned from Ingmar when I did that movie. For me to have been an actress was the best of schools to be a director because I know what it feels inside and I started to respect acting so much more. While I was still an actress I sometimes felt a little ashamed of being an actress. . .

SD: *Why?*

LU: I don't know. Because here I am, and there's so much going on in the world, and here I am an actress and people sit with you at dinner and they think they have to ask how it is to act, and how you learn your lines and things like that. . .

SD: *Nothing very substantial. . .*

LU: No, because they think you don't. And so I almost felt ashamed. But I knew deep down, when it didn't have to be me, that actors are so creative and actors are so fantastic, the really good ones, to build on their own life and to use that, without being themselves, but to use the best and the wisest thing that they know about life.

And the movie you have just seen (*Faithless*), to see Lena Endre give so much of her life so freely, I think it is the best performance in a movie. When you think of films and theatre you can take away the lights and the stage, everything, but you can never do without the word and the actors.

SD: *I would imagine that actors want to work with you because you come from that background, because you understand. There is a level of trust established there immediately.*

LU: There has to be a lot of trust. First of all you have to be very open with who you are so that they know you are not hiding something. Then they really have to trust you so that they know whatever they give you, you are not going to misuse them. They must feel that, while you are sitting there with the camera, you are like a lover. If you are with someone who really loves you, and they look at you and they show you that you are the most wonderful person in the world, you will suddenly bloom. If you are a kind of rose, which these people are, they will be the best of roses if you allow them to be roses, and don't try to make them into a blue copy of some idea you had in your own workroom.

SD: *Did you ever feel close to cinema as a whole, were you a film fan? Did you feel passionately involved in the film world, or was it more isolated, because you were in Scandinavia?*

LU: But, you know, we see films in Scandinavia too.

SD: *I'm from Australia. We just got them last year.*

LU: When I was in Australia, Doris Day was still the icon.

SD: *She's a big pinup for all of us. There's that sense, in the sixties and seventies, of an enclave up there, making a very specific kind of cinema that doesn't appear to be influenced by French cinema or Hollywood cinema. It was a parallel cinema.*

LU: That is true. Although I must say that we saw a lot of films undubbed. We saw Italian films, and French and Russian and from Czechoslovakia and from Poland, so we had a fantastic education in foreign films. Our films in the end did not look like these films, though these films really inspired us. When I was young and saw Vittorio De Sica's films, like *The Bicycle Thieves*, my whole view of life changed seeing these films.

That's why it's so important the type of films young people see today. They sneak into your fantasy, maybe even more so today than before, because today people seem more isolated, and there are very few places where they are face to face with others, and cinema is one of the few places now that they can still be influenced. That is why it is so sad today that they are getting all these cartoon movies and slice movies, when in my time we had much more grownup movies. It is cut-cut-cut-cut, you never get to see what life is about, what your heart is about, what your pulse is about. When you look at people you don't look back and forth; you look at people and movies should reflect that, and they don't do that anymore.

SD: *With DVD and video, even the communal experience is declining. There is a breakdown of that community. Do you feel endangered by Hollywood in Norway? Is that as strong there as in the rest of Europe, and is the push to resist that as strong?*

LU: It's like, I'm sure, it is in England. I think something like eighty percent of the films that we see are Hollywood movies, and the more people see these kinds of movies the harder it is to get them in to other movies, because they don't want to see it, because it's long, and slow. People have this haste: "It can't be too long because then I have to go out and. . ." What do they have to do? Life is long! Can't they give two hours, or more, and see if something changes in their life? Or maybe they'll have something to talk about with someone? Or maybe they are shocked and they decide something is going to be different in their life. It is good to be influenced.

It's great to be in a movie house and be a participant. In so many movies you are not a participant. But to be a participant, even if you don't like the movie, something is somehow shaken within you. That is good. We need to be part of life, we can't just be watching a screen, and watching what is happening, and watching the politicians, and watching everything. We have to be part of it. Not passive. So much in our time is making us passive because we don't know what's going on anymore. Wars happen and we don't know what the war is about. Politicians are elected and people don't even know how to elect them!

SD: *The core of Bergman's films is a watchfulness and almost a nineteenth century view that character decides destiny. Yet that is so unpopular and radically unfashionable. Do you get depressed in terms of whether you can keep making films, or if the films will find an audience? Do you just make something and hope it will connect with an audience somewhere?*

LU: Yes, I hope. But then I'm sixty-two years old. If I was thirty I would be more worried because I would wonder whether I could continue to make films this way. But I am not worried for me or for what my future will be, but I am worried for the audience and the film-makers. It is tough for film-makers if they want to make a more serious, or even a comedy, done seriously. But most of all I am worried for young people because they cannot go to the cinema and experience the wonder when the bell rings and the curtain goes and something is happening there On the plane nowadays, the Farrel brothers?

SD: *Farrelly brothers.*

LU: They were raping a chicken! It's not even fun!

SD: *I know. In Australia you have to take what you can get.*

LU: I was in Australia and they have a very different way of seeing things. Many years ago I did this Cocteau play called *The Human Voice*. It's about a woman, and she's on the phone, and that's all you see. She is on the phone with her lover who is apparently breaking up with her and she just cannot let him go. It's a really sad monologue. And she says, "Please don't hang up, don't hang up." And she's struggling for her life. It had been a success everywhere we'd been, and then we came to Sydney. On the second night, people had come because I was a star in Australia at that time, I was saying, "Don't hang up, oh, please, don't hang up." And I hear from the gallery, "Oh, please hang up!" And that's what I felt.

Liv Ullman, Part II

SHANE DANIELSEN/2001

SD: *Tell me the story of the meeting between Woody Allen and Ingmar Bergman that you managed to engineer . . .*

LU: *Oh, yes. I was performing in New York doing* The Doll's House, *and this was in the middle of the women's liberation in the seventies in the United States. Can I just tell you this story first?*

SD: *Er . . . yes.*

LU: I was doing it with Sam Waterston. I was Nora and he was Helmer. Sam always played the nice guy. And this was women's liberation. We did the rehearsals and Sam was very happy and I was happy and then we had the audience there for the first time two days before the premiere. They started booing when Helmer, my husband, came in. Each time I said something it was, "Oh, wonderful! Wonderful!" Anything I said! When he said something it was, "Boo!" It was terrible. And in the end, when I left the stage, they applauded, and he had one line, "I don't understand," and they really booed him.

Sam was so shaken afterwards he almost didn't want to do it anymore. So to pep him up I said we should do yoga before. So the day before the premiere we did some yoga and Sam stretched his toe a little, so he had to go onstage with a stick. And, you know, they really didn't boo because he had this stick. They still said, "Bravo! Bravo!" when Nora said something, but they were much more quiet. And when I left the stage they kind of felt sorry because he was sitting there with a stick.

From the *Guardian*, January 23, 2001. Reprinted by permission of the author.

Now this is the honest-to-God truth I am telling you. The next day was the premiere. Sam Waterston came in on crutches.

He did the whole run on crutches and nobody applauded when I left anymore. It was a success and it was a new way of doing the play.

So Ingmar wanted to come to the United States to see this. But he is very isolated. Woody Allen kept inviting me out for dinner because he admired Ingmar so much. References to Ingmar all the time.

So I told him that Ingmar was coming to town. Woody said, "Aaah! Can I meet him? I can't believe it." So I called Ingmar and said that Woody Allen wanted to meet him, and he said, "That would be a pleasure."

So Ingmar came for two days only and on one day he would see the play and the next day he would have dinner in his hotel suite because, you know, he is a genius and so he doesn't go on the streets and things . . . So we would have dinner with Woody in his suite. So Woody collected me from the theatre the second day in a limo with a chauffeur who wore white gloves who you couldn't address—he's also a kind of genius! So we sat in this limo and Woody was so nervous. We got to the suite and the door opens. The two look at each other. You should have seen their eyes: they just looked at each other. "Hello." "Hello." And that was the only thing the two of them said, hello, hello. That is true.

So we sat down at the dinner table and they didn't talk to each other! And Ingrid, who is Ingmar's wife, who is not normally allowed to talk when there are artists there, she was talking!

SD: *But you have a bit of a problem with Ingrid . . .*
LU: We didn't have that contact, we didn't share that much . . . but . . . you know, she's a great cook! So we talked about the meatballs! This is really true. And when we said something really silly, the two geniuses would look at each other and, you know, think, "Hmm. Little women." You know.

And for dessert, to put hurt upon hurt, she had an envelope with my child support—I got $1,500 a year in child support—and she gave that envelope to me over the table. So it was a strange dinner. And then it was over, and I'm not even sure they said goodbye. They kind of looked at each other with this knowing smile. Then I went back with Woody in his limo and he said, "Thank you Liv. That was an experience."

Ingmar then called me when I got back to my room and said, "Thank you Liv. He is really special." They didn't say a word to each other the whole dinner.

SD: *Let's open it up to some questions from the audience.*

Q: *What recent films have you seen that you liked?*

LU: I get all these movies that are nominated for Oscars and I see them on tapes which really is not how you should see them. I saw Hitching Dragon . . . Flying What . . . That one by Ang Lee [*Crouching Tiger, Hidden Dragon*]. I thought that was fantastic. I don't know about the story, but the images and these people fighting but flowing through the air . . . I thought that was fantastic. And I saw another movie, the script was not so good, but I saw an actress I have admired for some years, Cate Blanchett. She is doing such an extraordinary performance in a movie that perhaps isn't the best. She is really, apart from Lena Endre, she is really . . . well she is younger than Lena, so I would say she is the best actor of her generation and Lena Endre of hers. It is very difficult if you are an actress to be good in a bad film, but she manages that.

SD: *Would you consider working with international stars like that, or is it important for you to work within Scandinavia?*

LU: No. It is important for me to work with something that is close to my heart, and it doesn't matter to me what language they speak. Cate Blanchett, she is a soul mate, I can see. Languages are no problem, but it would be a problem if it was a Hollywood film because you don't get the last edit, and you can't have people editing your film. They haven't asked me either.

Q: *Why isn't there a Bergman retrospective at the NFT so young people can see Bergman, and what was it like acting with Ingrid Bergman?*

SD: *I'll answer the first part. Bergman prints are very hard to get hold of. Even to get the extracts we showed tonight.*

LU: I did hear that there may be a retrospective here. Maybe people could demand it. Working with Ingrid was an incredible joy. I admire her so much. What was good with her was that she was so honest, she came out with everything she felt, and that is sometimes difficult if you work with somebody like Ingmar. You respect him so much, and I'm using this word genius, and I mean it from my heart, but sometimes I am also using it in a special way . . . to explain . . . Ingrid was important because she did not qualify him as anything other than a director. I used to sit there and admire her, that she said everything that she did. We played a mother and a daughter, and we said to Ingmar, "Why are you making the mother so unsympathetic, just because she also wants to have a career. Can we change the words?" And Ingmar said, "No, you cannot change the words." We said, "Can we play against the character?" And he said, "Yes, you are actresses, you can do that."

Then there was this incredible episode happening when we did *Autumn Sonata*. I am the daughter and I am blaming my mother for everything I am in life. I am more than forty years old, and there comes a time when you cannot blame your mother anymore. Somehow you are living your own life. But she goes on blaming her mother. So it is this scene where the mother is blaming her daughter and I had three pages of a monologue telling the mother how terrible she'd been, look at the misery of my life and it's all your fault. I go on and on and on through a whole night. And in the morning, Ingrid Bergman, as the mother, has two lines. "Please, hold me. Please, love me." And I thought that was beautiful. If I had to do that, I would really make people cry, I would do it tenderly.

So I did all my lines, and Ingrid just sat there, and I did the hate and the anger and everything. The camera was turned on to Ingrid and she was to say, "Please, hold me. Please, love me." But she says, "No! I'm not going to say that. I want to slap her in the face and leave the room." And it was incredible—no one has talked to him in that way. He was red and he said, "That is your line." "I'm not doing it." So they started to yell and went out of the studio. We all looked at each other and thought, "The movie is going to end here." We heard the voices out there, really high voices—the genius and the actress.

Then suddenly the door opens and they come in and, of course, he has won; and he should win, they are his words. But she, she was saying the lines . . . but if you look at that, she says, "Please, hold me. Please, love me," but her face was mirroring every woman who has gone through their lives saying, "I'm sorry" and "What can I do for you?" And she has the face of somebody who is so fed up of saying,

"Excuse me for being alive." I think it was masterful. So Ingmar got what he wanted, he got the lines, but he also got a really incredible performance. Maybe the whole thing was staged by him. That I don't know. But the result is fantastic.

SD: *Would he do that kind of thing? Destabilizing you on set?*
LU: *No, he wouldn't . . . Well, what do I know?*

SD: *Well I was wondering how you get the pain in those performances? It's hard to switch that on and off.*
LU: He creates that kind of atmosphere where what you do is suddenly part of life the moment you are doing it. I was doing a suicide scene in *Face to Face*. I was told by him, "You're sitting on your bed and you take these pills and then you lie down on the bed and then you die. And we'll do it in one take." And I thought, "Is this all I'm getting?" He didn't say more. But then just before he said for the camera to go he said, "Oh, we did change the real pills for sugar pills?" And that was so fantastic, I knew he was doing it with me, but my fantasy allowed him to do it with me.

So the camera went and I knew that maybe these are the real pills, and I started to shiver a little on my hands. And I took the pills, more and more, and it became some kind of reality for me. I lied down and I was starting to experience it, and he never said cut. So I had to lie there and what do I do now? Yes. This is my childhood room and look at the tapestry, those beautiful flowers, and don't you think that if she was dying she would put her fingers on those tapestry flowers as she must have done when she was a little girl and I did that. I was moved by that. That was also set by Ingmar, the flowers, but he never said it. And he still didn't say cut. What is happening? And I had a watch, and I have to look at the watch because I have to know what time I am dying and I was so moved by that fantasy that I almost died. And I closed my eyes! And it was over. And Ingmar said, "Thank you. Now I don't have to commit suicide."

It's really hard to tell you, but a masterful audience will put you in that kind of mood, where everything suddenly becomes reality. The audience is quiet and listening to you, and you want to give more. That's where he was so good. He gave you great blocking and great atmosphere and the space to try things.

Q: *How do you bring out the performances in your actors?*

LU: It really has to do with trust. I must be trustworthy so that they can create. I am not going to ask them to do less of more unless it's really true. The fantastic scene you saw (*Faithless*) when Lena Endre is sitting in the window and she is talking about leaving her child. It is an eight to ten minute take on her face. The first time she did it, it was magnificent—it was an actress; you could see the technique and if anyone saw it they would say, what a fantastic actress. But I knew she could do more. So I said, that was fantastic, everyone will praise you, but I want more. Just think of that little child walking out and think of her back and her head that doesn't turn towards you, and that is going to be an image that you will carry with you for the rest of your life. Be Lena.

Then she did it one more time. And magic happened. And it wasn't like this big applause they say you get from people in the studio when something is good. There was a fantastic silence and she left the studio and some of the workers were patting her on the shoulder. She allowed herself to be the person, she wasn't doing the person. It is hard to explain.

SD: *Would you say a lot of screen acting is about forgetting that technique?*

LU: Yes. If you see the technique, it is good but it is not there. When you see a naked face then it's really there. When you are moved to the inner core of yourself, it is really there. If you cut away from that face four times you will lose that.

Q: *Was it a coincidence that both your films have featured Jewish families?*

LU: In a way it was coincidence. In *Sofie*, that was about a Jewish family, so everyone except the painter was Jewish. I do not really know why the husband in *Faithless* was Jewish. It probably belongs to the way Ingmar sees family and he believes that no one represents the family as well as a Jewish man and woman, but I'm just guessing now, coming from a long family history. But it was a coincidence. But I elected to do the first film because it was a Jewish story and I wanted to do that because, maybe for the same reasons. I wanted to show a family with traditions. Erland Josephson, who played the lead in that, was the only

Jewish person in *Sofie*, and he had forgotten so much about his child-hood. Since he was a child had not eaten kosher food and had forgot-ten the songs. But while we did the movie he remembered everything: the songs, the Hebrew language. It is also where my personal story has come from, although I am not Jewish.

Q: *You talked about Ingrid's struggle with Ingmar's text. How was it dealing with Ingmar's text as a director?*

LU: I didn't change a word. Of course a lot of things were taken away, otherwise it would have been six hours long. I had the freedom to do that, but I never changed words that were being said. I also had a free-dom because not having written it myself I didn't have to defend the words because they were already there. Ingmar may have had pain when Ingrid was talking that way, but I had the freedom to do the shooting script because he had written it as a monologue. He wanted me to do the shooting script because, just like in the film, he wanted a woman to come in and give her [point of view on] what had happened to him once. I allowed myself to take that freedom and not to ask him whether I had done what he wanted.

SD: *Did he come on set?*

LU: No. Never. He came on the last day and took some photographs. That was fantastic—that is full of trust. The pre-production was one year and he never asked anything. He never came on the set and he never came to the editing table and I admire him a lot for that. I don't think I could have done that. But he did it. He dares to show trust. I was faithful, I didn't do things that I thought would be wrong against who he is.

Q: *Why did you change from acting to directing? Why aren't you acting in any more films?*

LU: Well, that has to do with age. Partly because they were not queu-ing up for me and partly because I had decided that I didn't really want to act anymore. There aren't that many good directors like Ingmar and sometimes, with a certain age, you get impatient while they are doing their homework on you. I really didn't want to do that. And life was good to me. It gave me a new opportunity that I'm so grateful for.

People say that your life is over at forty, and my life was fantastic at forty. People say life is over at fifty, and I went into a new career. Now I'm more than sixty and that is why I want to take a pause, in case there is something else to do.

It doesn't have to be a career. Life is there whatever. If you are there in the garden or whatever. Life is very generous if you allow it to be generous, for us who are privileged to have choices.

SD: *What did you mean by "taking a pause"? From making films or from acting in films?*
LU: Acting, that's over with.

SD: *Completely? Nothing would coax you back?*
LU: Well, I never know about tomorrow, but I don't think so. I don't want to worry about the way I look, I want to worry about the way I live. To know that whatever happens, if I am to spend two-and-a-half years on a film, it must be life affirming. Or I can say I want to see my grandchild on a trip. To be free to say, "Yes, why not?" I never did that.

SD: *There's no project at the moment?*
LU: I have scripts lying there, but I'm so far . . . I want to take a pause and see what I want to do.

Q: *What was the experience like, of acting with and directing Erland Josephson?*
LU: Well, he is one of my best friends and we've known each other for thirty-five years. He was the only one I was nervous of directing because we are used to talking in breaks and talking bad about the director, sharing all these wonderful secrets. Suddenly I was isolated. I don't know if they were talking bad about me, but I wasn't part of that group anymore. But he was fantastic, he switched from being my playmate to listening to me as a director and honoured me with that. And he gave in a new way that was very different to what he gave me when I was an actor. He has been in all four films I have done, and I cannot really see a filmset without him. He is a very good man. It worked very much because of him, because he allowed me to change my part.

SD: *When you and Bibi Andersson were lying in bed in that classroom talking about what you wanted to achieve, have you surpassed your expectations?*
LU: Oh, yes. I could never have imagined. I think life is wonderful and I am tremendously grateful in that I still have Bibi and we can still lie down on the sofa and talk about what we want to do next. That friendship has lasted. If I have nothing else to do, I can be an icon!

Interview with Liv Ullmann

GERALD PEARY / 2001

"TODAY, I TALKED TO Ingmar in Sweden on the phone and asked him what I should say about *Faithless*," Liv Ullmann said, as we sat for a hotel-balcony interview at the Cannes Film Festival last May. There, the Ingmar Bergman-written and Ullmann-directed film was having its world premiere. Bergman told Ullman not to worry, and to say what she wanted about the movie: "When I gave it to you, I gave it to you with trust."

Ullmann had felt an unbearable responsibility, being handed, in 1998, this frighteningly honest, guilt-ridden screenplay based on an incident of infidelity in Bergman's life half a century ago. She tried to convince Bergman to direct *Faithless* himself, or, minimally, to oversee the pre- and post-production. No, he insisted that Ullmann, who starred in *Persona* and other Bergman masterpieces and has a grown daughter from their long-ago relationship, make the movie, interpret it her way. He would watch *Faithless* only when it was finished.

Bergman's stipulations: the remarkable Swedish actress, Lena Endre, must play Marianne, the married woman with a daughter who becomes embroiled in the affair. Erland Josephson, featured in such Bergman classics as *Hour of the Wolf, Fanny and Alexander*, and *Scenes from a Marriage*, should be cast as "Bergman," the forlorn octogenarian thinking back, via flashbacks, to the key indiscretion of his thirties.

The actual happening was in 1953. Ullmann: "He made *Summer with Monika*, and fell in love with the actress, Harriet Andersson. They went

From *Boston Phoenix*, March 2–8, 2001. © 2001 by *Boston Phoenix*. Reprinted by permission.

together to Paris, he came back to Sweden. He was married, had children, and said to his wife, 'I'm leaving you.' *Faithless* is about living through betrayal, loss."

The script germinated for decades, until Bergman found the actress who made sense for him as the object of his adulterous desire. Lena Endre had performed for Bergman at Stockholm's Royal Dramatic Theatre in *Romeo and Juliet, The Misanthrope*, and *Peer Gynt*. "I think he didn't know what face he needed to write this story of a woman's emotions," Ullmann said, "but the memories of Lena were with him. She has everything he needed: discipline, experience, and she's a great actor. If he hadn't picked her, I would have picked her anyway.

"I'm a woman who has known Ingmar the most, thirty-seven years. Erland has known him for more than fifty years and is the closest to him." So close that Josephson could embody "Bergman" and the filmmaker could escape without having to play himself on screen. "That way, Ingmar isn't sitting here in Cannes," Ullmann said. "He's scared of being found out, like we all are." Most important for Ullmann was that Bergman really liked the film when he saw the finished version. "Ingmar cried twice. First, when Marianne looks at her image in a mirror, a shot like the double mirror in *Persona*. Second, when Marianne comes home from the night of lovemaking."

But where Bergman and Ullmann really differed in interpreting the material, and where Ullmann's direction took a personal turn, was in dwelling on the daughter, Isabelle, nine, caught up in the dire consequences of her mother's adultery.

Ullmann hinted that there might be a repressed memory from Bergman's boyhood: "Maybe he was that little child. I think that one time when he was very young, something bad happened to him."

In Bergman's script, the little girl is talked about in a monologue but never appears on screen. "He didn't think of putting in the child. He didn't see the scale of suffering. I asked him about the children he had abandoned. But his generation didn't see it as havoc.

"Though I had to be truthful to him, I also had to be true to myself. The scene I'm most proud of for Lena is when she talks to the child and cries about leaving. The first take she did as an actress, the second as the character."

I wondered if the little girl cast as Isabelle, Michelle Gylemo, was sheltered from this episode's traumatic implications. Ullmann said, "I told the child that your parents are divorcing, your mother is leaving you. When we shot, I saw her tears. But she's an actress! She screamed, 'Did you like it? Should I do it again?' "

Actress Behind the Camera:
An Interview with Liv

RICHARD PORTON/2001

IN CHANGING, LIV ULLMANN'S remarkably frank memoir, the distinguished actress recalls the shooting of *Persona*, her debut film with Ingmar Bergman, as "the first time I met a film director who let me unveil feelings and thoughts no one else had recognized . . . a genius who created an atmosphere in which everything could happen—even that which I had not known about myself." At a time when film stars have almost become interchangeable commodities, Ullmann's famous collaboration with Bergman serves as a needed reminder that actors need not be obsessed with fat paychecks and the whims of their agents.

Although Bergman worked with a number of brilliant actors throughout his career—Max von Sydow, Bibi Andersson, and Erland Josephson are merely among the most famous—Ulmann's distinctive blend of vulnerability and self-assurance was ideal for Bergman's purposes, and her compelling presence in films such as *Persona*, *Scenes from a Marriage*, *The Passion of Anna*, and *Autumn Sonata* was a catalyst for some of his most powerful and innovative work. These films explored themes that would resurface in the Bergman scripts that Ullmann herself eventually directed—the chasm between esthetic brilliance and personal inadequacy and the rancor, and often irreparable damage, wrought by marital strife.

While Ullmann's first two features as a director—*Sofie* and *Kristin Lavransdatter*—were lavish and slightly leaden period pieces that were

---

From *Cineaste*, Spring 2001, p. 32+. © 2001 by *Cineaste*. Reprinted by permission.

far removed from the concerns of Bergman's chamber dramas, her subsequent decision to direct two Bergman scripts, *Private Confessions*, and her most recent effort, *Faithless*, tacitly acknowledges both the burdens and advantages of being an artist whose legacy will always be discussed in tandem with the career of her mentor and former lover.

Both *Private Confessions* and *Faithless* examine the marital entanglements that have often inspired Bergman's films (as well as the plays of his beloved August Strindberg). *Private Confessions*, however (a film that features characteristically brilliant performances by Pernilla August and Max von Sydow), inspired by the unhappy marriage endured by Bergman's parents, is safely rooted in a conservative, early twentieth-century past. Despite the rage on display in the protagonists' stormy marriage, a tentative sense of moral uplift is achieved at the film's conclusion.

Faithless, on the other hand, does not evoke the distant past; this portrait of love gone awry, while compassionate, is also unrelenting and does not offer any facile solace. In other hands, this chronicle of the devastating impact of an apparently harmless affair upon a marriage would seem moralistic and old-fashioned. Yet Bergman, the unrepentant agnostic, is not interested in traditional Christian mores or family values. Instead, his film, loosely autobiographical, is both an agonizing self-indictment and a detached inquiry into how minor deceptions can spiral into personal catastrophe.

The framing story of *Faithless* depicts a film director (straightforwardly called Bergman and played by the director's old friend Erland Josephson) who is attempting to formulate a screenplay based on painful memories of a youthful love affair. Marianne, the young actress he engages to help him (brilliantly played by Lena Endre, whose undiluted intensity bears comparison with the young Liv Ullmann) eventually embodies a character who resembles the old man's ex-lover as his scenario coalesces into a full-fledged film clef. Avoiding finger pointing, Ullmann and Bergman incisively demonstrate how all of the protagonists are—at least to some extent—victims of self-deception. We are never encouraged to entirely condemn or wholeheartedly embrace any of the characters. Markus (Thomas Hanzon), Marianne's infinitely patient husband and a brilliant musician, becomes, by the film's end, subservient to his own suppressed rage. Marianne's lover, David (Krister Henriksson), although often abrasive and childish, is also blessed with an impish charm. And Marianne herself, an enormously sympathetic figure, seems irreparably stymied by her own indecisiveness.

Cineaste interviewed Ullmann last September, shortly before the American premiere of *Faithless* at the 2000 New York Film Festival. Without denying her artistic debt to Bergman, she cogently pointed out both his strengths and weaknesses, while also sharing her thoughts concerning acting technique and the direction of actors.

CINEASTE: *Unlike* Faithless, Scenes from a Marriage *appears to end with at least a partial reconciliation between the estranged protagonists. Given the current film's downbeat ending, can we conclude that Bergman is growing increasingly pessimistic?*

LIV ULLMANN: I'm not sure if he's growing more pessimistic, but I think that, somehow, he's come face to face with himself in this last screenplay. That's tough—a priest isn't listening to him, no one else in fact is listening to him. The optimistic part of this is that he now will be able to put all this behind him. Unlike *Private Confessions*, Bergman finds himself (in the part played by Erland Josephson) completely alone—except for a woman who comes and helps him, lending him a woman's voice and relieving his isolation a bit.

CINEASTE: *Does this explain why Bergman didn't want to direct the film himself?*

ULLMANN: It might, because it's tremendously personal. He didn't know what choices I was going to make as a director, but he didn't interfere. He knows me so well, though, that he probably expected that I would make certain choices—and maybe he wanted me to make them. I told him that perhaps he should direct it, precisely because the script was so personal. But he dismissed this, and told me that he was excited about the choices I might make as a director. It will always be considered a Bergman film—if it's good it's still a Bergman film. It's a privilege, but it's still a difficulty.

CINEASTE: *Although you made many distinctive choices as a director, you didn't change any of Bergman's dialog, did you?*

ULLMANN: No, I didn't change a word or a comma, because I knew from acting with him that he's very protective of his lines. But, since it was a five-hour script, I had to do a lot of cutting. The film is mainly composed of Lena Endre's monologues, but people don't seem to notice this. Since she's so alive, they almost have the impression that they're listening to a dialogue between two people.

It was obvious that some things had to go because he wrote three drafts. The first one was magnificent, and because I was acquainted with that I could also incorporate some parts of it in the second script. Then he made changes and produced what became the final script. I believe that he's publishing the first script and that's fine.

CINEASTE: *And the Josephson character—who is called Bergman—essentially functions as a script editor. He wants to transform raw autobiographical confessions into art. And this, of course, is what Bergman the director always did.*

ULLMANN: Yes. In a certain sense, the film resembles what Bergman did with his script. He imagined a woman, and since he draws from reality, he had me in mind. Bergman says, "Come here and sit in my window, these are my lines—what do you want to do with them?" And I continued this process by providing my own images and my own experience. That's where Lena comes in; during pre-production, she contributed her own experiences to the script.

CINEASTE: *Did it then become important for you to develop a close collaboration with Lena Endre?*

ULLMANN: Yes, it was a real collaboration. Very few actresses are able to do what she did. She's superb, because you don't really feel that it's an actress—you feel that it's a woman. During the filming, if she seemed too much like an actress I would have her redo the scene. It was as if she was saying, like some method actors, "Aren't I clever?" When I pointed this out to her, she would immediately recognize the problem and rely on herself rather than acting technique.

CINEASTE: *This is interesting in light of your own work, because you've written of your early interest in Stanislavski. Of course, Stanislavski's techniques are not necessarily identical with what has been termed "the method" in the United States.*

ULLMANN: Stanislavski's technique is great and it really isn't the same as the method. The method is more artificial—at least for me. I know it works for some people. I did a play once on Broadway and the person rang the doorbell and never came into the living room where I was sitting on stage. Later I found out that both the person ringing the doorbell and the actress playing the maid were method actors. They hadn't seen each other for a long time and talked among themselves, while I sat alone on stage for what seemed like an hour. I don't believe in this. When Lena performs, I think she follows Stanislavski's approach. She knows her lines, but she just uses herself as the cloth from the weave— she becomes the cloth.

CINEASTE: *And what is your role in this process?*
ULLMANN: My role is to do the blocking, create a proper atmosphere and to think of things that will inspire her. I try to be a great listener, and if there is something she wants to do I can just say one word— because I've been an actress myself. A word is good, but long discussions are never good. I never overpower them with my own emotions. I've thought out the emotional structure for the entire movie, but the person in front of the camera at a particular moment is the one who is creating something. If they're good enough, they will always add something to what you've given them.

CINEASTE: *This is reminiscent of a famous, if perhaps apocryphal story, that Bergman asked you to focus on your lips during one of your most famous scenes with Bibi Andersson in* Persona.
ULLMANN: To my recollection, he didn't even say that, though. If you say to someone, concentrate on your lips, you get too self-conscious. We talk about experiences. Men are sometimes better directing women, because they have a certain openness and can make themselves naked in ways women can't.

CINEASTE: *Bergman, of course, has always elicited very strong performances from women, and many of his most memorable protagonists, such as the characters in* Persona, *are women.*
ULLMANN: Yes, but if at the time of *Persona* he hadn't met me, and hadn't sensed that I understood him and the part, I think my role

would have been written for Max von Sydow. He uses actors who he thinks understand him.

CINEASTE: *There's also quite a sharp contrast between this tone of* Faithless *and* Private Confessions.

ULLMANN: *Faithless* is much more despairing—that's in the writing. I tried to add grace and forgiveness. But there is only so much that you can do through the control of the images. In *Private Confessions*, the priest is the listener; that's taken away in *Faithless* and replaced with the figure of Bergman. Bergman is the listener; he's guilty and won't forgive himself and doesn't believe in God. Although he doesn't believe in God, he believes that "holiness" will set you free.

CINEASTE: *What do you mean by "holiness"?*

ULLMANN: If you look at the husband, who is a composer, you see a figure who also resembles Bergman. For him, great art, in those rare moments when you achieve something special, approaches holiness. Of course, I am volunteering my interpretation. I am guessing that this is what he would say. That's not my view of life. But we shared many things in common; although we lived together once, our friendship has lasted much longer. But I have done so much more than just working with him; I've worked with many other people.

CINEASTE: *There's a reference to Strindberg in* Faithless, *and you've played Nora in* A Doll's House. *What is the importance for you of the Scandinavian theatrical tradition?*

ULLMANN: I put a little picture of Strindberg in Bergman's workroom. Bergman is much closer to Strindberg than I am; somehow they are two twigs from the same branch. I'm sure that there are differences as well, but he's much closer to Strindberg than to Ibsen. He's directed Ibsen, but now more frequently goes back to Strindberg. For me, Strindberg is very negative. He can be wonderful, but I'd much rather work in an Ibsen play because I think his work is very modern. Some lines may be old-fashioned, but he's a writer who, like Shakespeare, continues to live, and I don't think that Strindberg does.

CINEASTE: *Of course, in* Faithless, *unlike Strindberg or Ibsen, it's hard to distinguish the victim from the victimizer.*

ULLMANN: Ingmar believes that the woman is the victim, but I don't agree with him. Neither does Lena. I do think that the child is a victim. If you make wrong choices, you will suffer; perhaps after seeing the movie you won't make those choices. The child can't watch a movie or make choices, which is why she's a victim and why I empathized with her.

CINEASTE: *The matter of making choices is also important for Nora in* A Doll's House.
ULLMANN: Exactly, and that's why she stops being a victim. She goes out the door, is face to face with herself, and makes a very positive, to me at least, choice.

CINEASTE: *Of course, in* Faithless *the characters' choices don't seem particularly deliberate. Marianne seems to view her relationship with David as frivolous. It's not a grand passion, but a mere fling.*
ULLMANN: Yes, she wants to have a little sugar in her life. Some of our worst choices are made that way. We think that we can just have a little fun and then go back to the way things were before. We didn't think that it would have these consequences. It's so stupid.

CINEASTE: *Although you didn't change the dialogue, you chose to emphasize the little daughter's role in ways that weren't apparent in the original script.*
ULLMANN: In *Scenes from a Marriage,* which Bergman wrote and directed, the couple has two children but you never see them. They didn't have any importance in the movie, but I wanted to do something different since I know how tough it is for children when people divorce. Very often it's good, since children shouldn't live with people who hate each other. But the people who are considering divorce should think how they're making the children part of their anguish.

I wanted to show that the child is, in many ways, invisible for these people. They're in pain and she says that she wishes that she hadn't done that to her child, but, despite her regrets, she does it anyway. When I speak to women about the scene when she's heartbroken after telling the children, they tell me that they don't feel sad for her. Whereas, I only feel sad for her. On the other hand, when young men look at this scene, all they can think of is the child's fate. They think, "Oh, my God

I can never allow my child to go through this." That is a great change, because much older men—even if they love their children, don't have the same "hands on" attitude that younger men have today. This movie was written by someone who never had a 'hands on' attitude. It doesn't mean that he's incapable of loving the child. He just has a different perspective, so it wasn't part of the script.

CINEASTE: *What significance should we attribute to the fact that the name of Lena Endre's character, Marianne Vogler, appears to synthesize two women you played in previous Bergman films—Elisabeth Vogler in* Persona *and Marianne in* Scenes from a Marriage?

ULLMANN: It hangs together. In *Scenes from a Marriage*, the husband says, "I'm leaving you, I'm going to Paris with a woman." And this story is recounted in *Faithless*, when David goes to Paris with Marianne. The Marianne that I played in *Scenes from a Marriage* is the wife that David left to go to Paris with this other woman. Both are called Marianne, so you can make all sorts of fantastic connections. Every viewer should have the freedom to do that.

Everyone also has the freedom to make connections with Elisabeth Vogler from *Persona*. When I played Elisabeth Vogler, I didn't know very much, but I just knew I was playing Ingmar. That's why I said that Max von Sydow could have played that part. I thought at that time, "I will just watch Ingmar and I will try to act like him." In the current film, the character called Bergman is like the character he made into a woman and I played as Elisabeth Vogler in *Persona*. You can have great fun with this.

CINEASTE: *Perhaps it's also attributable to the fact that, since Bergman hits upon many of the same themes in all his films, all of these motifs seem part of one ongoing narrative.*

ULLMANN: That's true, but this is the last one, because he's never been as face to face with himself as he is in this one—although he called one of his movies *Face to Face*. He was not face to face with himself in that movie—I don't know who was face to face with whom in that movie.

CINEASTE: *There's a striking moment when, after being discovered in bed by Markus, David and Marianne laugh. Was that present in Bergman's script?*

ULLMANN: We wanted to do it that way, because, in one of her monologues, she tells Bergman that this was like something out of a Feydeau
farce. We had a great time doing it; it was almost like a sitcom. The
strange thing was that, when the actor playing Markus first came in, he
never noticed that they were laughing. It was tough for him to do it
somehow. When we did it again and the camera was on him, he finally
noticed that they were laughing. He stopped and exclaimed, "Why are
you laughing?" He became so angry during his close-up as they continued to laugh. Not only was his character angry, he was also angry with
me and with the other actors. It provided him this horrified look; part
of this, of course, has something to do with the fact that he's a great
actor. They laugh out of nervousness; just as in church you sometimes
want to cry but start laughing hysterically. I've also had this on stage—
when I've started laughing and couldn't stop. It's something that actors
dread. It's a worse fear than forgetting your lines.

CINEASTE: *As in many Bergman films, much of the power in* Faithless
derives from your use of sustained close-ups.
ULLMANN: The cinematographer knows how close I want things to be.
I will always film a two shot and a long shot first and then go to the
close-up. We don't usually rehearse this, but often the cinematographer
will know when I want a close-up. Unless something is wrong technically, I try not to ask for more than one take. Sometimes the actor asks
for another take, but this seldom happens.

CINEASTE: *Some directors exhaust actors by demanding take after take.*
ULLMANN: I don't understand that. With these actors, it's not necessary. In my experience, I usually find that actors are best on the first
take. During the second, they repeat themselves. I did a second take,
however, in the scene when Lena is sitting in the window and crying
over her child. It was incredible the first time she did it. But it seemed
too clever. After the second take, it was amazingly quiet in the studio.
Nobody applauded, but when she went out all the technicians congrat-
ulated her. The first take was a great performance, but the second one
told us what the character was really thinking and feeling. Of course,
you have to work with the cinematographer and ensure that she has
the best lighting and that no one says "cut" before I do.

CINEASTE: *You worked with Sven Nykvist on* Private Confessions. *Are there differences between his approach and the choices favored by Jorgen Persson, the man who shot* Faithless?

ULLMANN: Nykvist and I speak the same language-we know each other so well. The man who shot *Faithless* is a great cinematographer, but is more technical and I was sometimes afraid that he'd talk too much. That's fine for him, but if he says, "Move a little, so we'll have more of the tree," the actors don't care. But he was really fantastic.

CINEASTE: *You also worked with Erland Josephson several times before, having directed him in* Sofie, *as well as acting with him in* Scenes from a Marriage.

ULLMANN: Yes, and we are very close. And if anyone knows Ingmar better than me, it's Erland. They've known each other since they were young. I think what he gives to this person called Bergman—Ingmar said he couldn't think of another name—is enormously touching. He shows us an elderly man who is longing to be kissed one more time, to be held one more time. And, in addition, having the fear of isolation and death.

CINEASTE: *On the one hand, he has an affinity with David, but also has the wisdom now to realize his folly.*

ULLMANN: Exactly.

CINEASTE: *Marianne says to David that, "We have an affinity in our misery," and that seems to be a key line.*

ULLMANN: Yeah, a lot of people have that. When they've done all of these things together, they're stuck together with their misery. In a way, it's a sad thing to be tied to someone merely because of the misery that you've shared. But that happens a lot. It happened to me. There's nothing in the film that I don't recognize from my life. And a lot of elderly and middle-aged people notice aspects of their own lives here. Maybe, after watching it, they'll be more careful.

CINEASTE: *So this film expresses your jaundiced view of contemporary society, as well as just marriage?*

ULLMANN: If we don't have any values anymore, if nothing we do means anything, then we'll end up feeling very gray. In the end, then, love is not important, other people are not important, and even you yourself are not important. When values decline, it takes all the fun out of living.

CINEASTE: *Have you considered acting in films or on stage again?*

ULLMANN: No, it's not part of my plan. Actually today somebody called me about a play on Broadway. Even though you say that you'll never act, something will come along to prompt you to say, "Oh my God, that's incredible." I probably won't, but to be offered this was tempting. I feel more fulfilled as a director. The only trouble is that it takes me two years to do a film—one year for preproduction and writing the screenplay, then we shoot the film, and then you travel with it. If you're thirty or forty, that's great. But now, to know that it's two and a half years of your life, you have to choose carefully because you don't want to waste any time.

Interview with Liv Ullmann:
Ullmann as a Director

ROBERT EMMET LONG/2004

REL: *I'd like to talk to you today about your work as a film director. In the past, directing films was pretty much a men's club, with here and there some quite brilliant women directors such as Leni Riefenstahl in Germany and Lena Wertmüller in italy. Lately an increasing number of women have become directors. There's Jane Campion and Mira Nair, and there's Soffia Coppola, who directed* Lost in Translation *recently and won an Academy Award.*

LU: But she didn't win for Best Director. She won for Best Screenplay. She was nominated for Best Director.

REL: *Oh, yes, of course. But let me ask you a double question. Have there been women directors whose work in the past you have admired, and do you see increasing opportunities for women to become film directors?*

LU: Well, there are increasing opportunities maybe specifically in Europe. The women there have a higher standard than they have had in the United States. You have a wonderful director in, for example, Barbra Streisand. I believe that maybe the one failing she has had in the past is that she has had a leading role in movies she herself directs. I don't believe that you can direct a movie where you play the lead yourself because sooner or later some vanity or something will take over when you are editing the film or when you are making decisions about

---

Published by permission of the author.

what you would like the theme to be. When you know you are going to be in it, there is no way you wouldn't then also think about yourself as an actress. But I think she's a wonderful director, and I hope that she will come back and make a movie when she is not an actress.

In Europe the women directors have been very strong. For example in France there are some very good women directors—please don't ask me about names because I'm bad at that. In Norway and Scandinavia there have been some good women directors; in Norway, in fact, there were better women directors than there were men directors. In Sweden, too, there have been women directors, although they were not better than the men because there were always very great men directors in Sweden. What happened in Norway is that if you are a woman director, and if you become strong and might even become successful, you don't belong to the boy's club; you lose friends and the film company that will give you your next movie. Some of these really good women directors in, for example Norway, will disappear. This has happened. I could give you the names of three wonderful women film directors, and none of them are making movies anymore. Yet at the time they did make movies, they were the best.

REL: *Well, I was just about to name two Swedish actresses who became directors. One is Mai Zetterling.*

LU: Yes, well, you see something like that, I think, also happened to her. She made beautiful films—I've seen two of them—very, very good films, and suddenly it became quiet; and I think it is the men's club taking over, not funding them, not allowing them to happen. They didn't have colleagues interested in their doing another film who were standing behind them. And the . . . what was the other Swedish actress who became a director?

REL: *The other was Ingrid Thulin, another Bergman actress. She made at least two feature films, I understand.*

LU: I don't even know that she did do that. Maybe she did, but I am not so sure that her professional life included directing films; at least I haven't seen the films. But somebody from the same school, Gunnel Lindblom, who had a lot of parts in Ingmar Bergman's films and was a wonderful actress . . . she made at least two, maybe three, very fine movies, and the same thing happened to her. She got acclaim, she got everything, and then suddenly it was quiet. What happens I don't know. And in the United states, look at Barbra Streisand. Suddenly it is quiet. She is not directing more films . . . Strangely enough, media attention when women make films is very negative, perhaps by the very fact that they are women. Even, for example, with Soffia Coppola. A lot of people are saying, "Oh, her father wrote the script, her father was over there directing her film, she didn't do it alone." Sometimes slighting rumors about women directors become so strong that in the end they are dismissed.

REL: *I've seen you described in print as a "feminist film director." Is this a good description of you?*
LU: I don't really know what a "feminist film director" is.
(REL laughs)

I am a woman and all my life I have been surrounded by women's issues. That is because I am a woman. Things happen within my body because I am a woman. I give birth because I am a woman. I fall in love in a woman's way. Even as a director I have a different way of approaching those I work with because I am a woman. I know because I have worked with so many male directors, I know that my language is at times different from theirs. And because I write most of the movies I direct, I know that the tone of these movies will be very much the tone of my personal experience. When I made my first movie, I tried at first to be very people pleasing so that I would be accepted, and that didn't work so well. I even asked the technicians, "Can I go out and get you some coffee," just so they would like me and respect me. When I began to speak on a set, I didn't have a commanding voice like a man's, and there were many practical things about filmmaking I had not yet learned. I'm not technically wonderful, because I'm not good with technical terms which maybe I should use with cinematographers.

I would say something like "slow down the camera"—it's almost like a dance in the way it slows down, a very slow, beautiful dance. And this is not the language a man would use. But if the crew wants me, they will accept the kind of language I use. It's maybe a kind of feminine language that we women should feel more free in using. If you work with a man, he will not have this language. His language is very technical, very appropriate, very right, very good; but personally I don't always understand it.

REL: *You must have learned a lot about directing from being directed by Ingmar Bergman.*

LU: Yes, of course I did, and I made so many films with him, but if I were to be very honest, the ones I learned from the most were the bad directors. Bad directors make you see, or feel, what you shouldn't do. They talk too much, they describe too much what is happening inside your character. They kill your fantasy and interfere with your ability to feel cleanly.

REL: *Was making your first film* Sofie *an intimidating experience for you?*

LU: No, it was a wonderful experience. I think the first week was intimidating, but that was because I allowed myself to be intimidated by myself. I was middle-aged, I was a former actress, or an actress, and I was a woman. I felt that these were three things that the crew would not like in a director, so I allowed myself to be intimidated by believing everybody had these negative feelings toward me. But once I threw these notions overboard, and once I stopped being people pleasing, I loved directing. I loved to be on the other side of the camera, and to watch great actors and actresses create; I knew that they would create if I allowed them to be who they were and just gave them the right light, the right movement, the right inspiration. I had written the script myself, and I knew what the framework was and where I wanted the camera, and I knew that I had a brilliant cameraman who knew how to put the light. I was surrounded by great people.

REL: *In all of the feature films you have made the focal figure has always been a woman, isn't that true? Sofie is depicted in very domestic surroundings throughout the film, and everything that occurs happens around her. She is a survivor, a strong woman, and one sees this particularly in the contrast she presents with her husband, who is emotionally tied to his mother and eventually loses his grip on life. She overshadows the other characters, I think.*

LU: Well, you can say that only because I chose to show her in a central way. I would think that if you were there and were part of the family, I don't think she would have overshadowed any of the others. If we were in the family, the father would seem to be dominant and we would see everything from his point of view. The wife would be seen largely from his point of view, and the very strong aunt. I believe you are saying that Sofie is the dominant one because she was "lifted out," you might say, and this gives her a larger size perhaps. We are more emotionally involved with her, so she may seem to have a dominance that she didn't necessarily have.

At the end she says good-bye to her son and he, he goes off . . . and she's standing there looking at the empty rooms, but she knows that her life with her son in these rooms has been extraordinary for her. She hasn't had an empty life. She even begins to dance in these rooms—dances for what she hopes for, what she dreams of. It's a lovely ending, the way I see it, although it is about somebody who, if you knew about her, you would never think of her as having had an extraordinary life in any way. It was just a unique life, like we all have, but nothing momentous really happened to her.

REL: *You've created her nineteenth-century Copenhagen world very meticulously. Did you do a lot of research in order to achieve the realism you do?*
LU: Yes, I did a lot of research, and that's part of why I love writing scripts. There were so many things to know about this circle of Jewish characters—and I'm not myself Jewish. I think my lack of knowledge at the beginning turned out in the end to be a strength for the movie. Because if I had been Jewish, many of the things in the story would have been so obvious that it wouldn't have seemed necessary to learn about them or to show them. To me, all the things I learned about Jewish life had a tremendous impact for me, and I wanted to show them. In fact, there was only one Jewish person in the cast, which was the actor Erland Josephson, who played the father, and he had never led a Jewish life since he was a little child with his grandfather. Now suddenly while he did the movie it came back to him—Jewish songs, for example. Suddenly he wanted to say certain things in Yiddish. When the family had their meal we had a real kosher meal.

REL: *Oh, you did!*
LU: A real kosher meal. It was fantastic!

REL: *You were very supportive of all the Jewish characters. You've treated them with consideration and kindness. Isn't there some special pleading in this? I mean, the movie seems to make an appeal to the viewer, as if to ask "how could people be so prejudiced against individuals as decent, and indeed lovable, as these people are?"*

LU: I don't know. I don't know how that is. At the end, I have the boy leave to go out into the world, and we know how the world will be with him. He may never come back again. I do not know and have never understood this prejudice. I wanted to show a family that had the family values that all different sorts of people would be able to recognize. They had traditions that if not recognizable specifically for those who are not Jewish are nevertheless loving and familiar. I think that we would be better off for knowing about these traditions. You know I would like to make a movie about an Islamic family. I am not speaking of extremists of course, and people who do hateful things.

REL: Kristin Lavransdatter *reminds me a little of Bergman's* The Virgin Spring, *which is set in the same fourteenth-century period.* The Virgin Spring *is very intense and concentrated, and* Kristin *is episodic. It's leisurely in telling its story. Did you have any trouble containing the sprawl of an epic film based on an epic novel?*

LU: Yeah . . . I wrote the film myself, and it was originally longer. I wish it could have been allowed to be longer. It was a three-hour movie, and I was forced to cut it down to two-and-a-half hours, and that's where the more shortened episodes came in. The strength of any movie like that is that it takes its time. I made the movies *The Emigrants* and *The New Land* many years ago . . . and they were . . .

REL: *Oh, yes, I know them very well. They're beautiful films.*

LU: They're beautiful, and you know they are both three hours long. I think *Kristin Lavransdatter* had to pay for having been cut down. I know Ingmar when he saw the movie, and it was three-hours-and-ten-minutes long, loved it. I wish it could have been three-hours-and-ten-minutes because there was so much I wanted to tell. There were so many things that were important for me. Maybe if I had been a more experienced director I would have known that I would be forced to cut; if I had known that I would be forced to cut, I would have gone into the script and decided about cuts there. I might have decided not to show Kristin's childhood, for example, because once I had shot such scenes I would love those things and it would be very hard for me to cut them away. So I cut a little bit away from this and a little bit away from that. And that's no good.

You asked me what I learned about directing from acting with Ingmar Bergman. I didn't learn about cutting at that point. But I did a movie for him as an actress last summer—a combination of *Scenes from a Marriage* called *Saraband*. I saw the way he was cutting the script again and again before we shot. I wish that knowledge had been clear to me before because I am always forced to cut and I hate it. You see the exciting things the cast and crew are doing, and suddenly you have to cut the scenes from the movie. It's like inflicting little deaths to their creativity.

REL: *How would you say that Kristin, as a person and as a character, compares with the heroines of your other movies?*

LU: Well, she has . . . there are independent women, and it was tough for Sofie to be independent the way Kristin was. She didn't dare to be as independent as Kristin, although she did things she shouldn't have done according to her family. I think that Kristin would compare to the other women in that she believed her life was *her* life, and that she couldn't live it according to the rules of the generation before her. So if you talk about feministic films, yeah, so maybe that's where feminism would come in—a way of thinking that "I have a unique life. I am a woman, and my life has to be lived according to who I am and not who my parents were."

REL: *Both* Private Confessions, *which appeared in 1997, and* Faithless, *which came out in 2000, are quite a bit alike inasmuch as they come out of Bergman's personal experience and writing. He wrote the scripts and then asked you to direct them. They both involve marital infidelity and tormenting guilt. In particular,* Private Confessions *is strongly reminiscent of the marital situation of Bergman's parents.*

LU: Yes, the scripts he wrote were in the form of monologues, and I . . . he gave me some books he had written while he wrote the script. They were a kind of diary and there were some wonderful things in them that I included in the shooting script. For example, the talk Anna has with the priest, Uncle Jacob, a great monologue he has at that point. And there's the scene where the sacrament is celebrated in the hall. Is sacrament the right word?

REL: *Communion?*

LU: The communion. I thought that was good. Ingmar loved that I had done that, because that tells so much more in some way, I feel, about the family than it would have if you merely told about it as a story. There again, celebrating the communion may be an everyday thing for Ingmar, so that he might not have included it in the script. But for me, you know, it was a revelation to show the whole thing and what happens between the people. Are they lying, or are they not lying? I just loved it . . .

(REL laughs)

LU: The couple's predicament was even more intense in *Faithless.*

REL: *I was just about to ask about* Faithless. *It's a very painful film that is filled with inner suffering. The film critic David Thomson in a recent book remarked that* Faithless *is far and away the best work you have done as a director. He calls it "a vital extension of Bergman's work, and a magnificent picture in its own right." Is it your favorite of the films you have made?*

LU: It is in some ways my favorite film, because I put so much of what I believed into the work. Ingmar's having written it in the form of a monologue made it in some way a very personal film for me. There was a story in it I wanted to tell—to tell about the director, whom I saw as Ingmar, and to tell about the actress, who was also me. I also wanted to put the child prominently into the movie. In all the movies I've done with Ingmar you only hear about the children, you never see them. But if you are to tell his family story, or if you are to tell about things that are special for Ingmar, you have to tell what happens to the children when the grownups are behaving the way they are behaving; because in *Faithless* he is telling a story about faithlessness that had once affected him as a child. I was really proud of that movie because it stirred up a lot of other people. It stirred up Ingmar to the degree (LU suddenly begins laughing) that he liked what I had done.

REL: *Oh, really!*

LU: I'd got a monologue and I had to interpret it in the way I wanted to. When you read the monologue—it's just in the beginning that the director, whom Ingmar calls Bergman, speaks. He's not part of the movie. She's the one speaking. I show them in the director's study, or workroom, and I first shot the whole movie, or the first half of the movie, in that workroom. You know, I think he would have done it in this way if he had shot it himself. But you know what? I shot the movie once more showing everything she was telling about; and in that way I could interweave her telling the story with what had happened—interweave views of the one who is listening, who is Ingmar, with the story of what's happened to him. To me, this interweaving of the two was important.

And then the other important thing is that after I received the script from Ingmar, we agreed that we wouldn't discuss it until I was finished with the movie. Otherwise I wouldn't do it. And he agreed absolutely. Yet I did talk to him about it when I got the script. "Shouldn't he be forgiven for what he had once done?" I asked him. "No," he said, "I don't believe in forgiving. I don't forgive myself." But I wanted him to include something where he does forgive himself. He wouldn't do it, but then I did this. In the workroom I had the younger Bergman sitting with the older Bergman, and telling the story of what he did to the woman . . . Do you know the passage I am talking about?

REL: *Yes.*

LU: Yeah. And then suddenly the older Bergman touches the younger one on the cheek, like it's o. k., you are forgiven, and then he leans back. I love that, because although Ingmar doesn't want to forgive himself, the older one really should do it. And *did* in my movie.

And you know, I believe that the reason Ingmar gave me these two scripts to do . . . I know that he gave me the first one because he said that I was religious. And he did not know anyone else who believed in God and was the way I was. That's why he wanted me to do that movie. About the other movie I really don't know why he wanted me to do it except that he must have liked what I . . . Actually, he loves *Private Confessions*, he loves that movie. But the other movie, I think there were things that he knows I know. He would never have made the film himself, he could never have done it, would have resisted doing it, but he knew maybe deep-down that I would do it, and he wanted it done. Do you know what I mean?

REL: *I think I do.*
LU: That is how I think it happened.

REL: *There is a rumor that you may be directing a new film version of* A Doll's House.
LU: Yes, in a way that's not just a rumor. I have written a script. It's now finished. Kate Winslet has said "yes" to do Nora and is very enthusiastic. John Cusack has said "yes" to do Helmer, and Stellan Skarsgård, a Swedish actor who lives and works in the United States is to do Doctor Rank. We are supposed to start the first of January in Norway.

And I've also written another script, which it would also be nice to direct as well. It is based on a work of Olaf Olafson, an Icelandic writer whose book *Coming Home* is out in the United States. It's an incredible book. I've written a script which he and the producer really like, and the movie should go into production at some time too.

REL: *Your movie of* A Doll's House *is something to look forward to. You've played Nora many times, I know. Wasn't it your Broadway debut with Sam Waterston?*
LU: Actually it was.

REL: *You played Nora at various times in your life. I wonder if Nora might be conceived in your film in a different way than she was when you played her on the stage.*
LU: Yes, absolutely, because even in the three times I've played her . . . I've played her once on the radio, once in the National Theatre in Oslo, and once on tour in Norway, in addition to playing her on Broadway. Each time it was different for me because with age comes new knowledge and new experiences of my own that I can use. So, when I wrote Nora now—when I was asked to write the script and to direct—I think I'm the best director for the play.
(Both LU and REL break out laughing)

REL: *You're an expert on the subject alright.*

LU: I'm an expert on the subject. I've done her, I know her, I'm an actress and I've directed movies. I can put so much in the script of what I know, and at the same time, for example, I can give an actress like Kate Winslet tremendous freedom to go with her experience. I haven't changed Ibsen because why should you change an incredible genius? I've done what I did with Ingmar, who I also think belongs to the genius family. I've added things that I believe maybe Ibsen couldn't do because the work was presented on the stage rather than on film. I've added the children. I have added things that are very much part of today, although the play takes place at the turn of the century in my movie. There are things that we know today that I am sure were part of those days too but that Ibsen didn't write about. I've also removed the stagy part: to be a doll today is not the same as being a doll then. (REL laughs)

To be a doll today is to be a people pleaser, a woman who will never reveal that she is too capable or too strong because she doesn't want to emasculate the man she is with. We women are playing the same game, only we use . . . we do it a little differently . . . I mean, look, I've spoken of what I did directing *Sofie* the first week. I ran around and I asked everyone if I should bring them coffee. That's a Nora. I mean, you get the big directing job and you . . .

REL: *You're still thinking like a servant.*

LU: I know it. I know it. This is what Nora does. She dances when she doesn't know what else to do to keep their attention, when she could sit down and talk about something more serious instead. She dances and dances until she has to say who she is. And then she is so surprised by who she is she has to leave the house until she has grown up herself.

REL: *I think my time is up, but I have to tell you that I not only admire you but that I also think you're a wonderful person to talk to.*

LU: So are you.

REL: *Thank you so much.*

INDEX

CONVERSATIONS WITH FILMMAKERS SERIES
PETER BRUNETTE, GENERAL EDITOR

The collected interviews with notable modern directors, including

Robert Aldrich • Woody Allen • Pedro Almodóvar • Robert Altman • Theo Angelopolous • Bernardo Bertolucci • Tim Burton • Jane Campion • Frank Capra • Charlie Chaplin • Francis Ford Coppola • George Cukor • Brian De Palma • Clint Eastwood • John Ford • Terry Gilliam • Jean-Luc Godard • Peter Greenaway • Howard Hawks • Alfred Hitchcock • John Huston • Jim Jarmusch • Elia Kazan • Stanley Kubrick • Fritz Lang • Spike Lee • Mike Leigh • George Lucas • Sidney Lumet • Roman Polanski • Michael Powell • Jean Renoir • Martin Ritt • Carlos Saura • John Sayles • Martin Scorsese • Ridley Scott • Steven Soderbergh • Steven Spielberg • George Stevens • Oliver Stone • Quentin Tarantino • Lars von Trier • Orson Welles • Billy Wilder • John Woo • Zhang Yimou • Fred Zinnemann